A COMPLETE GUIDE

The Charleston, Savannah & Coastal Islands Book

Classic house south of Broad Street, Charleston

A COMPLETE GUIDE

5TH EDITION

THE CHARLESTON, SAVANNAH & COASTAL ISLANDS BOOK

Cecily
McMillan

The Countryman Press
Woodstock, Vermont

ISBN 1-58157-071-6
ISSN 1550-252X

Front cover photo © Jim Hargan
All other photos by the author unless otherwise specified © 2004
Book design by Bodenweber Design
Composition by Melinda Belter
Maps by Mapping Specialists Ltd., Madison, WI © The Countryman Press

Published by The Countryman Press, P.O. Box 748, Woodstock, Vermont 05091

Distributed by W. W. Norton & Company, Inc., 500 Fifth Avenue, New York, NY 10110

Manufactured in the United States of America

10 9 8 7 6 5 4 3 2 1

No complimentary meals or lodgings were accepted by the author and reviewers in gathering information for this work.

To the memory of George McMillan, who first brought me to the Lowcountry and turned my eyes to its subtleties, and to our son, Tom, with whom I continue to love it.

Contents

6

Acknowledgments

This book gathers together for readers both a sense of Lowcountry history and all the details that make for a successful visit. Such a project required the efforts of friends and assistants.

In Charleston, Langhorne Howard and Nina McCully have given me valuable insights into their native city. Working for many years with the photographer Wade Spees has allowed me to see the Lowcountry through his gifted eye, as a place of serene beauty, humanity, and vitality. Suzy Little and Dorothy and Grant Dugdale always keep me posted on the ways in which Charleston is changing, and how it remains the same.

In Beaufort and on St. Helena Island, my home, Dale Friedman provided great help, and I also relied on Cheryl and Roger Steele and Mary Mack.

Beth Scott deepened my knowledge of Savannah and Hilton Head. Steve Wise, author, museum curator, and military historian, kindly critiqued my History chapter.

Jenny Stacy and, now, Erica Backus at the Savannah Area Convention and Visitors Bureau and Chris Nobles at the Charleston Area Convention and Visitors Bureau are thorough, professional, and full of good suggestions.

Thanks to Philip Rich at Berkshire House for previous editions, to Susan Minnich who polished everything, and to my new editors at Countryman Press. Also especially to Priscilla Johnson McMillan who continues to nurture my Lowcountry life.

INTRODUCTION

There are some places about which we have such strong impressions that when we finally go there they seem familiar. The Lowcountry seems to have lodged itself so securely in so many imaginations that I often find, when I am asked about it, that what I have to say matters less than the opportunity I may be giving someone to fine-tune the picture they already have.

Where these clustered impressions come from, whether learned in a history lesson on the Civil War, gathered from a friend, understood in a novel, or viewed on a movie screen, seems less important than the fact that they feel fully conceived. This isn't surprising: The Lowcountry has earned our permanent attention. It is a compelling world. Like other places that have witnessed tremendous historic upheavals and whose residents have had to adjust to changed circumstances, it evokes a natural sympathy in us for its stories.

I first visited the Lowcountry in the summer of 1979, and have been listening in on its history ever since. I return to where I feel the presence and rituals of the past: the shores of St. Helena Sound, where I catch crabs on a string or dig for oysters much as Native Americans might have done; Drayton Hall where beds of lilies bloom as they did in Jefferson's Monticello garden; Penn Center, where descendants of slaves honor their heritage and the strength of their forebears in song; the squares of Savannah, laid out more than 250 years ago and still possessing a power of geometry that untangles nature and orders the pace of urban life.

The region's physical beauty is just as evocative. The landscape is soft, uninterrupted by hills on land, carpeted with marsh grass and flowing waters at its edges. The air itself seems to press down, weighted by all the humidity, wrapping the Lowcountry like a package. There are distinctive seasons here, which bring their own changes in color and light, in bird migrations and blossoms. Every day the shoreline is redefined by the tides.

This book is intended to both introduce you to some of the long-standing pleasures and pastimes found in the Lowcountry and point you to where you might discover ones of your own. Individual chapter openings lay out a broad context into which you may place yourself, as a traveler looking to plan a day or as a reader adjusting the imaginary pictures you arrived with to those you observed first-hand. Sometimes, your efforts may be studious—admiring architecture, exploring sites of historic and cultural significance. At other times, you will be content to satisfy your senses: to feel the beach between your toes, smell the salt marsh, watch a pelican dive, taste fresh shrimp. Don't neglect to listen for old stories, either.

It may turn out that, having come to the Lowcountry for a vacation, you end up joining the ranks of those who return for good. The glossy residential resorts on the developed islands like Kiawah and Hilton Head have drawn national attention to the area; Beaufort has appeared on so many "Best Small Town" lists and attracted so many new visitors that it is possible to walk down its main street and see only unfamiliar faces. The Spoleto Festival has put Charleston on an international map.

Yet the inexorable need in many of us for community, for a sense of continuity that comes from bringing the past forward, keeps the Lowcountry alive, keeps it from resting solely on the life of its past for vitality. Today, restaurants, bookstores, jazz and blues clubs, clothing shops, art galleries, and B&Bs are embedding themselves in the old Lowcountry places. They are enlarging the remnant world, just as spats fasten on oyster banks and make them grow.

Cecily McMillan
St. Helena Island, South Carolina

THE WAY THIS BOOK WORKS

This book is divided into six chapters. Several of them cover specific regions of the Lowcountry. But, like a shelf of individual volumes, it encourages browsing: You may want to thumb through the opening sections of individual chapters, for example, to get an overview of the subject. Or you may want to start with the Chapter One, *History*, then pick and choose among the others as your visit unfolds and your needs become apparent.

If you're interested in finding a place to eat or sleep—and during the high season in spring you're encouraged to consider advance planning—look over the restaurant and lodging charts in the Index (organized by area and price); then turn to the pages in the general index and read the specific entries for the places that most interest you.

Some entries, most notably those in the Lodging and Dining sections of chapters, include specific information (telephone, address, hours, etc.) organized for easy reference at the beginning of each listing. All such information has been checked for accuracy as close to the time of publication as possible, but details change so it's best to call ahead. Wherever possible I have included web sites for planning and reference. For year-round tourist information see the sources listed in Chapter Six, *Information*.

Prices

Prices change, too, and for that reason we've avoided listing specific prices in favor of noting their range. Lodging price codes are based on a per-room rate, double-occupancy in the high season months. Low season rates, which generally apply in December and January, are usually about 20 percent less. In the high season many places, small and large, require a minimum two-night stay and may also have specific rules regarding adequate notice and refunds in the event of cancellation. Check ahead.

You might also confirm information that we've provided about policies in effect concerning such things as handicapped access and smoking.

Restaurant prices indicate the cost of a meal including appetizer, entrée, and dessert, but not bar beverages, tax, or tip. Prix-fixe menus are noted. Here again, the season of your visit may bring on special conditions: When there are crowds, most restaurants extend their hours of operation, serving meals both earlier and later. In the winter, they may shut down for a day or two.

Price Codes

	Lodging	*Dining*
Inexpensive	Up to $60	Up to $15
Moderate	$60 to $120	$15 to $30
Expensive	$120 to $200	$30 to $50
Very Expensive	Over $200	Over $50

Credit cards are abbreviated as follows:

AE—American Express	DC—Diner's Club
CB—Carte Blanche	MC—MasterCard
D—Discover Card	V— Visa

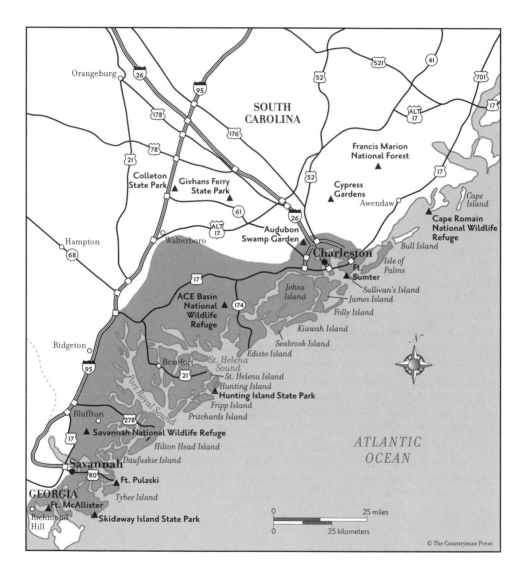

THE CHARLESTON, SAVANNAH & COASTAL ISLANDS BOOK

1

History

"No Fayrer or Fytter Place"

Toward the middle of the 16th century, European adventurers were spreading across the Atlantic Ocean in a wild burst of exploring, hoping to claim for their sovereigns and spon-sors vast territories of land and the riches they believed to flourish there. Aboard what now seem to be preposterously small ships and guided by hopeless maps (few of these expedi-tions ever landed where they intended), they arrived, established forts, and set to their business. One of the places they landed—Spanish, French, and English in succession—was the region we now know as the Lowcountry of South Carolina and Georgia.

The next 150 years was a period of settling and retreating, of establishing colonies and defending them—from one another, from the Native Americans who lived there, and from the twin scourges of disease and deprivation. Motivated by religious zeal and political unrest at home, as well as by the drive to acquire real estate, slaves, or converts to Christ-ianity, the Europeans kept returning to build, to trade, to map, to start life over in new places on which they imposed an Old World order. In the end, it was the English who dominated the Lowcountry.

While the accounts of these years outdo one another in their use of superlatives to describe God and king, they contain even richer praise for the new country. Captain Jean Ribaut, a Frenchman who led a group of 150 Huguenot colonists to the Lowcountry in 1562, claimed in a report (translated into English the following year) that there was "no fayrer or fytter place" than the area of Port Royal Sound, near present-day Beaufort, one of the "goodlyest, best and frutfullest countres that ever was sene"; where egrets were so plentiful the bushes "be all white covered with them"; where there were "so many sortes of fishes that ye may take them without net or angle."

On a site now at the edge of a golf course at the Marine Corps Recruit Depot on Parris Island, Ribaut and his settlers built Charlesfort. It was a basic defensive structure measur-ing 96 feet by 78 feet, barricaded with palisades, and surrounded by a moat. There were gun platforms at its corners and, inside, a rude house with a straw roof. Modest though it may have been, Charlesfort represented the first attempt by the French to establish a colony in what is now the United States. The effort took place three years before the found-ing of St. Augustine by the Spanish, and 45 years before the English settled Jamestown. Impressed with the Lowcountry and confident of its potential, Ribaut quickly returned to

The marsh overlooking the bridge to Parris Island

France, intending to return with supplies and recruits. He never made it back; the colony itself collapsed soon afterwards. The well-situated site did not lie fallow for long, however. In 1566 the Spanish expanded their reach north from St. Augustine and constructed Fort San Felipe on the ruins of Charlesfort. It seemed inevitable that a place so plentifully endowed would not go begging.

To a modern traveler who chances upon a rookery in Hunting Island State Park, or to the youngster throwing a cast net and needing the strength of two to draw it in, perhaps nothing has changed. Today, as centuries ago, the natural resources of the Lowcountry are breathtakingly impressive wherever you go. There will be schools of dolphin by your boat off Hilton Head, dozens of shrimp from casting your net in Edisto Island's creeks, hundreds of eggs in the loggerhead turtle's nest on Pritchard's Island, and thousands of terns, which—when they rise all at once off Egg Bank in St. Helena Sound—appear as a cloud of smoke on the horizon. There will be late-afternoon light so intense and golden it makes the dun bark of the grayest sycamore shimmer.

And remember: When Ribaut called the Lowcountry a place "where nothing lacketh," Charleston, Beaufort, and Savannah had not even been invented.

By 1740, each of these towns had developed the intense self-consciousness—the spirit of place—that is apparent here today. You can find it in the watercolors of a native artist, in the concert of an African-American chorus, in the words of a docent, in the tales of a fisherman. Before the first roads were laid, the wharves constructed, or the means of governance fully conceived, the continuity of culture that characterizes all the Lowcountry was begun. It is the rare American place to have evolved intact, with its monuments and houses and symbols of achievement still pointing to a documented and recognized past.

So overwhelming is the sense of place in the Lowcountry I have often felt of people I know that if they ever left the city limits of Charleston or Savannah they would vaporize.

There's no doubt, to read from their accounts, that visitors from the earliest days of settlement have shared the feeling that the Lowcountry is a special place, a dramatic place apart. Looking backward, it is hard to pinpoint precisely when the term "Lowcountry"—or even, as it is sometimes spelled, "Low Country"—became widely used. It is certainly an apt geographical description for an area that is hill-less and hardly above sea level. But to accurately define the Lowcountry, to comprehend it at its broadest, you must consider that it is many things: a place of dozens of distinctive, interconnected natural communities and ecosystems; a site where historical forces have been converging, sometimes with disastrous consequences, for 400 years; a region whose tiny society influenced national culture; a self-conscious political subdivision of the United States.

Technically, the Lowcountry is divided from what is known as the South Carolina Upcountry by the fall line, that feature of geography which bisects the state from the Georgia border at Augusta, approximately 90 miles from the coast, to North Carolina. Upland of the fall line the soil is red clay, and it is hilly; downward the land flattens and spreads, creating broad alluvial plains, which meet the sea.

As for other defining attributes, the Lowcountry that stretches from Charleston to Savannah and the Sea Islands in between seems to enjoy an enduring sense of pride: Old families, old houses, old customs, and old loyalties remain, if not as guiding principles, then ones whose legacy is passed on, as one might give a quilt to the next generation. As the writers of the classic WPA Guide, "South Carolina, A Guide to the Palmetto State," wrote in 1941, the Lowcountry inhabitant "may live in Charleston, a city that competes with the New Jerusalem in his dreams; or he may live in a drafty Georgian country house" but he "recalls his past glory with a pride that surpasses his ability to appreciate thoroughly the good things of the present."

Today residents do appreciate the present but they are aware they must protect what they have, even at a price. Lowcountry residents were willing to pay it once, to take the drastic measure of firing on Fort Sumter, and they are continuing that commitment. Maintaining Historic Districts, scenic vistas, two-lane island roads, Gullah communities, marine sanctuaries comprising tens of thousands of acres—these are among the accomplishments of present-day preservationists who seek to insure the presence of the past in everyday life. Their victories are for you to savor, too.

NATURAL HISTORY

The coastline that defines the Lowcountry was, until about 245 million years ago, still more or less attached to the eastern rim of what became present-day Europe and Africa. The shifting of geologic plates that caused the movement of the landmass and created the southern Appalachians, among other mountain ranges, led to the formation of the Atlantic Ocean and the Lowcountry coastal plain.

In the geologic history of the southeast region, the coastal plain is a rather new development. Long before the present-day coastline obtained its shape (toward the end of the Miocene—third epoch of the Cenozoic Era) the upcountry regions already were well established. They were formed in an earlier era, the Mesozoic (220–70 million years ago, the time when the dinosaurs came and went), and their ancient mineral formations contrast sharply with those of the coast.

Sand Hills

I continued through this forest nearly in a direct line towards the sea coast, five or six miles, when the land became uneven, with ridges of sand hills, mixed with sea shells, and covered by almost impenetrable thickets, consisting of Live Oaks, Sweet-bay, Myrica, Ilex, . . . The dark labyrinth is succeeded by a great extent of salt plains, beyond which the boundless ocean is seen. Betwixt the dark forest and the salt plains, I crossed a rivulet of fresh water, where I sat down a while to rest myself, under the shadow of sweet Bays and Oaks; the lively breezes were perfumed by the fragrant breath of the superb Crinum, called by the inhabitants, White Lily. This admirable beauty of the sea-coast islands dwells in the humid shady groves, where the soil is made fertile and mellow by the admixture of sea shells . . . and the texture and whiteness of its flowers at once charmed me.

—From *Travels of William Bartram*
(First published in 1791; New York: Viking Penguin, 1988)

Over time, a cycle was begun. Eroded material from these highland ridges was carried by streams draining the Blue Ridge and Piedmont uplands and deposited, again and again, to the south and east. This Cretaceous material extended the landmass. Periodic inundation by the sea followed, covering the sediment and creating distinctive geologic layers of clay, sand, and gravel. At least seven such terraces have been identified, ranging in elevation from 25 feet to 270 feet. Mining activity near Charleston has unearthed fossils of shark teeth and mammoth vertebrae.

In short, millions of years ago much of the present-day Lowcountry was under water, while as recently as thousands of years ago, the Native Americans who lived here probably collected oysters and shellfish from beds that, were we to locate them today, would lie some 95 miles out to sea.

Today, well beneath the sandy soil, ranging in thickness from 1,000 to 3,000 feet, lie the sandstone, siltstones, shale, and limestone that were dumped there. They undergird the land and stretch well beyond it into the ocean to form the continental shelf and the upper slope. The oldest rocks of the coastal plain lie in scattered sections under these layers and it is activity in their faults that can, and has, caused earthquakes, such as the one that damaged Charleston in 1886.

The geologic history of the Lowcountry has given its farmers, residents, and for a time its phosphate-mining industry, some unique advantages. Unlike northern coastal areas such as New England, the area is free of surface rocks. Preparing a field never required the building of a stone wall beside it. The nature of subterranean rock formations has provided some especially good soils for timber cultivation. More important, the deeper layers of rocks serve as aquifers to provide potable water for agriculture, industry, and homes—not an idle resource given the near sea-level elevation of the Lowcountry.

Finally, if the Lowcountry were without the plentiful deposits of easily eroded rock that tumbled from the highlands over the years, the region would have no beaches. The sand you traverse, across miles of coastal and barrier beach, is their legacy.

The phenomenon of rocks-into-sand is one piece of the Lowcountry's geologic history. Another is the transformation of one massive ocean into a landscape of sculptured sounds, estuaries, and marshes. Their evolution has defined the Lowcountry as the site of one of the nation's most productive fisheries, a home to dozens of species of native and migratory birds, and a habitat for mammals small and large. Even the trees and plants of the coast flourish in direct response to these various bodies of water.

The Marine Environment

The Lowcountry marine environment includes several distinctive parts: swamps, estuaries, marshes, maritime forests, dunes and interdune meadows, tidal creeks and sounds, alluvial and blackwater rivers. Their functions are interdependent; to all, tidal action—about 6 to 9 feet throughout the region—is significant. Evidence of the complexity of the marine ecosystem is best seen at any number of points where the land meets the sea, for it is here that some of the most dynamic and subtle dramas of nature are played out. To witness them, a traveler need do no more than lean over a bridge at low tide, step out of the car by a rural creek, or walk the beach.

Perhaps the most common sight of the Lowcountry is the field of smooth cordgrass (*Spartina alterniflora*) that makes up the salt marsh and the muddy banks and flats that cut through it. Rimmed by wax myrtle and Carolina cherry laurel on its banks, overshadowed by huge live oaks whose limbs are draped with Spanish moss (an air plant, member of the pineapple family) and dotted with resurrection fern, the salt marsh is probably nature's most productive nursery.

What you will see here is this: filter-feeders such as snails, crabs, oysters, shrimp, and mullet ingesting the detritus—a potent mixture of decomposed marsh grass, animal matter, algae, and fungi. Or something larger, a heron, say, or a bottlenose dolphin, or a raccoon eating its smaller prey. The fiddler crabs with their lopsided claws will gather and disperse by the hundreds, a muddy cavalry. Look up and there are the shrimp boats, nets dragging at their sides. Behind them flock the gulls scavenging for cast-off fish. As the tide recedes, you will hear the marsh release oxygen and pop like 100 pricked balloons. The earthy smell of "pluff mud" will fill the air.

In brackish marshes slightly farther inland, along the tidal rivers, there will be more sediment, flushed from the upland, and greater plant diversity. In the shelter of the vegetation lie the nests of waterfowl; in the highest trees is, perhaps, the nest of a bald eagle. Three of the rivers, the Ashepoo, Combahee, and Edisto, form one of the largest estuarine systems on the East Coast— the ACE Basin, located in and around US 17 south of Charleston. Protection and expansion of the basin is assured by a consortium of federal, state, and private interests. Farther south, the Savannah Wildlife Refuge offers another opportunity to see these natural forces at work.

A Pleasing Music

A beautiful green frog inhabits the grassy, marshy shores of these large rivers. They are very numerous, and their noise exactly resembles the barking of little dogs, or the yelping of puppies: these likewise make a great clamour, but as their notes are fine, and uttered in chorus, by separate bands or communities, far and near, rising and falling with the gentle breezes, affords a pleasing kind of music.

—From *Travels of William Bartram*,
(First published in 1791; New York: Viking Penguin, 1988)

The Worlds of Islands and Cities

The barrier islands offer another view of the marine ecosystem. Developed or not, they maintain a sense of isolation and fragility at "the edge of the world." Even as they appear solid, they are in fact changing shape all the time: their dunes migrating, growing, eroding, their forests shaped by the unforgiving winds and salt spray. The lives of the birds and mammals that make their homes here are impacted daily by the elements. If the beach has suffered from erosion, oak-tree roots and upended palmettos will obstruct your path. As if to mock this rough beauty, dozens of sanderlings play at the water's edge, while overhead the big brown pelicans impose an order of their own as they fly in unerring formation.

Voluptuous Charm

Picket life was of course the place to feel the charm of the natural beauty on the Sea Islands. We had a world of profuse and tangled vegetation around us, such as would have been a dream of delight to me, but for the constant sense of responsibility and care which came between. Amid this preoccupation, Nature seemed but a mirage, and not the close and intimate associate I had before known. I pressed no flowers, collected no insects or birds' eggs, made no notes on natural objects, reversing in these respects all previous habits. Yet now, in the retrospect, there seems to have been infused into me through every pore the voluptuous charm of the season and the place; and the slightest corresponding sound or odor now calls back the memory of those delicious days.

—From *Army Life in a Black Regiment*
by Thomas Wentworth Higginson
(New York: W. W. Norton, 1984 [First published in 1869])

You may be lucky enough to participate in a late-night "turtle watch" when groups of residents observe the 300-pound loggerhead sea turtles drag themselves up the beach, dig holes, and lay eggs. On several barrier islands, teams of people are charged with marking the nests and moving the eggs to a secure hatchery, away from predators, poachers, and high tides. At the time of release, the hatchlings make their way to the ocean in groups of two and three, and then somehow, miraculously, paddle with their tiny fins to the open sea.

Precisely where these turtles go is not known. From Lowcountry marinas, it takes a big fishing boat several hours to reach the Gulf Stream, where, as every fisherman knows, the big, fighting fish swim—creatures that might eat a turtle in a second. And there are other giants in this marine wildness—the right whales and the manatees.

Coastal refuges show life in abundance; but even in the cities, away from the water's edge, you will be surrounded by natural beauty. In downtown Savannah, the parkways are filled to bursting with azaleas and flowering dogwood in the spring. Honeysuckle, jessamine, wisteria, and trumpet vine tumble wildly over garden walls or race up tree trunks. And then there are the birds: the tiny Carolina wren, practically domesticated as it makes its nest in a flower box; mourning doves cooing on telephone wires, and the ever-present mockingbird.

Mark Catesby, the naturalist who "discovered" the mockingbird in this region over 250 years ago, noted its fantastic ability to mimic. Today it is said that the bird can imitate 39

The Mock-Bird

This ancient sublime forest, frequently intersected with extensive avenues, vistas and green lawns, opening to extensive savannas and far distant Rice plantations, agreeably employs the imagination, and captivates the senses by scenes of magnificence and grandeur. The gay mock-bird, vocal and joyous, mounts aloft on silvered wings, rolls over and over, then gently descends, and presides in the choir of the tuneful tribes.

—From *Travels of William Bartram*,
(*New York: Viking Penguin, 1988 [First published in 1791]*)

songs and 50 call notes, not to mention the cackling of hens, the creak of old gates, and the croaking of frogs. Given the diversity and abundance of Lowcountry life, the mockingbird has songs enough for a lifetime.

Social History

Early Human Inhabitants

The Native Americans who ranged along the coast from the earliest days—as far back as 10,000 BC—have left the merest impression of their lives in patterned pottery shards, woven reed baskets, huge shell middens and rings, cypress-log canoes, and the remains of burial or religious sites scattered throughout the region. They also left their names, now anglicized in common usage, to confirm their presence in a dozen Lowcountry places. Some of the most prominent archaeological remains have been found on coastal islands— Hilton Head, Callawassie—suggesting that these early inhabitants possessed both geographic agility and a sense of territorial significance. Their population is thought to have numbered 50,000 at its peak.

Their society in the Lowcountry was divided into loose tribal confederations, each of which may have communicated in its own tongue. Summers were spent along the coast and on the coastal islands, farming and harvesting fish and shellfish; in winter they retreated inland, where they hunted deer and small game. An apparently abundant food supply and an absence of harshness in the climate or geography seem to have helped insure the stability of these native societies. Communal farming produced several crops a year of corn and bounteous harvests of beans, peas, pumpkin, and watermelon. The forests yielded wild fruits, nuts, berries, and other plants for food; roots and barks for medicinal drinks. Well-fortified towns, rimmed with circular stockades and enclosing an ever-burning ceremonial fire, established their home base.

Houses had the appearance of Quonset huts, long and domed. They were constructed of wooden frames over which mats, woven from palmetto fronds, could be draped, or, during hot weather, removed. Inside the walls were lined with benches for sleeping. Some houses were grander than others, featuring rooms and pillared platforms usually reserved for a chief or tribe member believed to have unusual wisdom or healing powers.

A larger structure, perhaps 200 feet in diameter, served as a community center for religious and social activities. Early European observers noted devout attention to ritual celebrations in praise of the harvest, accompanied by singing, dancing, and playing of instruments—cane flutes, drums, and rattles made from shells and seed pods. Some Native American games included forms of bowling and lacrosse. They laid their dead to rest, wrapped like swaddled babies, atop high scaffoldings.

Encounters with Europeans

By the time of their first encounters with white men, the coastal Native Americans had sorted themselves into various confederacies. From Charleston to the Savannah River lived a group of tribes known collectively as the Cusabo, including the Combahee, Ashepoo, Edisto, Stono, Wando, Kiawah, and Etiwan.

Their responses to the incursion of Europeans were mixed: Some were generous and open to trade, teaching the newcomers how to fish and make secure shelter, and in so doing probably saved their lives. Some Native Americans also shared farming techniques. One white settler told of his success in cultivating with one tribe such crops as grape vines, pomegranates, orange and fig trees, barley, onions, and garlic. Some Native Americans and their chiefs, known as caciques, helped the Frenchmen of Charlesfort build a ship, caulked with moss, for a return voyage to Europe. Some delivered to English explorers the prime high-bluff settings on which the newcomers laid the cities of Charles Town and Savannah. Some boarded ships and went abroad, or to Barbados.

Other accounts, however, report canoe flotillas fleeing in shock, the villagers hiding for days in the woods. Fighting and massacres were not unknown. Among the Europeans, the toll was largely on French and Spanish settlers, who were the first to land.

If the settlers faced an uneasy alliance with the Cusabo, the Cusabo themselves knew an even stronger enemy in the Westo, a vigorous inland tribe. Over time, the Westo dominated until they in turn were swept out by stronger tribes and the English settlers of early Charles Town.

By the time of persistent English colonization, toward the end of the 17th century, another tribe, the Yemassee, had gained prominence in the region. Once friendly with the Spanish explorers to the south and educated in their ways of civilization, this group shifted its allegiance to the English as its members migrated north. They proved to be loyal supporters of Colonel "Tuscarora Jack" Barnwell, a flamboyant Irishman who had recently come to the Lowcountry, in a campaign to subdue hostile North Carolina tribes. Barnwell, who is buried in St. Helena's Episcopal Churchyard in Beaufort, proved to be a diplomat, as well: In 1719, he was called on by the settlers of Charles Town to represent their grievances to the Lords Proprietors, an action that resulted in the formal establishment of a royal colony.

The Yemassee carried on a healthy deerskin trade with the new Europeans, and there developed over time a far-ranging network of agents, outposts, and agreements. Yet, finally, the very success of the enterprise and the pressure of increased migration onto native lands proved to be the colonists' undoing. Long-simmering resentment of unscrupulous traders, unfair taking of land, and abuse of their people led to a gathering of 15 Native American nations, who directed an assault from the Yemassee town at Pocotaligo. They attacked on Easter Sunday, 1715, killing as many traders as they could and sending the residents of Beaufort to their ships. The bloody Yemassee War lasted two years. At times, hundreds of warriors were dangerously close to Charles Town, reminding its residents of their isolation and pitiful protection under the crown. Eventually, the Yemassee forces disbanded and moved out of the region for good. By the middle of the 18th century, the last remnant tribes near Savannah had left the area.

The Settling of Charles Town

Carolina was originally known to Europeans as "Carolana," and it was the dream of the kings of Spain and France to have it. Their struggle for domination, played out on lands far distant from their own among native inhabitants who had been there for centuries, marked the earliest days of settlement.

The Spanish arrived first, in 1521, under the leadership of Francisco Gordillo: He named the Sea Island area Santa Elena. Further colonization was planned for but never materialized. Five years later, another Spaniard, Vasquez de Ayllon, having heard marvelous stories of the rich, vast land of Santa Elena, gathered 500 settlers and established his party at a point farther north along the coast. Their hopes, too, were to be dashed—by illness, a revolt among the slaves they had brought, attacks by Native Americans, and unusually harsh winter weather.

In 1562, Captain Jean Ribaut established Charlesfort, the first Protestant colony in North America, in the area he named Port Royal. Charlesfort, too, soon petered out and by 1566 the area belonged to the Spanish, who commenced to build a string of forts along the coast. In 1629, Charles I of England announced his intentions of ownership. In the end, it was the English claim that stuck, although the early residents of Charles Town faced Spanish, French, and Native forces several times before they were secure.

Time passed, however, before the English pursued their claim by actually settling. It took a monarch pressed to return favors—and a group of men with means, entrepreneurial spirit, and a keen sense of the market—to reap the benefits imagined for so long by so many. The monarch was Charles II, King of England during the Restoration. The group of men was Carolina's Lords Proprietors: Sir John Colleton, the Duke of Albermarle (George Monk), Lord Craven, Lord Berkeley, Sir William Berkeley, Sir George Carteret, the Earl of Clarendon, and Lord Ashley (Anthony Ashley Cooper).

The familiar nursery rhyme that calls Old King Cole a "merry old soul" might aptly have applied to Charles II. By 1663, restored to the throne after the dispatch of Cromwell, Charles found himself short of cash and facing obligations to those who had helped him in the late civil war. As a token of his appreciation, he gave to his loyal friends the territory "described in the parts of America not yet cultivated or planted, and only inhabited by some barbarous people who have no knowledge of Almighty God." This was to be the Carolina Province. Its development, particularly along the lower coast, was to define a society that exists today.

Planning for colonization began immediately. Sir John Colleton, who had lived among the planters in Barbados, convinced his associates of the need for expansion of the society there (already nearly 40 years old) and of the profits to be made in overseeing its relocation. In the summer of 1663, Captain William Hilton sailed the ship *Adventure* into Port Royal Sound, and their project began in earnest.

Hilton's successful foray and contact with friendly natives led to another exploratory trip three years later under the leadership of Captain Robert Sandford. This time, the English left behind Henry Woodward, a surgeon whose interest in the culture, language, and habits of the Native Americans was to ease the way, several years hence, for the first settlement at Charles Town. That day finally came in 1670 with the arrival of the ship *Carolina*, the only one of three ships to complete the voyage from England via Barbados.

It was at first unclear precisely where to settle—whether in the vicinity of Port Royal Sound, which Hilton had explored, or farther north, along the North Edisto River, where Sandford had ventured. Finally, after further viewing of both sites under the piloting and careful guidance of the *"cacique,"* or chief, of the Kiawah tribe, the colonists established a fort at Albermarle Point in the lands of the Kiawah, at Old Towne Creek up the Ashley River from present-day Charleston.

The earliest years of this colony have been brought to life at Charles Towne Landing which today offers a true sense of the importance of siting—high on a bluff from which unfriendly Spanish ships might be seen—and evidence of agricultural successes and failures. Small-scale farming worked; large cash crops, upon which rested the hopes of the Barbadian planters, didn't as yet.

In 1671, another shipload of colonists arrived, including more from Barbados, accompanied by their slaves; by the following year the colony consisted of 30 houses and 200 people.

The colonists prospered and gained confidence, such that by 1680 they had removed themselves from Albermarle Point to a site on the peninsula at the mouth of the harbor, where they laid out their city. From this time forward, the development of Charles Town—indeed of the entire Lowcountry of which it was the capital—proceeded rapidly.

Early Growth and Prosperity

Between 1690 and 1720, according to the historian Carl Bridenbaugh, the population of Charles Town tripled. New immigrants included French Huguenots and Irish, who established themselves in business and government. Wharves, churches, protective sea walls, defensive bastions, and homes were built. Streets were named (Church, Broad, Meeting, Tradd, and Queen are among those you can see today) and some of them were paved with oyster shells. Trade with the Native Americans was lively, and exports thrived: Deerskins and fur were shipped to England; pork, corn, naval stores, and lumber went to Barbados and the southern islands. The vast natural networks of creeks and rivers opened up the countryside to planters who raised beef and pork, cultivated cotton, rice, and indigo, and harvested lumber. And of course the waterways were crucial to transporting all these goods to Charles Town.

In governance, the influence of the Barbados colony continued to be felt in the key areas of law and representation by parish, and in the adoption of the slave code. The settlers from Barbados also imposed their architecture—the classic design with its raised basement and upstairs piazzas—and their intent to develop plantations outside the city limits. The increasing importation of slaves followed, an absolute essential in making large-scale agriculture a success.

Thus, from the very beginning, Charles Town was a society in which profitability and expansion—not to mention ease of living, even among the less grand—were inextricably tied to slaves and their management by law and custom. The historian Peter Wood estimates that by 1715 the slave population exceeded the European population.

Prosperity did not guarantee security, though. Charles Town faced threats from outsiders: There were skirmishes with Native Americans, Spanish soldiers, even pirates such as Blackbeard (Edward Teach) and Stede Bonnet. In 1718, 49 pirates were hanged.

Success in trade and a growing, more diverse population did, however, embolden the citizens to improve their lot. Prompted by resentment toward England (which refused to help pay for the defense of the city, attempted to enact trade restrictions, and raised the colonists' quitrents, among other heavy-handed actions), the citizens challenged the very form of proprietorship under which their colony had been established. In 1721, after much to-and-fro with England, the Carolina Province became a royal colony. By the 1730s, it was

Beaufort's cotton planters built homes to rival their Charleston peers

referred to by its new name, Charlestown. Only after the Revolution, when it was incorporated as the new state of South Carolina's first city, would it finally adopt the now-familiar spelling as Charleston.

Expansion in Colonial Lowcountry

Once people were settled, once they were safe, once they had established their markets and their means of production, and their slave workforce, the Lowcountry around colonial Charlestown started its meteoric climb to achieve what it eventually became: person for person, the wealthiest region in the colonies. It started with rice; continued with indigo, and finally came cotton. The fact that all these crops were suited to Lowcountry cultivation, that there was land to support them and slaves to work them, that there was desire abroad for their harvest (in some cases a bounty paid for it), and hefty profit to be made on it, left only a need for a class of men to seize the opportunity to grow rich. As was the case in other colonies, there were plenty of them, and they promptly did so.

The world they began to establish, the ways they embellished it, the physical order they imposed on it, and the choices they made to keep it alive defined Lowcountry culture right up to the Civil War. Even after that, even today, the echoes of those efforts resound in Lowcountry political, social, and economic life. In the deepest way, they form the basis of the stories people tell themselves about who they are.

As planters and their families spread out—and as new colonists continued to arrive from Barbados—they ventured across the Ashley River to Magnolia and Drayton Halls and Middleton Plantation; they went to Goose Creek and points inland; to Beaufort, across the Sea Islands of Kiawah, Seabrook, John's, Edisto, St. Helena, Lady's, and Hilton Head. In addition to their main house in the city, planters might establish a "big house" on one plantation and then own several others that were far more rustic, run by overseers and a slave crew. Profits were turned to acquire new land and more slaves. A merchant, having amassed a fortune in town, would follow a path similar to the one taken by this newly land-ed gentry. Planters were businessmen, and vice versa.

Thus emerged a small society that was at once far-flung across the Lowcountry but glued together by shared aspirations, tastes, assumptions about plantation life and the treatment of blacks, and very strongly by marriage.

The relation between city and country was intimate. Charlestown, already the throb-bing commercial heart of this society, came to display all its wealth. There were theatrical performances, clubs of every variety, subscription concerts followed by elaborate balls, racetracks, even a "season" that included "Race Week" in February. Some refinement had been brought to the wilderness. In fact, there was still a lot of wilderness: To the south, it was just being tamed. By 1742, when there were nearly 7,000 people living in Charlestown, Savannah's population numbered only in the hundreds.

The Founding of Savannah

By comparison with the settling of Charlestown, the founding of Savannah in 1733 was seen as a far less ambitious enterprise—and perhaps a morally loftier one. The colony began as the idea of a group of 20 Englishmen, who petitioned the Crown for a grant of land. They were known as the Trustees, and they had idealistic, philanthropic goals: Land would be held communally, settlers would be selected from "impoverished classes;" Trustees would pay for passage of settlers; there would be no liquor, slavery, or land speculation. The Trustees were given executive and legislative powers for 21 years. They could distribute land to settlers, but land was held in the Trustees' name.

The 114 or so settlers who arrived under the flag of King George were mostly of modest means, and their goal—as outlined by the Trustees—was the development of exports, including wine and silk. They were also supposed to defend the colony from the Spanish, and thus provide a buffer for prosperous Charlestown.

They were led by General James Oglethorpe, a high-minded Englishman with a caretak-er's concern for his flock, many of whom addressed him as "Father." Such was his sense of mission that when the ship *Ann* arrived in Charlestown harbor for consultations with the royal governor, the passengers were required to remain aboard and fish for their supper, so as not to have their heads turned by the glamorous city.

Continuing south, the *Ann* stopped at tiny Beaufort. Here passengers were allowed to fraternize with the residents, whose standard of living probably appeared to be more in line with what the newcomers, in the best of circumstances, might hope to accomplish. General Oglethorpe chose as his site for Savannah a place where "the river forms a half-moon, along the south side of which the banks are about 40 feet high, and on the top a flat, which they call a bluff." He was assisted by Colonel William Bull, a engineer from Charlestown with local surveying experience, and guided by Tomochichi, a friendly Yamacraw chief. The site was about 18 miles from the river's mouth on the Atlantic, on water sufficiently deep for ships drawing up to 12 feet to navigate within 10 yards of the shore.

Oglethorpe and Bull immediately addressed the task of planning the city, and it is the legacy of their inspired effort that distinguishes Savannah today. The city was, and is, a meticulously planned urban environment stretching back from the river in a series of squares and boulevards, which, then as now, are landscaped focal points. The basic form consisted of blocks of five symmetrical 60- by 90-foot lots encompassing 21 squares. Space was designated for public buildings and market areas, as well as for secure retreats, where settlers living outside the city limits could take cover in the event of Native American uprisings. The plan has been designated a National Historic Civil Engineering Landmark.

As things turned out, relations with the Native Americans remained friendly. Tomochichi supported the colonists' work throughout his life and was instrumental in winning the trust of tribes in the area. He was also willing to support Oglethorpe in battles with the Spanish, which were to occur sporadically over the next 10 years. The existence of a trading post nearby—run by John Musgrove, from South Carolina, and his wife, Mary, who was part Creek—also smoothed the way for natural contact.

Given such a propitious start, it was up to the settlers to clear and build, hunt and farm, and establish the Trustees' Garden. This they did, on the grants of 50 acres received by heads of families (five acres in the city, 45 outside it for farming). The settlers were also the beneficiaries of hundreds of head of livestock from their South Carolina neighbors, as well as rice and horses. For quite some time, even after Savannah got on its feet, South Carolina, and the port of Charlestown in particular, was to dominate the commercial life of the southern coast.

More settlers, including Irish, Scots, Swiss, Germans, and Italians, came very quickly. Jews and Protestant Salzburgers from the German-Austrian border area sought refuge from religious persecution. By 1741, there were 142 houses, a courthouse, jail, storehouse, market building, and a 10-acre, fenced public garden. By 1742, the liquor ban was repealed by popular demand.

Soon enough the settlers found that some of the original restrictions intended to guide development were hampering it. By 1749, the ban on slavery was repealed because settlers felt they could not compete with South Carolina's productivity and overseas trade. In 1750, the Trustees relinquished their hold on land (again, by popular demand): private property ownership ensued.

In 1752, when the original Trustee Charter was up for review, Parliament refused further aid. As a result, in 1754, the colony became a royal province with governance by a royal

A Savannah square

Built in the style of a Greek temple, and destroyed during the American Revolution and again in the Civil War, only the ruins of the Old Sheldon Church remain today

council appointed by the King. As such, the province was subject to all the taxes, levies, duties, etc. that the other American colonies endured.

Thus in a sense released from Oglethorpe's idealism, the colonists proceeded to develop plantations as their neighbors had. However, it took until the close of the French and Indian War in 1763 (when Florida was ceded to England) for Savannah to begin to flourish as a colonial city and primary port serving the Georgia backcountry. By the time of the Revolution, the South Carolina and Georgia colonies had settled lingering border disputes, were engaging freely in trade, and were communicating through four Lowcountry newspapers. The region had pulled together, united by shared commercial and social goals, and a culture deeply affected by slavery.

In 1775, a Provincial Congress was called because Savannah residents were as fed up with English governance and taxation as the rest of the colonies. In a show of solidarity and goodwill, the colony joined the Revolution.

The American Revolution

Ten years before reports of the battles of Lexington and Concord reached the Lowcountry, its residents were taking independent action to defy British rule, especially its methods of colonial governance and taxation. By the time of the Stamp Act in 1765, they had become wealthy, self-confident, and better organized in their own military defense. Having built their cities from scratch, they were in no mood to be further subjugated, and their responses were violent. In Charlestown, long-festering political disagreements between the colonists and the royal governor burst to the surface. They bitterly resented his order to move the Assembly and center of government to Beaufort, a day's journey by boat. In Savannah, where relations between colonists and governor had been more cordial, groups of Liberty Boys nevertheless were openly challenging loyalists and destroying British property.

By 1774, many colonists had become defiant. The merchants of Charlestown refused to buy tea that had been taxed, preferring to let it mold in the Exchange Building (which you can see today at the foot of Broad Street). British products were boycotted. Five delegates were sent to the First Continental Congress. In Savannah, leaders gathered at Tondee's Tavern to sign a petition denouncing the acts Parliament had passed in response to the Boston Tea Party (the Intolerable Acts) and insisting on their independent rights.

At this point, war seemed inevitable, even though there were loyalists throughout the Lowcountry who urged negotiation and reconsideration of non-importation policies. In 1776, four South Carolinians and three Georgians signed the Declaration of Independence. Colonial rule was over, but the fighting had just begun.

In the first significant victory of the Revolution (June 28, 1776, a day that is still celebrated in Charleston), General William Moultrie, outnumbered and outgunned, defeated an invading fleet of 50 British warships from his position on Sullivan's Island, in a fort built of palmetto logs. Visitors to the site today are impressed by the degree of risk and bravery that battle entailed.

But the Lowcountry was not yet secure. In December 1778, the British captured Savannah, and in May 1780, after a one-month siege, they finally subdued Charlestown. The British avenged the colonists by imprisoning and executing patriots. When they finally left the Lowcountry, in 1782, they were loaded down with war booty.

The American Revolution had a profound effect on stable Lowcountry society. It was nothing less than a civil war dividing families and generations. Robert Rosen points out in his book *A Short History of Charleston* that William Bull was for the king but his nephews for the revolutionaries. Daniel Heyward was a Tory, but his son Thomas signed the Declaration of Independence. Similar clashes of ideals and politics occurred in other prominent Lowcountry families such as the Draytons, Pinckneys, Manigaults, Horrys, and Hugers.

The political questions raised by the conflict sensitized new classes of people to their own self-interest. The governments that came into place afterwards reflected these diverse new motivations. No longer were mechanics and other artisans—"the little people"—satisfied with government dominated by the planter class, especially when planters' slaves soaked up most of the available work. As for the wealthy, they were forced to read the writing on the wall; fortunately, some of the Lowcountry's planters were themselves ardent patriots, and they adjusted to democratic government, though their influence remained out of proportion to their numbers.

The years following the Revolution saw a boom in population, in building, and in commerce. Many of the houses of the Lowcountry date from this Federal period, when new fortunes were made and old ones even further enhanced. If the architecture of the Lowcountry can be read as a book, this is its first great chapter.

Entrepreneurs, ship captains, military people, and merchants from New England came to the cities and Sea Islands to build their plantations. While the bounty on indigo was a casualty of war and led to a decline in that crop, the invention in 1793 of the cotton gin, on a plantation near Savannah, meant that the process of removing seeds from cotton could occur with greater ease and speed. Slaves working in the ginhouses still hand plucked seeds from the most highly prized strain then being grown: Sea Island cotton, whose long, silky fibers would be broken by the action of the gin. These seeds were saved, talked about, compared, and the best of them used for the following crop. Despite ups and downs in the cotton market and competition from the rest of the new American republic, for most of the next 60 years the Lowcountry flourished.

Plantation Life and Gullah Culture

The first African-American slave came to the Lowcountry to stay in 1670. Ever since then, slaves, freedmen, and their heirs have defined in the most essential way imaginable the politics, growth, lifestyle, culture, language, and habits of the Lowcountry. The complexity of relations between blacks and whites—who, in city or country, lived in close quarters and experienced daily contact but were governed by strict social codes enforced by penalties— has informed all Lowcountry history. Fear of black uprising, especially after the ill-fated Denmark Vesey rebellion in 1822, made for a regulation of life unknown outside the South.

For the best overview of slave life, visit The Charleston Museum. Or drive to Middleton Place, another site that, with its landscaped gardens and farmyard, offers splendid evidence of the world the slaves built. Imagine the daily bustle of slaves around what is now Charleston's Market Area, or in Savannah's waterfront warehouses, now restored.

When out and about in the Lowcountry and thinking about its past, probably the two most significant things to recognize are the immense enterprise that characterized plantations (where they now may be silent and grand, they were once fantastically busy places with dozens of buildings) and the isolation the slaves endured there.

The world of the plantation was self-sufficient, marked by dozens of specific activities taking place according to the season: gathering marsh hay for fertilizer; harvesting, clearing, and burning the fields; building and repairing; growing food crops; moting and ginning cotton, packing it in the cotton house, taking it to the landing to be shipped on barges. Within that world of action, and responding to its often-crushing demands, there arose a culture among slaves, now generally called the Gullah culture, which included elements of their African past. Scholars have identified these remnant "Africanisms" in religious and mythical beliefs; in patterns of speech and dress; in basketry, art, dance, and song. In its totality, Gullah is a way of life that informed—and still informs—the manner in which slaves and their descendants managed their relationship toward white people and kept intact some expression of their own identity.

From the earliest days, black slaves from certain rice-growing regions of the West African coast were prized for their knowledge of that crop's cultivation. Rice-growing is a delicate business. It requires periodic flooding of fields; the design, building, and maintenance of a dike-and-gate system; and hundreds of people, including children, to protect the rice plants from birds, gather it in, separate the grain from the chaff by means of seagrass "fanner baskets," and clean it with mortar and pestle. In all of these areas, black people were experienced, and they taught what they knew.

Indigo and cotton crops demanded other kinds of hard labor—in preparing the fields with usually nothing more than a hoe and a plow-dragging ox; in building pits to soak the indigo or in chopping weeds to free the cotton plants; in extracting the dye or in picking tufts from spiky bolls. Labor was apportioned by "tasks" of land, a task being about a quarter of an acre, for which slaves were responsible. Plantation ledgers were organized around work completed according to this system. In addition, slaves were used as carpenters, blacksmiths, cooks, loggers, boat-builders, butchers, and house-servants. While planters left at the onset of "the sickly season" to escape malaria, blacks were immune to this fever and worked through the miasmic heat of summer.

A caste system grew up within the population that served the needs of the plantation master: slaves associated with domestic life were at the top and field hands were at the bottom. Becoming a black "driver" meant that a slave would work with an overseer to direct crews; it also meant meting out punishment and whippings to fellow slaves. With blacks outnumbering whites by vast majorities, keeping order through work and brutality was essential to the plantation system.

The treatment of slaves varied widely in the Lowcountry. It is important to remember that while the majority of white people in the city and the country owned slaves, only a very small portion of them owned more than a dozen. Some planters bought and sold families; some kept them together, some did not. Some allowed friendships or marriage to occur between plantations; some took skilled slaves to the city and hired them out. Some planters allowed slaves to hunt and fish, keep gardens, raise fowl, and sell eggs. Some gave them staples—molasses, cloth, tobacco, shoes—on a periodic basis.

Slaves lived in cabins or slave rows that shared a common wall and had dirt floors. On the plantations they worshipped at praise houses—usually small, clapboard buildings lined with benches—where services were marked by recitations of the gospel, praying, and the singing of spirituals in which an elder "deaconed out" a line and the worshippers respond-ed in unison. They buried their dead in separate slave cemeteries, dozens of which are in still in use today.

Whatever the specific case, a slaves' identity (and that of his family) was tied to one place, which he might never leave during his lifetime. If ever he did travel it was under a strict pass or ticket system. His fortunes were often tied to one white family, and his heirs to its heirs. Education of slaves was either haphazard or strictly forbidden.

It is not possible to overestimate the way in which the Civil War disrupted the order imposed by the plantation world and the society it held in check. When recovery was to come to the Lowcountry, it would come to the countryside last.

The Civil War and the Years of Poverty

If the Lowcountry is seen by visitors as a place rich in references to the Civil War, both physical and spiritual, perhaps it is because there was such a difference in the "before" and "after." The cataclysmic changes wrought by that great conflict are well known.

Perhaps less well known is the fact that even before the Civil War, the Lowcountry already had been undergoing a slow transformation. Historians point to a definite drift of the Lowcountry after the 1820s, from occupying a place at the center of colonial and post-Revolutionary commerce to becoming just one of many prosperous regions in the South.

The Lowcountry's golden age was, in fact, the now-distant time of relative innocence and optimism long before the antebellum era, a time of cosmopolitan outlook and quiet accommodation with the rest of the country that was lost during the overheated days immediately prior to the Civil War. (It has only been in the later years of the 20th century— some might say as recently as the great resort booms, the "second Yankee invasion"—that the Lowcountry has been able to consider itself as reentering the mainstream of American culture.) The nostalgia for long-lost days, which most every visitor to the Lowcountry feels, is probably for a time more nearly 200 years ago than 140.

By the 1850s, due to a number of factors, including the price and availability of cotton elsewhere, protective tariffs for new industries in the north, and the emergence of the abolitionist movement, the Lowcountry had lost its position of national preeminence. As a result, its outlook became more narrowly regional. Political positions hardened; tolerance for a national view of things receded. The institution of slavery was viewed less as a neces-sary evil—possibly temporary—and more as a positive benefit, one from which Southerners could not turn back. And there were politicians, like John C. Calhoun, who made an eloquent case for this vision. As Mary Boykin Chesnut wrote in her diary at the time of

> Secession is the fashion here. Young ladies sing for it; old ladies pray for it; young men are dying to fight for it; old men are ready to demonstrate it.
>
> —From a dispatch to the London *Times*, April 1861, sent from Charleston by English journalist William Howard Russell

secession: "South Carolina had been rampant for years. She was the torment of herself and everyone else. Nobody could live in this state unless he were a fire-eater."

Of course, life did go on, populations increased, profits were made. Charleston and Savannah grew, with the addition of magnificent mansions in the Greek Revival style—such as Charleston's Edmondston-Alston House—or in the Regency style—such as the William Scarbrough House in Savannah. Small towns like Beaufort raised their own gentry. Nonetheless, planters' societies that might, in the past, have discussed nothing more ominous than crop yields, seed types, and the accounting practices of their agents and cotton factors, now found their attentions turned to defensive matters concerning their slaves, their fortunes, and their state's rights.

In December 1860, led by Lowcountry Secessionists, South Carolina separated itself from the Union. The following year, Georgia followed suit. Soon, the harbor forts that watched over both cities—Fort Sumter and Fort Pulaski—were battle sites. Both of the forts can be visited today, and the story of their defense is a dramatic one.

Additional glimpses of the Civil War period are poignantly on display at the Confederate Museum in Charleston, with its frayed uniforms and flags, and in the Green-Meldrim House in Savannah, headquarters of General Sherman, who, having completed his victorious March to the Sea in 1864, not only celebrated Christmas in Savannah but also offered the city itself as a gift to President Lincoln.

Born into slavery, Robert Smalls was a Civil War hero and prominent Reconstruction-era congressman from Beaufort.

A less well known chapter of Civil War history, having Beaufort as its center, concerns the efforts on the part of Northern abolitionists to live among the newly freed slaves and prepare them for full "citizenship." The enterprise followed by several months the Union invasion of Port Royal in November 1861. Over the next several years, a hundred or so men and women took up residence in the abandoned plantation houses, managed the plantations for the government, which looked to cotton crops for revenue, and set up schools for slaves young and old in front parlors and cotton houses.

After the Civil War, the Lowcountry, now impoverished, turned in upon itself.

It was as if people simply went home and stayed there, hoarding their gentility in their city homes as they might their last pennies, taking in sewing, teaching, and boarding guests. In the country they concentrated on making a living again as farmers, albeit far more modest ones. People were thrown back on their resources—fishing, hunting, and farming—and they made do. Only small numbers of freedmen actually received, and were able to hang on to, land they had been promised.

Although phosphate mining, timbering, and shipyards emerged as centers of postwar activity, the economy was slow to repair itself. An idea of just how poor conditions were, right up until World War II, can be glimpsed in the work of Walker Evans, Marion Post Wolcott, and other photographers sent by the Farm Security Administration to document Lowcountry life.

As it turns out, the legacy of poverty was just as crucial in preserving the built environment of the Lowcountry as prosperity had been, in the early years, for bringing it to life. As early as the 1920s, Charlestonians were organizing to save their old buildings. In 1931, the city passed the nation's first Historic District zoning ordinances; some 20 years later, the Historic Savannah Foundation was founded to oppose the demolition of the Isaiah Davenport House.

Ever since, these cities' Historic Districts and properties in the country nearby have been central attractions to generations of tourists. They have provided architects, landscape gardeners, historians—even novelists—with material for inspiration. It is a remarkable testament to the Lowcountry's enduring legacy and powers of regeneration that, despite all this scholarly trawling, the region doesn't seem fished out.

The Lowcountry Legacy

Through all its changes, the Lowcountry landscape has retained its immense allure for those who have lived and traveled here, from roving early settlers to today's nomads of the bus tour. Perhaps this is because a sense of history and a sense of place intersect at so many points in the Lowcountry. There is no high ground here. History itself provides the only vantage point, the only way to detach oneself from an insular sense of place that is always responding to forces—of wind and tide, of society and war—greater than itself. It was and is a place to be desired. Whether your quest is satisfied by filling a bucket with oysters, paddling a canoe in the marsh, or visiting an old home accompanied by nothing more than your imagination, the Lowcountry offers a rare chance to enact and to observe the subtle rituals of the past, and to take from them, for yourself, the pleasures they've delivered for so long to so many.

To describe our growing up in the lowcountry of South Carolina, I would have to take you to the marsh on a spring day, flush the great blue heron from its silent occupation, scatter marsh hens as we sink to our knees in the mud, open you an oyster with a pocketknife and feed it to you from the shell and say, "There. That taste. That's the taste of my childhood." I would say, "Breathe deeply," and you would breathe and remember that smell for the rest of your life, the bold, fecund aroma of the tidal marsh, exquisite and sensual, the smell of the South in heat, a smell like new milk, semen, and spilled wine, all perfumed with seawater.

—From *The Prince of Tides* by Pat Conroy
(Boston: Houghton Mifflin Company)
©1986 by Pat Conroy

A joggling board in a hidden Charleston garden

2

CHARLESTON

A City of Stories

Charleston is one of the nation's oldest urban environments. It has been the site of some
of the most dramatic and significant events in American history, and it has an architectural
inventory that is more varied and abundant than any other city in America. As a colonial
city, and then as a regional capital for more than 300 years, it has a continuity of culture.

To a visitor, awareness of this cultural legacy may seem quaint or idiosyncratic. It is in
fact a meaningful and pervasive sentiment, one that informs the smallest turn of phrase
and the largest civic hopes of people who have long viewed their city as a place apart, a
place with values so closely held that residents would, and did, die for them. In such a
world (Charlestonians have called their home "The Holy City" with only a trace of irony) it
is not surprising that when residents talk with visitors about Charleston's history—about
its essence—they begin by talking about relationships: Those between the races, between
and among individuals and families, between the region and the rest of the country.

Compounding this sense of intimacy with the past is its indisputable physical expression in the city's man-made and natural landscape. For while it is one thing to tell a story
of times gone by, it is quite another to be able to locate that narrative, and to read it, in an
urban setting that still exists and reverberates with meaning. This quality is at the core of
the city's cultural identity, more important than buildings or objects, although are plenty
of them, too. Charleston is a city of culture because people still believe that a sense of history and of place distinguishes their lives.

Charleston has stayed small—some might say defiantly so—in a way different than any
other region in the United States. Unlike many American places, it was not compelled to
reinvent itself over time. The traditional cultural pleasures to be had in dress balls, small
concerts, the cultivation of gardens, card playing, church picnics, and literary societies
continued for generations. The life of the plantation, in which families would be absent
from the city except in seasonal bursts, heightened the importance of domestic culture: It
has been said that without the plantations, set at some distance from each other, there
would have been no tradition of Southern hospitality, nor the development of the domestic
art of "visiting," so significant to this day.

Most obviously, Charleston stayed the same for so long because it liked what it was. It
preferred its provincial insularity to what it perceived as vulgarity elsewhere. And, especially in the early years of this century, it was too worn down to do much but carry on in the
old ways, its people too habituated to the familiar social roles they inherited long after the
society which had assigned those roles had been wiped out. They couldn't step out of their
skins, and, for the most part, didn't want to.

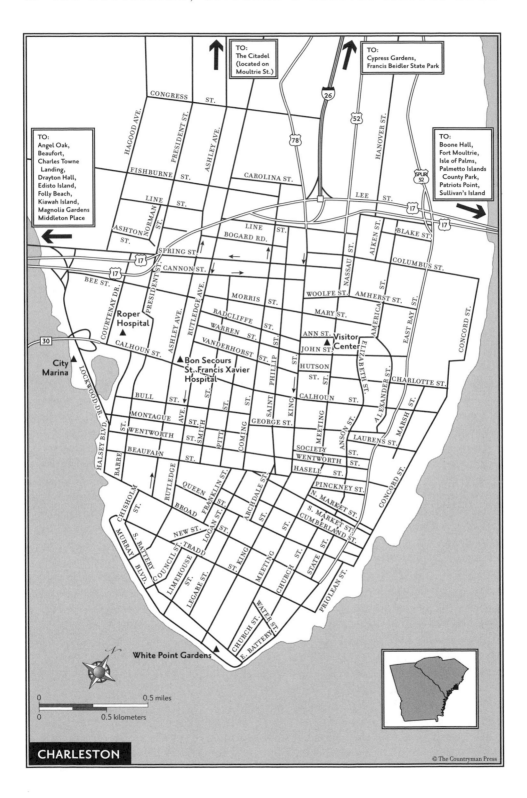

TO:
The Citadel
(located on
Moultrie St.)

TO:
Cypress Gardens,
Francis Beidler State Park

TO:
Angel Oak,
Beaufort,
Charles Towne
Landing,
Drayton Hall,
Edisto Island,
Folly Beach,
Kiawah Island,
Magnolia Gardens
Middleton Place

TO:
Boone Hall,
Fort Moultrie,
Isle of Palms,
Palmetto Islands
County Park,
Patriots Point,
Sullivan's Island

Roper
Hospital

City
Marina

Bon Secours
St. Francis Xavier
Hospital

Visitor
Center

White Point Gardens

0   0.5 miles
0   0.5 kilometers

CHARLESTON

© The Countryman Press

King Street house, Charleston

But when the time came, in the 1920s, to protect the life they knew and valued, Charlestonians acted. They did not do so violently, as in the case of Fort Sumter, but using political talent, hard work, and a potent sense of what mattered residents enacted the country's first historic preservation ordinance, protecting buildings and sites that otherwise might have been destroyed in the name of "progress."

The success of preservation efforts in the ensuing 75 years has meant that the past has been brought forward for all to see: in individual houses, in neighborhoods, and in whole districts. The city has become a colorful tapestry and a magnificent backdrop for all sorts of cultural activities.

Like the historic sections of the city, cultural activities keep brushing themselves up, reinvestigating the old, and cultivating the new. For every historic house there seems to be an art gallery; for every plantation house tour, a much deeper investigation into the life of slaves. Where blossoming gardens were once celebrated informally, now programs and walks guide a visitor's appreciation. The spirituals of the praise houses and the blues of the cotton fields are performed for bigger audiences. Modest sailing regattas have become Water Festivals.

Perhaps no event showcases Charleston like the annual Spoleto Festival, held for several weeks in May and June (for information see the Spoleto entry in the **Culture** section). Dozens of operatic, theatrical, dance, and musical performances transform the city. Fine art exhibits and lecture series proliferate. Performers and artists with international reputations take up residence and flock to restaurants and parks. The city itself sponsors a companion arts festival, Piccolo Spoleto, made up of free events at outdoor sites.

Putting aside all of the activity that enlivens Charleston, it is enough to say that it is a marvelous city because it has escaped the trend that architectural critic Ada Louise Huxtable calls the "theming of America" in which "authentic reproductions" of the past are constructed from scratch based on selected remnants: Charleston has no need to be replaced by a neater version of itself to be understood.

GETTING THERE

Charleston International Airport (www.chs-airport.com) is your destination, served by major airlines (Continental, Delta, Northwest, US Airways, and United Express) with direct flights from cities across the United States. It's an easy place to negotiate, well-designed, with few of those anonymous spaces and corridors that make traveling endless and tiresome. Rental cars from several agencies are available; when returning your car, there's convenient, no waiting, parking lot check-in. Expect to pay about $10 per person for shuttle service to peninsular Charleston, about $22–$25 for a cab (for two passengers; $10 extra for a third.) The larger hotels offer their own shuttle service—ask when you book your rooms. **Greyhound** (843-744-4247 or 1-800-231-2222; www.greyhound.com; North Charleston) serves the area with a depot about 20 minutes from downtown. **Amtrak** (843-744-8264 or 1-800-872-7245; www.amtrak.com; 4565 Gaynor Ave.;) travels the north-south corridor, making daily stops at North Charleston about 25 minutes from downtown. By car, Charleston is located at exits off I-95 via I-26 heading east, about 30 minutes to downtown. Parking downtown may be non-existent, difficult, or costly. Check with your B&B, inn, or hotel about parking.

The distance from Washington to Charleston is 512 miles; from Jacksonville to Charleston is 241 miles; from Asheville via I-40 to I-26 is 265 miles. From Charlotte, take I-77 south to I-20 at Columbia; follow I-20 for a few exits to link up with I-26 east. Distance to Charleston: 200 miles. From Atlanta take I-75 to I-16. When it crosses I-95 go north for Charleston, 286 miles.

LODGING

When President George Washington toured the states of the new nation in 1791, he was determined to observe life as it was lived on all levels of society. In the Lowcountry, he accepted the enthusiastic hospitality of the planters—he was rowed in their barges by slaves dressed in finery, and took meals in their mansions—but he preferred to spend the night in the "public houses" that existed along the main highways, in the simple places frequented by messengers and mail carriers, small farmers and merchants. He even paid his own way when he was permitted.

The public houses of Washington's day are long gone, but the modest style of overnight lodging they offered, of clean rooms, shared bathrooms and communal meals, existed well into the 20th century. It was a custom, like most, that had its roots in necessity: During the years of poverty following the Civil War, taking in guests provided income for families or Confederate widows, who still lived in the commodious old houses.

These days, if you stay in an old home that has been transformed into a glossy bed & breakfast—and they are among the most romantic lodging options—the only Confederate widow in evidence will be in a portrait on the wall. They are elegant places, with Jacuzzi tubs and fireplaces: You are likely to hang your clothes in an antique armoire or view from your window walled gardens rimmed with flower beds and dense with camellias and azaleas.

Charleston also has first-rate luxury hotels; several inns and hotels renovated from larger commercial buildings; modest chain hotels; and, on its outskirts, dazzling beach resorts. The lodgings included here represent a sampling of offerings in all of these categories. The list is by no means complete because building and remodeling go on apace. Places at the beach—a house in a neighborhood or a villa in a gated resort—are plentiful, and generally handled by agents or through individual resorts.

Each option carries with it unique possibilities for you to consider. Although the distance between Charleston and the beach is not great, if you intend to spend most of your time in the city, to shop and eat out and take part in cultural life, you may not want to travel 25 to 35 minutes to the beach for a night's sleep. Alternatively, if golf, tennis, boating, and being on the ocean are at the center of your vacation, or especially if you're traveling with children, it might be wise to make a resort or rental home your base, and travel to Charleston by day. Of course, for trips lasting several days, many combinations of lodging are possible.

The hospitality industry is highly evolved here: More than 3 million people visit the area each year. The large hotels provide every amenity you'd expect. The luxury inns outdo each other in finishing touches: chocolates at bedtime, daily newspapers delivered with your breakfast, afternoon tea or refreshments served gratis in gardens, parlors, or courtyards. Even the B&B units, where a home's owner is your host, offer helpful extras like jogger's maps, a selection of restaurant menus, tips on neighborhood sights, even history lessons from the house-proud.

If you're traveling with children, some hotels and inns can recommend on-site baby-sitting services. You should inquire and make specific arrangements in advance. Some places discourage guests traveling with children; others have rules as to minimum ages and the placement and cost of extra beds in the room. At the resorts, well-staffed activity programs occupy the younger set.

If you have special needs, ask to see if they can be accommodated. Pets, for example, are sometimes allowed; smoking is always regulated, often allowed only on balconies or in courtyards, sometimes forbidden on the property. Wheelchair access, by ramps or elevators, in bathrooms or bedrooms does vary. Off-street parking is usually provided by larger establishments. Confirm the arrangement or fee with smaller ones and private-home accommodations. Respect deposit/cancellation policies, as they are strictly followed in smaller inns and B&Bs. For more information website addresses have been included where applicable.

Rates

Inexpensive	Up to $60
Moderate	$60 to $120
Expensive	$120 to $200
Very Expensive	$200 and up

These rates do not include room taxes or special service charges that might apply during your stay.

Credit cards
AE—American Express
DC—Diner's Club
CB—Carte Blanche
MC—MasterCard
D—Discover Card
V—Visa

Hotels and Larger Inns
Charleston Place
843-722-4900 or 1-800-611-5545.
www.charlestonplacehotel.com.
205 Meeting St., Charleston, SC 29401.
Price: Expensive to Very Expensive.
Credit Cards: AE, D, DC, MC, V.

The construction of this luxury hotel nearly 20 years ago, with its own elegant shops and

Fountain at Charleston Place

the cachet to draw brand-name stores to the neighborhood, signaled a fateful change in the look and feel of downtown historic Charleston. It's a microclimate now, with Saks, Talbot's, and the like, a part of but slightly apart from, the old Charleston. It hums by day and night with well-dressed tourists and conventioneers, and offers a premium and convenient Charleston address. There are two restaurants, a popular bar, a sensational pool and spa. Its dramatic decorations—a grand curved staircase, a huge chandelier, massive pots of flowers, shiny marble floors, and rooms of polished furniture—make it a destination. Special rate packages, which include tickets to Spoleto performances, and very reasonable off-season rates, are worth looking into.

Embassy Suites—Historic District

843-723-6900 or 1-800-362-2779.
www.charleston-hotels.net.
337 Meeting St., Charleston, SC 29403.
Price: Moderate to Expensive.
Credit Cards: AE, D, DC, MC, V.

This large chain has managed a fine makeover of the 19th-century Citadel building where generations of Southern boys attended military school. It still looks formidable, with massive, theatrical palm trees, a courtyard, and crenellated turrets, but the outdoor pool and sundeck soften the institutional edges. The two-room suites allow for flexibility (the living rooms have a sleeper sofa) if you're traveling with children or need a workspace, and also convenience, with mini-kitchens and televisions. Located near the Visitor Center where many tours and trolley service originate.

Francis Marion Hotel

843-722-0600 or 1-877-756-2121.
www.francismarioncharleston.com.
387 King St., Charleston, SC 29403.
Price: Expensive to Very Expensive.
Credit Cards: AE, D, DC, MC, V.

Newly restored and awarded membership in the Historic Hotels of America (affiliated with the National Trust for Historic

Preservation), this was a solid 1920s hotel to begin with: wide stairs and hallways, wood paneling, plaster moldings covered in gold-leaf, a lobby with big windows and club chairs, and high ceilings. Today there are 226 guest rooms, including suites of various configurations for extended families. It overlooks Marion Square (with great views of Charleston from rooms on the upper floors), and from the snazzy new coffee bar you can watch the goings on in the upbeat College of Charleston neighborhood.

Harbour View Inn
843-853-8439 or 1-888-853-8439.
www.harbourviewcharleston.com.
2 Vendue Range, Charleston, SC 29401.
Price: Expensive to Very Expensive.
Credit Cards: AE, D, DC, MC, V.

Just steps from the Waterfront Park and featuring many rooms with stunning views and harbor breezes, this new hotel has the right mix of elegance and understatement. The minimalist feel to the rooms empha-sizes volume and light over decoration: sea grass/rush carpeting, cream-colored walls, big windows (some with broad slatted "plantation" shutters), perhaps one framed print, and an armoire made by a local woodworking company. Many of the rooms have fireplaces, some have balconies, some have whirlpool baths. A good deal of atten-tion is paid to details here, even in the choice, framing, and hanging of art in the hallways, and it really shows.

King Charles Inn
843-723-7451 or 1-866-546-4700.
www.kingcharlesinn.com.
237 Meeting St., Charleston, SC 29401.
Price: Moderate to Expensive.
Credit Cards: AE, D, DC, MC, V.

A Best Western choice for visitors on a budget. An outdoor pool is located on an elevated, screened terrace, affording good privacy for an establishment that's in the heart of downtown. It may be modest but the service is attentive, there's parking, and the location is unbeatable.

The Mills House
843-577-2400 or 1-800-874-9600.
www.millshouse.com.
115 Meeting St., Charleston, SC 29401.
Price: Expensive to Very Expensive.
Credit Cards: AE, D, DC, MC, V.

This is a big, bustling hotel with marble floors, glittering chandeliers, and a mid-19th century feel where you can relax and people-watch from the cozy "Best Friend Bar" or from a banquette in the lobby. (Nightly entertainment increases the foot traffic.) There are 214 guest rooms and 19 suites, decorated with reproduction furni-ture, loosely Victorian in style to recall the original Mills House Hotel, which dated from 1853. After a day of walking, you may want to relax in the courtyard, take a few laps in the pool, or stretch out on the deck with the newspaper.

Renaissance Charleston Hotel
843-534-0300 or 1-800-468-3571.
www.renaissancehotels.com.
68 Wentworth St., Charleston, SC 29401.
Price: Expensive.
Credit Cards: AE, D, MC, V.

A large hotel (166 rooms) with an outdoor heated pool and fitness center, in a good location just north of Market St. and the hipper location of upper King Street. Luxury, yes, with granite counters, wireless Internet, two-line phones, and decor a lit-tle more mainstream than other hotels (more colors, valances, and dust ruffles), but locals send their business here—management is well known to be thoughtful about its small-business neighbors and has recommendations for shopping and dining that are not obvious.

Smaller Luxury Inns

Ansonborough Inn

843-723-1655 or 1-800-522-2073.
www.ansonboroughinn.com
21 Hasell St., Charleston, SC 29401.
Price: Moderate to Expensive.
Credit Cards: AE, D, MC, V.

This circa-1900 stationer's warehouse two
blocks from the City Market was given new
life as an all-suite inn, but reminders of
its past use—including huge beams, plank
floors, and walls of exposed brick—remain
to good effect. Each of the 37 suites has a
wet bar including microwave and mini-
refrigerator, modem hookups, and varieties of bed sizes so that your suite can
accommodate comfortably everyone in
your party.

Battery Carriage House Inn

843-727-3100 or 1-800-775-5575.
www.batterycarriagehouse.com.
20 South Battery, Charleston, SC 29401.
Price: Expensive.
Credit Cards: AE, MC, V.

The main house at Number 20 South
Battery was built in 1843, and today's visitors stay in rooms beneath and behind it, in
the old carriage house. South Battery
defines the edge of the historic residential
district known as "South of Broad." This is
the neighborhood that comes to mind when
most people think of Charleston, a place of
iron gates entwined with jasmine, houses
with massive columns set on high founda-
tions, narrow streets, and families like your
innkeepers, the Hasties to whom the house
has belonged for several generations. There
is one suite and 11 rooms, whose small
dimensions are alleviated by access to a
narrow piazza and a lovely back garden.
Continental breakfast and the newspaper
arrive at your door, or you can start your
day under the rose arbor.

Fulton Lane Inn

843-720-2600 or 1-800-720-2688.
www.charminginns.com.
202 King St., Charleston, SC 29401.
Price: Moderate to Very Expensive.
Credit Cards: AE, D, DC, MC, V.
Handicap Access: Two rooms.
A non-smoking inn.

This inn is located between King and
Meeting Streets amid the downtown antique
and gallery district. The 27 rooms have a
refreshing, airy, look: sisal, wicker, and
muslin decorating accents; louvered shutters; wall-coverings and paint in soft, liquid
colors like celadon, pale peach, and lemon.
The feel is summer in the Lowcountry—all
year long. You can go simple or go deluxe,
with canopied beds and fireplaces, kitchens,
and cathedral ceilings; all rooms have either
one king-sized bed or two queen-sized beds.
Part of a local consortium of inns with good
service and referrals.

Governor's House Inn

843-720-2070 or 1-800-720-9812.
www.governorshouse.com.
117 Broad St., Charleston, SC 29401.
Price: Expensive to Very Expensive.
Credit Cards: None.

The Governor who lived in the Governor's
House was Edward Rutledge, who at 26
signed the Declaration of Independence and
at 30 was a patriot under arrest. He may have
suffered at the hands of the British, but the
stunning restoration of this grand home
suggests he appreciated the finer things in
life. There are 11 guest rooms—the nicest
among them have 12-foot ceilings and their
own verandah access with rooftop views of
the South of Broad neighborhood—including
two suites (one on each floor) in the kitchen
house dependency, featuring its original
1760 fireplace, now converted to gas. With
over-the-top marble bathrooms, it's an
excellent spot for an indulge-yourself weekend; it's not a place for kids.

John Rutledge House Inn

843-723-7999 or 1-800-476-9741.
www.charminginns.com.
116 Broad St., Charleston, SC 29401.
Price: Expensive to Very Expensive.
Credit Cards: AE, D, MC, V.

Tradition has it that John Rutledge (who later signed the U.S. Constitution) built this imposing house around 1763 for his bride, Elizabeth Grimke. The antique furnishings, parquet floors, high ceilings, carved mantelpieces, and rich fabrics that characterize the house today suggest its original opulence, such as might have impressed President George Washington when he visited. Nineteen rooms are offered to guests, either in the main house or in two carriage houses. Suites in the main house include an additional sitting room and fireplace; some have Jacuzzi tubs. Continental breakfast is included and full breakfast is available. A big plus to staying here is the use of a charming courtyard, sheltered from the street, where you may gather to relax, eat, have a cocktail or late-night snack.

Planters Inn

843-722-2345 or 1-800-845-7082.
www.plantersinn.com.
112 N. Market St., Charleston, SC 29401.
Price: Expensive to Very Expensive.
Credit Cards: AE, D, DC, MC, V.

A location at the intersection of N. Market St. and Meeting St. makes this 62-room inn superbly convenient to nightlife, shopping, the Gibbes Museum, and the historic residential areas. You can walk in any direction and find something going on—the closest Charleston comes to having a "big city" feel. The service is superior and the rooms elegant, many with fireplaces and four-poster beds. The acclaimed Peninsula Grill restaurant is located here.

Two Meeting Street Inn

843-723-7322.
www.twomeetingstreetinn.com.
2 Meeting St., Charleston, SC 29401.
Price: Expensive to Very Expensive.
Credit Cards: None.
A non-smoking inn.

This Queen Anne mansion, with its wraparound porches and rocking chairs, has passed the age of 100, but may never have looked better. (Given Charleston, it's young almost to the point of new.) Its oak-paneled sitting rooms and guest rooms are filled with Oriental rugs and period accessories, and highlighted by fabrics and wall-coverings in rich, deep colors. There are nine rooms on three floors, all with private baths (some with Victorian-style tubs), some with private balcony access. This is the place for honeymooners and celebrating couples who often book a year in advance—especially for those rooms with canopied four-posters needing a special set of stairs to reach. Continental breakfast is served, and there is an elaborate afternoon tea. Minimum stays are required on holidays and weekends. Children over 12 are welcomed.

Wentworth Mansion

843-853-1886 or 1-888-466-1886.
www.wentworthmansion.com.
149 Wentworth St., Charleston, SC 29401.
Price: Very Expensive.
Credit Cards: AE, D, DC, MC, V.

Visitors worship Charleston's 18th-century and antebellum architecture, but this Second Empire–style mansion (built in 1886 for a cotton baron) will turn your head. For sheer per-square-foot, Gilded Age extravagance, it has no peer: carved plasterwork ceilings, marble fireplaces, Tiffany glass, mahogany paneling, intricately tiled floors, and a cupola accessed by a stairway for the brave, which yields a panoramic view of the city. And that's what was there before millions were spent on deluxe renovation and antiques. Today there are 21 sumptuous guest rooms and suites, many with separate Jacuzzis and walk-in showers, some with private porches, almost all with fireplaces. A continental breakfast buffet is set on a sun porch; a classic gentleman's library is a late-night refuge. One of Charleston's best restaurants, Circa 1886, is in the Carriage House.

Bed & Breakfast Lodgings in Private Homes and Gardens

A central reservation service, **Historic Charleston Bed and Breakfast** (843-722-6606 or 1-800-743-3583; www.historiccharlestonbedandbreakfast.com; 57 Broad St., Charleston, SC 29401) offers some 50 listings of rooms with private baths in homes or their garden dependencies in Charleston's historic neighborhoods. Their phone lines are open weekdays from 9–5. Credit cards (MC, V) can be used to book a deposit, but the balance is usually cash or check only. Other useful sources of information are provided by the **South Carolina Bed & Breakfast Association** (1-888-599-1234; www.southcarolinabedandbreakfast.com), whose on-line listings provide the information necessary to make a choice and www.bbonline.com, a national listing service. There are bargains, especially if you're willing to leave the South of Broad/Market neighborhood, but flexibility and adventure might be the real draw—the chance to feel like a local, sit in a courtyard and read, bring a picnic home at midday. Some accommodations are well suited to larger parties, families, or couples traveling together, and they may also have their own kitchen facilities, gardens, and bicycles for you to use. The service makes a good match if you have some sense of what you want.

You may also contact individuals directly or book lodgings that are not owner-occupied but not exactly commercial,

either. Places of this sort may be as large as four rooms and quite private. Credit cards that are accepted are noted. Otherwise, cash, personal check, or traveler's check is acceptable.

Bed, No Breakfast (843-723-4450; 16 Halsey St., Charleston, SC 29401) Two no-smoking rooms with shared bath—a reliable basic value. Off-street parking in Medical University neighborhood. Inexpensive to Moderate. No credit cards.

1837 Bed and Breakfast (843-723-7166; 1-877-723-1837; www.1837bb.com; 126 Wentworth St., Charleston, SC 29401) Nine guest rooms, porches with rockers, full breakfast. College of Charleston area. Moderate. AE, D, MC, V.

Fantasia B&B (843-853-0201; 1-800-852-4466; www.fantasiabb.com; 11 George St., Charleston, SC 29401) Rooms in a carriage house or the main house, with kitchenettes, private baths, balcony access and cable. Internet available in main house living room. In the Ansonborough neighborhood, about a ten-minute walk to Broad Street. Moderate to Expensive. AE, D, MC, V.

4 Unity Alley (843-577-6660; www.unitybb.com; 4 Unity Alley, Charleston, SC 29401) Three suites with bedroom and sitting room, and communal dining area, located just off East Bay St. in the French Quarter neighborhood, a mix of commercial (galleries, fancy restaurants) and residential uses. Expensive. AE, MC, V to hold your reservation but payment due in cash or by check.

The Hayne House (843-577-2633; www.haynehouse.com; 30 King St., Charleston, SC 29401) A native Charlestonian familiar with the world of historic preservation and his family are your hosts: six rooms in both a kitchen house and a main house, private baths, and the use of garden and piazza; full

Southern breakfast in the main house. No television, great location, kids welcome. Expensive. MC, V.

36 Meeting Street Bed and Breakfast

(843-722-1034; www.36meetingstreet.com; 36 Meeting St., Charleston, SC 29401) Three suites with cooking areas and private baths—one in an 18th-century home and two in an adjacent carriage house. Children welcome. Moderate to Expensive. D, MC, V.

The Thomas Lamboll House (843-723-3212 or 1-888-794-0793; www.lamboll house.com; 19 King St., Charleston, SC 29401) Open the French doors from your bedroom onto the piazza of this pre-Revolutionary house located steps from the Battery. Two rooms with private baths and fireplaces. Expensive. MC, V.

27 State Street (843-722-4243; www .charleston-bb.com; 27 State St., Charleston, SC 29401) Enter your private suite (with kitchenette) through the court-yard of a foursquare, circa-1800 house in Charleston's "French Quarter," a block off East Bay St. and the harbor. Expensive to Very Expensive.

Charleston Environs

If you prefer to stay outside Charleston, near a plantation or one of the Sea Islands, you'll find plenty to choose from. Here are some possibilities, arranged by location, with separate sections on resort and rental accommodations and beach rental agents.

The Inn at Middleton Place

843-556-0500 or 1-800-543-4774.
www.middletonplace.org.
4290 Ashley River Rd., Charleston, SC 29414.
Price: Expensive to Very Expensive.
Credit Cards: AE, MC, V.

The Middleton Inn, located on a bluff adjacent to the beautiful gardens at Middleton Place, is about 25 minutes from downtown Charleston. For serenity and privacy, for long walks along the Ashley River or at Middleton Place (admission waived for inn guests), for kayaking and horseback riding, come here. Ask about weekend packages. Designed by W. G. Clark about 20 years ago and winner of architectural awards, it's handsomely modern on the outside, splendidly understated on the inside. There are 53 rooms in four buildings, each with working log fireplaces, custom-made furniture, soft colors, and large bathrooms. Some are handicapped accessible. Floor-to-ceiling windows with louvered shutters filter the light and air in the woodland setting. The restaurant at Middleton Place serves lunch and dinner daily.

Folly Beach

Charleston on the Beach (843-588-6464 or 1-800-465-4329; www.charlestonon thebeach.com; 1 Center St., Folly Beach, SC 29439) A 132-room oceanfront Holiday Inn hotel, with game room, pool, fishing pier, restaurant, and bar. Handicap access and non-smoking rooms available. Moderate to Expensive. AE, D, DC, MC, V.

Holliday Inn of Folly Beach (843-588-2191 or 1-800-792-5270; www.hollidayinn follybeach.com; 116 W. Ashley Ave., Folly Beach, SC 29439) This modest motel, one block from the beach, is as reliable as the chain hotel with the similar name, but it's much more inviting. Moderate to Expensive. AE, D, MC, V.

Isle of Palms

Holiday Inn Express (843-886-3003 or 1-800-465-4329; www.hiexpress.com; 1126 Ocean Blvd., Isle of Palms, SC 29451) There are 69 rooms, including 18 suites, situated in a great location with all the beach amenities—including microwaves and mini-refrigerators. Moderate to Expensive. AE, MC, V.

Seaside Inn (843-886-7000 or 1-888-999-6516; www.seasideinniop.com; 1004

Ocean Blvd., Isle of Palms, SC 29451) A 51-room hotel, basic but all you need, located next to the Windjammer, the beach area's most popular bar/restaurant.

Resorts and Rentals—Charleston Area Sea Islands

The Sea Island resort areas around Charleston are 25 to 35 minutes from downtown. They are, by themselves, fully self-contained destinations from which you can travel to the city by day to sightsee and shop, and to which you can return for recreation, dining, and relaxation. You can play golf and tennis and walk on the beach twelve months a year, and swim in the ocean from May to November. Each resort has a well-supervised children's activity program.

What follows is a list of the resorts and an outline of their lodgings. If you are interested in longer stays of a week or more, you may also want to contact some of the rental agents who specialize in private beach properties, including villas and houses located both within the resorts and outside of them. Note that rental rates for some especially fancy private homes within the resorts can be as much as twice the average rates quoted below.

Rental accommodations are fully furnished, including washer and dryer, but you should check to see if you need to bring anything, if there are special features like handicap access, or if a fee for cleaning after your departure is included. Deposits are necessary, and if you need to cancel, you must often do so up to three weeks in advance to have your deposit returned. During summer months, minimum stays of three days (in a villa) to a week (in a house) are often required.

Typical summer rental prices for a two-bedroom, oceanfront house ranged from $1,300 to $2,900 per week. The farther you are from the beach—by a lagoon or in the woods—the less expensive the rate. January through mid-March, and October through December are generally considered low season and rentals are priced accordingly. The resorts offer numerous packages covering a long-weekend or week's stay to attract golfers, honeymooners, Thanksgiving get-togethers, and visitors coming for the tours of historic homes in the fall and spring. There may be bargains, such as there would not be in downtown Charleston, for larger family reunion groups.

Kiawah Island Golf Resort

843-768-2121 or 1-800-654-2924.
www.kiawahresort.com.
12 Kiawah Beach Drive, Kiawah Island, SC 29455.
Price: Expensive to Very Expensive.
Credit Cards: AE, D, DC, MC, V.

There are many ways to enjoy Kiawah: in the 150-room inn, a rambling building with decks, breezeways, ceiling fans, and plenty of places to sit in the shade; in one of some 300 villa accommodations, fully furnished with kitchens, which come in several sizes; or in a private, architect-designed "beach house" that is not, by the way, anything like the faded house on stilts where you played board games in your bathing suit. The beach is private and 10 miles long. Thirty miles of paved bike trails wind around five golf courses and recreational areas, ultimately linking two distinct resort villages. The Sanctuary, a self-enclosed luxury hotel complex at Kiawah, will open in 2004.

Seabrook Island Resort

843-768-1000 or 1-800-845-2475.
www.discoverseabrook.com.
1002 Landfall Way, Seabrook Island, SC 29455.
Price: Expensive to Very Expensive.
Credit Cards: AE, D, MC, V.

Seabrook is a 2,200-acre private country club community now controlled by property owners (there are about 900 permanent residents), which means that it's very low key and means to stay that way. Visitors stay in rented villas or in homes. Its unique asset is its equestrian center, but it also provides resort amenities like golf (two courses), tennis (13 Har-Tru courts), a beach and beach club, pool, and fitness center.

Wild Dunes Resort
843-886-6000 or 1-800-845-8880. www.wilddunes.com.
5757 Palm Blvd., Isle of Palms, SC 29451. Price: Expensive to Very Expensive. Credit Cards: AE, D, DC, MC, V.

Wild Dunes is just 15 miles north of Charleston, a small resort located on the northeast end of the modest Isle of Palms. It's the place to stay if you want beach resort life (two golf courses, tennis, pools, water sports, kids' recreation program, beach club) and the advantage of the city an easy ride away. Sullivan's Island is close by, too. Guests choose accommodations in the 93-room Boardwalk Inn or in fully outfitted villas, townhouses, and cottages.

Beach Rental Agents
Beachwalker Rentals (843-768-1777 or 1-800-334-6308; www.beachwalker.com; 3690 Bohicket Rd., Johns Island, SC 29455) Accommodations on Kiawah and Seabrook Islands.

Carroll Realty (843-886-9600 or 1-800-845-7718; www.carrollrealtyinc.com; 103 Palm Blvd., Isle of Palms, SC 29451) Homes and villas by the week, month, or year on Isle of Palms, Wild Dunes, and Sullivan's Island.

Great Beach Vacations (Kiawah: 1-800-870-4059; www.kiawahinfo.com; Seabrook: 1-800-845-2233; www.seabrookinfo.com; Wild Dunes, Isle of Palms: 1-800-346-0606; www.isleof palmsinfo.com) A clearinghouse of information with a deep inventory of investment/rental properties.

Island Realty (843-886-8144 or 1-800-905-6290; www.islandrealty.com; 1304 Palm Blvd., Isle of Palms, SC 29451) Wide selection of rentals and golf packages on Sullivan's Island, Isle of Palms, and the more remote Dewees Island.

Pam Harrington Exclusives, Inc. (843-768-0273 or 1-800-845-6966; www.kiawah exclusives.com; 3690 Bohicket Rd., Suite 2-C, Johns Island, SC 29455) Homes and villas on Kiawah.

Seabrook Exclusives (843-768-0808 or 1-888-718-7949; www.seabrookexclusives.com; 3690 Bohicket Rd., Johns Island, SC 29455)

DINING

Dining is one Lowcountry ritual that remained important, even through hard times. Schoolchildren released for an hour from class and fathers home from the office gathered daily at the midday meal. It honored family, tradition, the art of conversation, and the resourcefulness of the cook. As the extraordinary Southern chef Edna Lewis said: "The birds are just the beginning. In the South you put everything you have on the table."

Indeed, accounts tell of hunting and fishing parties that delivered marsh hen, dove, quail, and crab by the dozens; that brought in pigeon and deer hunted by torchlight; that landed huge drum, a beast of a fish that pulled at hook and line and dragged a *bâteau*, or boat, as a whale might. Add to these hunters' trophies the harvest from garden and field—okra, corn, peas and beans, turnips, beets, greens, and, of course, rice, first introduced to the Lowcountry in the late 1600s—and you had, and have to this day, a traditional Southern meal, flavored as always with meat marked by "a streak of lean and a streak of fat."

It was not only the natural bounty of the land and the availability of labor for several harvests that led to a Lowcountry dining tradition. The plantation operation and its physical layout—including detached kitchens and smokehouses—gave rise to a separate world of cooking. Slaves were in charge here and they contributed their own sense of spicing, texture, ingredients, and method. The influence of their African and West Indian heritage, combined with European preferences, produced a distinctive regional style that today is being self-consciously redefined at restaurants like Cypress and Circa 1886, and examined by acclaimed food writers like John Martin Taylor. Taylor gave up his signature store in Charleston to sell his books, food products, and other food-related items online from his website (www.hoppinjohns.com), where you can also learn about Lowcountry cuisine from an insider with opinions.

The sign that Charleston has come of age may be the prices in the restaurants, but there are still plenty of modest places that serve local specials and are best known to local people. The list below reflects a range of prices and styles; more and smaller places are listed at the end of the section under "Faster Food."

Here are some suggestions. Many of them have on-line sites where you can check menus and make reservations. The general price range we list is meant to reflect the cost of a single meal, usually dinner, featuring an appetizer, entrée, dessert, and coffee. Cocktails, beer, wine, gratuity, and tax are not included in the estimated price. Lunches are generally less expensive, and in some cases, noted as a bargain.

Dining Price Code

Inexpensive	Up to $15
Moderate	$15 to $30
Expensive	$30 to $50
Very Expensive	$50 or more

Credit Cards

AE—American Express
DC—Diner's Club
CB—Carte Blanche
MC—MasterCard
D—Discover Card
V—Visa

During Spoleto, most Charleston restaurants relax their hours, serving lunch as late as 3 PM, early supper at 5:30, and full meals at midnight. The crowds pile up, so make reservations. If you're rushing between performances, picnic in the open-air pavilions at the Waterfront Park at the foot of Queen Street, in the shady grove of Washington Square, or on a bench at the Battery.

Anson

843-577-0551.
www.ansonrestaurant.com.
12 Anson St.
Open: Daily.
Price: Expensive.
Cuisine: American.
Serving: D.
Credit Cards: AE, D, MC, V.

The cooking technique here is last-minute sautéing: The dish arrives at your table sizzling hot, with crispy vegetables, meat, fish from that morning's catch, or fowl glistening with juice. The produce comes from local farms growing Charleston "heirloom" vegetables that were cultivated in the 19th century; the rice is "Carolina Gold," growing again after a 100-year hiatus; the lamb, duck, quail, and squab are free-range. There are comfy banquettes and lots of smaller tables for four or six, done up in heavy linens. The Market area in which Anson used to stand out as an attractive oasis is a little more care-worn and Anson less a local favorite, but still full of brio.

Basil

843-724-3490.
460 King St.

Closed: Sun.
Price: Moderate.
Cuisine: Thai. Serving: L, D.
Credit Cards: MC, V.

Downtown merchants,professionals, gallery owners, and professors are flocking to this corner restaurant on the booming section of King St. north of Calhoun. Sometimes there's a line, no reservations are taken, but Charlestonians have been waiting for an excellent Thai restaurant for a while: now they have it. Standards like crispy duck and spicy noodle soups, dishes with peanuts and coconut and curries. The grill is open, with seating at the chef's counter, or at tables, in booths or at a tiny bar. Lunch is a bargain. A welcomed place, simple and elegant.

Boathouse on East Bay

843-577-7171.
www.boathouserestaurants.com.
549 East Bay St.
Open: Daily.
Price: Expensive.
Cuisine: Seafood.
Serving: D and Sun. Brunch.
Credit Cards: AE, D, MC, V.

A big space whose teak and mahogany paneling and nautical decor recall the small craft and "mosquito fleet" heritage of the harbor. The staples of Lowcountry kitchens plain and fancy—like coleslaw, shrimp and grits, or fried green tomatoes, are given a welcome here, as are sushi and oysters from far above the Mason-Dixon Line. There's a happy-hour scene around the raw seafood bar. It gets full—make reservations.

Bookstore Cafe

843-720-8843.
412 King St.
Open: Daily.
Price: Inexpensive.
Cuisine: American.
Serving: B, L
Credit Cards: MC, V.

Fried oysters, roasted half-chicken, ham-and-eggs, and the blue-plate specials make this a top local choice, especially for its all-day breakfast. Near the Visitors Center, Manigault House, Charleston Museum, and Upper King shopping area.

Charleston Grill

843-577-4522.
www.charlestongrill.com.
224 King St., at Charleston Place.
Open: Daily.
Price: Expensive to Very Expensive.
Cuisine: New Southern.
Serving: D.
Credit Cards: AE, D, MC, V.

Astonishing menu or manifesto? Acclaimed chef Bob Waggoner makes his convincing case for a Lowcountry cuisine (with some French guidance) that reaches beyond home-grown ingredients and local imaginations. He stuffs the homely hushpuppy with caramelized figs and gives it self-confidence. He marries escargot to truffled grits. The entrées are good, but you can make a meal of appetizers and salads. The atmosphere is relaxed, a broad, generous clubroom feel, even though it's in a big hotel.

Circa 1886

843-853-7828.
www.circa1886.com.
149 Wentworth St.
Closed: Sun.
Price: Expensive to Very Expensive.
Cuisine: American.
Serving: D.
Credit Cards: AE, D, MC, V.

The Wentworth Mansion and its carriage house were built in the late 19th century and Circa 1886 resurrects all of the opulence of that time with contemporary flair. Once common local ingredients like conch, quail, and fresh beets turn up with fruit and sweet accents, and spicing inspired by the West Indies. There's a vegetarian entrée, but big servings of beef tenderloin and lamb chops, too. Set in a quiet garden corner, with the garden itself off the beaten track, the lovely building is set up with two rooms (about 50 seats), handsomely decorated with remnant beadboard, heart pine, and original stall-door details.

Cypress

843-727-0111.
www.magnolias-blossom-cypress.com.
167 E. Bay St.
Open: Daily.
Price: Expensive to Very Expensive.
Cuisine: American with Asian accent.
Serving: D.
Credit Cards: AE, MC, V.

The makeover of this once rather typical exposed-brick, warehouse-style place is nothing short of awe-some. It includes soft lights that change colors like a mood ring and a three-story glass wall behind which are stored thousands of bottles of wine lined up in perfect rows of black racks (actually, they look like they're in jail). You can eat downstairs at huge banquettes or beautifully dressed tables, or in the upstairs bar. The idea is sumptuous elegance with a surprising light, lively, minimalist feel. The food is superb, ranging from a sampler of sushi, benne-seed shrimp, and oysters to filet of hickory-smoked beef and braised leeks.

Fish

843-722-3474.
www.fishrestaurant.net.
442 King St.
Closed: Sun.
Price: Moderate to Expensive.
Cuisine: Southern.
Serving: L (Mon.–Fri.); D (Mon.–Sat.)
Credit Cards: AE, MC, V.

Located in an 1837 single-house with its side-to-the-street entryway used for outdoor dining, this is an intimate place full of customers who live in the Upper King St.

neighborhood or who choose it for an off-the-beaten-path feel. The owners have cultivated relationships with local growers and fishermen so that the menu, in winter, may be full of root vegetables, and when the shad are running in the Edisto River, sweet roe. Near the Visitors Center, so it's a good stop for lunch (more of a bargain) before or after a tour.

Fulton Five

843-853-5555.
5 Fulton St.
Closed: Sun.
Price: Moderate to Expensive.
Cuisine: Northern Italian.
Serving: D.
Credit Cards: AE, CB, DC, MC, V.

It's said Gian Carlo Menotti chose Charleston for his Spoleto Festival USA because it had a Mediterranean feel, a serene charm as easy to appreciate and as softly worn as stucco walls. Fulton Five wasn't open then, but its romantic setting fits the description. This restaurant, which seats perhaps 40, inside or on a patio, exudes quiet confidence and lack of pretension, both in the menu and in the decor: green walls that seem murky and lustrous, recessed windows set off by dark brown shutters, brocade fabrics that are velvety to the touch. It's comfortable to eat here alone. The Northern Italian menu includes clams with Tuscan beans, carpaccio, paper-thin veal, risotto dishes, and osso buco.

Gaulart & Maliclet

843-577-9797.
98 Broad St.
Closed: Sun.
Price: Inexpensive to Moderate.
Cuisine: French.
Serving: B, L, D.
Credit Cards: AE, D, DC, MC, V.

Known by its nickname "Fast and French," this bistro is the most popular, enduring little place in the Historic District. Seated on high chairs at a counter that juts out into tiny bays, your neighbors are likely to be Broad St. lawyers, Legare St. dowagers, and Queen St. artists (in Charleston, that may describe one family). You'll find platters of pâté, sausages, selections of cheeses, and French bread; hearty soups; fondues; excellent wine. Vegetarian options. Open late after house tours and Spoleto performances.

Hank's
843-723-3474.
www.hanksseafood.com.
10 Hayne St.
Open: Daily.
Price: Moderate to Expensive.
Cuisine: American; Seafood.
Serving: D.
Credit Cards: AE, D, MC, V.

This warehouse in the Market area used to be an eccentric "club" (if you needed to ask you didn't belong); now it houses Hank's Seafood, a handsome, self-conscious (the building has been properly "aged" with faux details), good-natured throwback to family seafood houses of the 1950s. Except in this incarnation, the shrimp cocktail actually tastes like shrimp, there's not sawdust on the floor, and the grilled fish entrées could come with beurre blanc. Were there rare seared tuna plates with lemon soy broth back then? Not in my town's Clam Box. The communal table draws its own crowd and is another way to be a part of a local scene.

High Cotton
843-724-3815.
www.mavericksouthernkitchens.com.
199 East Bay St.
Open: Daily.
Price: Expensive to Very Expensive.
Cuisine: New American.
Serving: D; Brunch Sat. and Sun.
Credit Cards: AE, D, MC, V.

Prosperity's high tide of restaurants surged on East Bay St., and this is one remarkable piece of sea glass it left behind. It's glossy, unabashed, and high energy: its intent, apparent in every detail from the smoked meat and home-brewed sauces to the paintings and potted palms, is to make you look good and feel good. And who are you? You are looking for quail or red meat or encrusted fish. On Saturday you'll go for eggs and barbecue duck hash. Come here for a robust dinner (in-house smoking and searing a specialty) and share a dessert soufflé with your friends. Jazz and entertainment nightly and at brunch.

Hominy Grill
843-937-0930.
www.hominygrill.com.
207 Rutledge Ave.
Open: Daily.
Price: Inexpensive to Moderate.
Cuisine: Southern.
Serving: B, L, D, Sat., Sun. brunch.
Credit Cards: AE, MC, V.

What is it about Charleston that an old barbershop with a tin ceiling in an offbeat neighborhood can be redone so simply, come alive as a full-service restaurant, serve terrific food, and not seem to break a sweat? Or burst into irony? The answer is probably the city's deep reserves of youth, and its appreciation of pleasure, gardens, nice weather, and frame buildings. There is still modesty and grace amidst the excess. A day that starts with butcher-paper tablecloths, thick mugs of coffee, biscuits, and bacon can proceed seamlessly to a turkey club, then move on to linens, catfish, and starlight in the walled garden.

Il Cortile de Re
843-853-1888.
193A King St.
Closed: Sun., Mon.
Price: Inexpensive to Moderate.

Cuisine: Italian.
Serving: L (Thurs.–Sat.), D (Tues.–Sat.)
Credit Cards: MC, V.

A storefront Italian bistro with an outdoor garden in the midst of the King St. antique district, an easy walk to the Gibbes Museum, the Nathaniel Russell House, and Church St. galleries. The lunch menu is small, maybe three salads, three panini sandwiches, three pastas; dinner is far more elaborate and features Italian entrées like boar, veal, and sausage. Local people who know food consider it a favorite, because it still feels like a neighborhood spot but the details, such as the balsamic dressings and amazing cheese selections, are not left to chance. A lunchtime bargain.

Jestine's Kitchen
843-722-7224.
251 Meeting St.
Closed Mon.
Price: Inexpensive to Moderate.
Cuisine: Homestyle Southern.
Serving: L.
Credit Cards: AE, D, MC, V.

Plain and simple Southern food, with lots of fried entrées (chicken, oysters, tomatoes, pork) and greens and grits on the side. Unpretentious room right on Meeting St. where, if you get nothing else, you can come for pie and the best sweet tea in town.

Magnolia's Uptown/Down South
843-577-7771.
www.magnolias-blossom-cypress.com.
185 E. Bay St.
Open: Daily.
Price: Moderate to Expensive.
Cuisine: "Nouvelle" Southern.
Serving: L, D.
Credit Cards: AE, MC, V.

This big and breezy place epitomizes the willing-to-please personality of the New South. It's energetic, with a menu that sticks to basic Southern foodstuffs—greens, black-eyed peas, grits, and shrimp—and dresses them up in unusual ways. It's very popular, with more visitors than locals during the high season, but has kept its touch and still delivers. Sunday brunch lasts past 3 PM for you late risers.

McCrady's
843-577-0025.
www.mccradysrestaurant.com.
2 Unity Alley (off East Bay St.).
Open: Daily.
Price: Expensive to Very Expensive.
Cuisine: New American.
Serving: D.
Credit Cards: AE, MC, V.

Award-winning for wine and food, expanded to include both a wine bar and lounge (entrance on E. Bay St.), and with its original space in a beautifully redone 18th century tavern, McCrady's is an understated, excellent restaurant. The menu features local fish, though more than the usual—tuna, grouper, and skate, for example—as well as local vegetables that are imaginatively paired and dressed up with sauce reductions. The cooking has classic French underpinnings with art-world presentation. Prix fixe options are sometimes available.

Peninsula Grill
843-723-0700.
www.peninsulagrill.com.
112 N. Market St.
Open: Daily.
Price: Expensive to Very Expensive.
Cuisine: American with Southern accents.
Serving: D.
Credit Cards: AE, D, DC, MC, V.

An elegant dining room, sometimes a bit noisy, never overbearing. The room has a great geometry, a square place punctuated by pillars and further softened by walls of

Relaxing at Vickery's café

It's simple and open: big plate-glass windows open onto a busy intersection just north of Saks. The salads are imaginative, many garnished with fruit relish, and plain choices for kids and the less adventurous: paninis, pasta, soups. Live music at night.

Vickery's
843-577-5300.
15 Beaufain St.
Open: Daily.
Price: Inexpensive to Moderate.
Cuisine: American; Cuban.
Serving: L, D.
Credit Cards: AE, D, MC, V.

A popular place for young locals and College of Charleston students, with tables and banquettes surrounding a horseshoe-shaped bar, and walls decorated with . . . stuff. Outdoor dining under the umbrellas is the place to be on a Friday afternoon in spring; inside it's noisy and friendly. Cuban and Caribbean spices warm up burgers, chicken, and pork; black beans and rice, with hot sausage, is the choice of regulars; three-dozen varieties of beer wash it all down.

Vintage Restaurant and Wine Bar
843-577-0090.
14 N. Market St.
Open: Daily.
Price: Expensive.
Cuisine: New American.
Serving: D; Sun. Brunch.
Credit Cards: AE, D, MC, V.

A restaurant and wine bar in a wonderful minimalist space (located via passageway) at the foot of the Market, across East Bay St. It has the feel and menu of a bistro for the new millennium—imaginative, pristine, not too fussy. A simple mix of textures, as in monkfish with foie gras emulsion and a root vegetable, is all you want. There are some 400 wines available, 70 by the glass; on

dark velvet dressed with 19th-century paintings. The light is suffused with soft gold overtones, as if the color had been rubbed on the air. Jell-O would taste good here. You may order "simple" entrées like strip steak, veal chops, or grouper and choose your sauces and sides; or go for the house specials (pan-roasted breast of duck is one). Champagne is always on the menu here. You may also eat in the courtyard or the bar, tiny and splendid and worth a stop.

Sermet's Corner
843-853-7775.
276 King St.
Open: Daily.
Price: Moderate.
Cuisine: North African, Mediterranean.
Serving: L, D.
Credit Cards: AE, D, MC, V.

This restaurant looks and acts like a real bistro, where students, children, grandparents, couples, and solo types feel at home.

Charleston's Vintage Restaurant and Wine Bar

Sunday nights several varieties are paired with offerings on a special, multi-course menu. It's probably a tad too expensive to become a weekly habit, but its intimate, fresh feeling would encourage one.

Charleston Area and the Sea Islands

If you are staying at a Sea Island resort, you will find a variety of dining choices offered in a range of prices and styles; but most of them, like the resorts themselves, are characterized by solid predictability. If you are more adventurous and want to eat with local people, you might try some of the following restaurants.

Bowen's Island Restaurant
843-795-2757.
1870 Bowen's Island Rd., 2 miles before Folly Beach.
Open Mon.–Sat.
Price: Inexpensive to Moderate.

Cuisine: Lowcountry seafood.
Serving: D.
Credit Cards: None.

If Huck Finn lived in the Lowcountry this is where he'd eat. It's basic: screen doors slamming, beat-up wooden tables engraved with initials, great breeze, offering hush-puppies, shrimp, roasted oysters cooked the old-fashioned way (throw them across a piece of metal sheeting above an open fire, and cover with wet rags until they steam open). A local tradition that has resisted any attempts at self-improvement.

Mustard Seed
843-849-0050.
1220 Ben Sawyer Blvd., Mt. Pleasant.
Closed: Sun.
Price: Inexpensive to Moderate.
Cuisine: New American.
Serving: L, D.
Credit Cards: AE, MC, V.

A casual, very popular local restaurant, often packed, but with a nice bar and a simple, robust menu. A hippie feel for a new century. Lots of pastas, seafood with light sauces, grilled portobello mushrooms, vegetarian specials. Other locations, equally charming, in Summerville and James Island.

Rosebank Farms Cafe
843-768-1807.
Bohicket Marina Village, Seabrook Island.
Open: Daily.
Price: Moderate to Expensive.
Cuisine: Seafood; Southern.
Serving: L, D.
Credit Cards: AE, D, MC, V.

Tucked among the shops of the marina village between Kiawah and Seabrook, and overlooking the berthed boats, this is worth a trip for lunch, if you're exploring, or for dinner to watch an incredible sunset. The seafood comes Cajun style or encrusted

with herbs; the pan-fried chicken livers are a specialty. There's always a blue-plate special at lunch. Murals depicting the natural world and the people in it make for a gauzy, tropical island feel—and so do the warm breezes off the creek.

Starfish Grille
843-588-2518.
101 E. Arctic Ave., on Folly Pier.
Closed: Sun.
Price: Moderate to Expensive.
Cuisine: Southern.
Serving: L. D.
Credit Cards: D, MC, V.

Attractive, reliable, and in a terrific spot on the pier at Folly Beach. A perfect place to stop in for lunch if you've been on the water or touring forts.

FOOD PURVEYORS

Bakeries/Coffee Houses
Baker's Cafe (843-577-2694; 214 King St.) A busy place especially for Sunday brunch, but ideal for a snack. Located at the head of the King Street antique district.

Cafe Café (843-723-3622; 177 Meeting St.) Opens at 7 PM, so just the place for a croissant and coffee after a morning run in the Waterfront Park.

Normandy Farm Bakery (843-577-5763; 86 Society St.) Carefully nurtured fermented starter yields incredible French loaves—get them while they're hot. Also focaccia, pastries, and coffee.

Port City Java (843-853-5282; 387 King St.) Smoothies, pastries, coffee, young people. Additional locations at 211 King St. and 261 Calhoun St. (at the Westin Francis Marion).

Saffron (843-722-5588; 333 E. Bay St.) The glass cases

Gourmet shops feature the best of Lowcountry

filled with daily specials like chocolate-chip scones and pastries, and the racks of fresh bread, could lead to a gourmet picnic if you don't want to eat here.

Candy and Ice Cream

Charleston Chocolates (843-577-4491; www.charlestonchocolates.com; 190 East Bay St.) It's Valentine's Day year-round here with hand-dipped chocolates and fancy trimmings.

Haagen-Dazs (843-723-9326; 43 S. Market St.) Sometimes it's far too hot in the Lowcountry for ice cream—it's a melted mess after a few licks—but this old favorite stays open after the sun goes down.

Lucas Neuhaus (843-722-0461; 73 State St.) If you're in the Market area and overwhelmed by all the shops and all the merchandise for sale, drop in for one fabulous Belgian chocolate or confection.

Pizza, Sandwiches, and Faster Food

Andolini's (843-722-7437; 82 Wentworth St.) The place for pizza in Charleston. Order as you enter, eat in a high-backed booth or on the back patio.

Joseph's (843-958-8500; 129 Meeting St.) A local favorite for breakfast, homemade soups at lunch, and courtyard dining.

Juanita Greenberg's Nacho Royale (843-723-6224; 439 King St.) The four food groups are represented here—hot, fresh, simple. Big burritos, handmade nachos in portions made for two. You can start with a margarita at 4 PM.

Kennedy's Market and Bakery (843-723-2026; 60 Calhoun St.) Hearty gourmet sandwiches, fresh bakery goods, soup, and wine.

The Kickin' Chicken (843-805-5020; 350 King St.) Fifteen flavors of wings so take plenty of napkins. Salads and sandwiches.

TOURING IN THE HISTORIC DISTRICT AND BEYOND

As in Savannah, opportunities for tours are plentiful and varied, including by carriage, bus, van, on foot, and by boat. The tour business has gotten so sophisticated that practically everyone has a special angle. Tour operators are licensed and amazingly patient with questions; they really know their stuff. Tours range from one to two-and-one-half hours, longer for out-of-town sites and scheduled stops at house museums, with prices in town starting at about $10 for children and $15 for adults and escalating quickly according to the length of the trip. Check the websites where available to find the one that best suits your interests. Tours that cover areas in the Sea Islands are more plentiful these days, with an emphasis on Gullah culture. Reservations are highly recommended for all tours. Note that some tours involving nature study or water trips are described more fully in the **Recreation** section later in this chapter.

If you're a generalist, start your day (and park your car) at the **Charleston Visitor Center** (375 Meeting St.) where there are lots of maps, helpful docents, and an audio-visual presentation that presents an excellent introduction to the city. From here, you may select a guided tour. Carriage tours, city shuttle buses, mini-van tours, and walking-tour

Church Street, Charleston

guides often collect and discharge passengers at this site. Sometimes a motorized tour is the most efficient way to review the city's deep inventory of houses—from the famous "single house" (one room wide, standing endways with its door to the street) to double-piazzaed mansions dominating their harborside sites. Or you may head out on your own. Any way you choose, you won't be disappointed. At the Visitor Center you may purchase a Heritage Passport ($34.95), which permits entry to Drayton Hall, Middleton Place, the Gibbes

Museum of Art, and three renowned historic houses in Charleston. It is a terrific bargain and it's good for one year from the time of purchase.

By Bus or Minivan

After all is said and done, the emergence of the "New South" has just as much to do with economics and enlightenment as with air-conditioning. There's no doubt that the comfort and cool of a minivan or bus tour—in which the guide is like your favorite classroom teacher and the atmosphere as fresh as a fine hotel room—has its virtues. The audio is high quality, the video may be on a laser disc, and extra-large windows offer great views. These tours also travel to sites out of the city limits, such as historic forts and plantations. But remember that comfort comes at a sacrifice—larger vehicles may not be able to navigate the old, sometimes alley-width streets of Historic Districts, and the pace is swiftly modern. They are a good choice for handicapped passengers, the eager visitor who wants to cover a lot of ground in a day, and groups of six or more.

Motorized tours generally pick up and deliver passengers from major downtown hotels and the Visitor Center.

Charleston Tours, Inc. (843-571-0049; www.charleston-tours.com)

Doin' The Charleston (843-763-1233 or 1-800-647-4487; www.dointhecharlestontours .com)

Gullah Tours (843-763-7551; www.gullahtours.com)

Sites and Insight Tours by Al Miller (843-762-0051; www.sitesandinsights.com)

Talk of the Towne (843-795-8199 or 1-888-795-8199; wwwtalkofthetowne.com)

Taylored Tours (843-830-6375 or 1-888-449-8687; www.toursofcharleston.com)

By Boat

Charleston Explorer Dolphin Tours (843-814-0544; www.charlestonexplorers.org)

Sandlapper History Tour (843-849-8687; www.sandlappertours.com)

Schooner Pride (84' tall ship) (843-559-9686; www.schoonerpride.com)

Spiritline Harbor Tour (843-722-2628; www.spiritlinecruises.com)

By Bicycle or on Foot

Discovering the nooks and crannies of the Historic Districts under your own steam is an intimate way to imagine the past. Furthermore, even though homes, churches, and ballast-stone streets have been preserved impeccably, they are still neighborhoods, not museums. Getting out from under the windshield or behind the tinted glass will help you understand the real, living context of these places, in which so much has occurred over time. Besides, it's probably dangerous to smell the jasmine and make a left turn at the same time.

There are bicycles, tandems (for two), and pedal carriages (for two or three people) for rent by the hour, the half-day, the day, or the week. The typical hourly rate is $10 for a bicycle and $15 for a pedal carriage. Personalized tours with a picnic might also be arranged. Helmets, baby-seats, and locks are provided at low or no cost. These shops can help you further.

The Bicycle Shoppe (843-722-8168; www.bicycleshoppe.com)

Mike's Bikes (843-723-8025; www.mikesbikescharleston.com)

Walking tours are a Lowcountry art form. Extolling the virtues of one's city in lacy prose comes naturally. There are many stories to tell, and an abundance of people to tell them.

As guiding has evolved, so have tours tailored to specific interests: architecture, gardening, the Civil War, African-American culture, religious heritage, ghosts, even sites of films or novels set in the Lowcountry. With sufficient advance notice, some private guides will craft a unique tour for your group, or offer bilingual service.

Walking tours generally last up to two hours and are scheduled in both morning and afternoon. Ask how large the group can get—smaller is better. Reservations are recommended, in some cases required. In the summer, wear a hat and sunscreen, and you may want to carry water. Prices range from about $14–$18 per person, reduced rates for children. Here are some ideas. Self-guided walking tours, with a cassette and headphones, can be rented at the Visitor Center for 24 hours ($17).

Anna's House and Garden Tours (843-853-2266; www.ghostwalk.com)

Architectural Walking Tours (1-800-931-7761; www.architecturalwalkingtoursof charleston.com)

Charleston Walks (1-800-729-3420; www.charlestonwalks.com)

Civil War Walking Tour (843-722-7033; www.civilwartours.com)

Ghosts of Charleston (843-723-1670 or 1-800-854-1670; www.tourcharleston.com)

Tourrific Tours (843-853-2500)

By Carriage

Carriages drawn by horses or mules pull you into the past while your guide tells colorful tales. The companies listed below are some among many. Tours generally last one hour and are scheduled throughout the day and evening. Prices per person are about $18; children ride at a reduced rate. Customized or private tours are often available if you inquire in advance. Tours depart from either the company stables or from pre-arranged pick-up sites.

Carolina Polo & Carriage Co. (843-577-6767; www.cpcc.com)

Old South Carriage Co. (843-723-9712; www.oldsouthcarriagetours.com)

Olde Towne Carriage Co. (843-722-1315; www.oldetownecarriage.com)

Palmetto Carriage Works (843-723-8145; www.carriagetour.com)

CULTURE

Architecture

Whether you have a serious or a layman's interest in architecture, you should approach the riches of Charleston and its environs with a game plan. Is it small rooms and thickly carved mantels of the colonial period you like? The fine lightness of touch and classical

decoration introduced by the Adam brothers? Do open-air living spaces afforded by
piazzas and walled gardens appeal?
Ironwork? Brick or clapboard? Small
country churches or city steeples?
Interiors or exteriors? Grand plantations
or modest row houses? Rooms adorned
with 18th-century furniture or ones that
remain bare, objects in and of themselves?
For suggestions on buildings that express
these aesthetic considerations, see the
"Historic House" listing later in this
chapter. Don't overlook the marvelous
decorative ironwork that adorns buildings
and streetscapes throughout the city. One
of the craft's most revered practitioners,
and a man whose work is seen throughout
Charleston, is Phillip Simmons. More
information about Simmons can be found
at www.phillipsimmons.org or through the
Phillip Simmons Foundation, 843-728-
8018, 91 Anson St., Charleston, SC 29401.

Art

Gibbes Museum of Art (843-722-2706;
www.gibbesmuseum.org; 135 Meeting St.)
The permanent collection presents
Charleston from the 18th century to the
present. Not to be missed are Charles

Double porches on a single house

Fraser's exquisite miniatures of prominent citizens during the city's early days, interpre-
tations of 20th-century plantation and rural life, including Alice Ravenel Huger Smith's
watercolors, or sketches and woodcuts by Alfred Hutty and Anna Hewyard Taylor. Also, a
very fine museum shop. Open Tues. through Sat. 10–5; Sun. 1–5. Closed Mon. and holidays. Adults $7; children $4.

Dance

Dance performances take place through most of the year, but are especially frequent during the Spoleto Festival. Call ahead for schedules and ticket information.

Charleston Ballet Theatre (843-723-7334; 477 King St.)

Robert Ivey Ballet (843-875-9308; 908 Bacon's Bridge Rd., Summerville)

Film

First-run movie houses tend to be located in malls away from downtown, and they account
for most of the region's audiences. In Charleston, the American Cinema Grill is a gem,
where you can order a simple meal and glass of wine and watch the movie from your table.
From time to time, especially during Spoleto, special film series are scheduled in college

auditoriums or libraries. Check local newspaper listings or look for handbills posted around town.

The new IMAX theatre offers a screen eight stories high, audio booming from every corner, and films well known for their "you-are-there" feeling.

American Cinema Grill (843-722-3456; 446 King St.)

Charleston Film Festival (843-722-1947)

Citadel Mall Cinema I-VI (843-763-7052; 2072 Sam Rittenburg Blvd.)

IMAX Theater of Charleston (843-725-4629; 360 Concord St.)

James Island Cinema Theatre (843-795-9499; 1743 Central Park Rd.)

Northwoods Mall Cinema (843-569-6794; 2181 Northwoods Blvd.)

Galleries

The recently organized Charleston Fine Art Dealers Association (www.cfada.com), whose members run ten galleries in Charleston, is a force for appreciation of both the work of the Charleston Renaissance artists of the 20th-century and of the New Renaissance artists in the Charleston of the 21st. Their Fine Art Annual each November, held in association with the Gibbes Museum, consists of lectures, demonstrations, and gallery receptions designed to educate and celebrate the enduring work of local and regional artists.

There are also galleries for contemporary art from national artists, as well as places where the collections are more intimate reflections of Lowcountry light and life. The French Quarter of Charleston, from S. Market to Tradd St. from the waterfront to Meeting St., is a thriving place for artists and galleries, too. An association of artists (www.french quartergalleries.com) holds quarterly walks there on the first Friday evenings of March, May, October, and December.

Here are some of the notable art galleries in the city.

Bernie Horton Gallery (843-958-0014; www.berniehortongallery.com; 111 Church St.) Here are the colors of the Lowcountry, from the fluorescent green of the summer marsh and the pink and purple at sunset, to the white boots of shrimpers. Originals and limited edition fine art prints of the countryside and the people and animals that live in it.

Carolina Galleries (843-723-2266; www.carolinagalleries.com; 188 King St.) The best place to see the paintings, etchings, pastels, drawings, and more, of the artists who made up Charleston Renaissance: Alice Ravenel Huger Smith, Anna Heyward Taylor, Alfred Hutty, and others.

The Charleston Renaissance Gallery (843-723-0025; www. fineartsouth.com; 103 Church St.) Located in a beautifully restored post-Revolutionary brick building, Robert Hicklin's gallery is at the forefront of renewed interest in Charleston's 20th-century art history—and it's worth going to for the education it offers. West Fraser's city scenes and Lowcountry landscapes, some in oil, some in watercolor, are showcased, as are 19th-century paintings and sculptures.

Coleman Fine Art (843-853-7000; www.colemanfineart.com; 79 Church St.) Members of the gallery include a number of artists working in a realistic style in oils and watercolors as well as the paintings of portraitist and illustrator Mary Whyte. Smith Coleman III, who owns the gallery, also restores damaged works of art and makes lovely frames. The gallery is located in the former studio of Elizabeth O'Neil Verner.

Eva Carter Gallery (843-722-0506; www.evacartergallery.com; 132 East Bay St.) Abstract oils, works on paper, and sculpture.

Gaye Sanders Fisher Gallery (843-958-0010; www.gayesandersfisher.com; 124 Church St.) Located in an 18th-century single house, featuring watercolors that burst with the feeling of Lowcountry landscape and architecture.

John Carroll Doyle Art Gallery (843-577-7344; www.johncdoyle.com; 54 Broad St.) A Charleston native, Doyle is one of the painters in the "new" Charleston Renaissance, capturing people in intense moments (like blues harmonica players) and teasing that intensity out of landscapes and animals.

Margaret Petterson Gallery (843-722-8094; www.margaretpetterson.com; 125 Church St.) Vibrant oil paintings of the city and its flora, as well as monotypes.

Martin Gallery (843-723-7378; 57 Queen St.) Contemporary art and elegant craft work, including jewelry incorporating precious stones and sculpted gold.

Nina Liu and Friends (843-722-2724; 24 State St.) Wonderful contemporary art in media such as fabric, collage, ceramic, paper and glass—it can be startling, magical and strong. The owner is an artist with a fine eye.

Smith-Killian Fine Art (843-853-0708; www.smithkillian.com; 9 Queen St.) Representing well-known painter Betty Anglin Smith and her accomplished triplets—painters Jennifer Smith Rogers and Shannon Smith, and photographer Tripp Smith. The best place to see the Lowcountry and Charleston itself being represented at this moment in time.

The Sylvan Gallery (843-722-2172; www.thesylvangallery.com; 171 King St.) Opened in late 2002, and representing 30 artists, the gallery features sculpture and 20th- and 21st-century representational art.

Wells Gallery (843-853-3233; www.wellsgallery.com; 103 Broad St.) Contemporary art of nationally recognized artists such as Susan Mayfield West, John Carroll Doyle, and Rhett Thurman. A good stop to see how the Lowcountry experience is being realistically brought to life.

Sculpture by Darrell Davis in the Smith-Killian Gallery, in the French Quarter

Historic Homes, Gardens & Religious Sites

It's hard to avoid historic sites in Charleston, but whether or not you visit one, and how much time you spend there will, of course, depend on your interest and schedule, whether you're traveling with children, and whether you have your own car. It may be preferable, for example, to do just one big thing in a day (a boat ride to Fort Sumter, a visit to a planta-tion garden) plus two smaller ones (see a house museum or church, take a walking tour, picnic in a park).

Distances are not great: to gardens and lighthouses and island sites from Charleston takes about 30 minutes. The sites in the following list are open all year, unless otherwise noted. Admission fees and hours are as of 2004; reduced admission generally applies to children 12 and under, seniors, students, and military personnel. Combination tickets offer savings at historic houses, sites, and museums, so ask at the venue or at the Visitor Center.

Keep in mind that the last tours of the day start approximately 30 minutes before clos-ing time. Visitors generally are welcome to enter religious sites, but are asked to observe the worship schedule and related courtesies of visitation, as few of the sites offer regular tour services. Handicapped access is sometimes limited in the old buildings, and there are usually rules regarding strollers.

Aiken-Rhett House

843-723-1159.
www.historiccharleston.org.
48 Elizabeth St.
Mon. through Sat., 10–5; Sun. 2–5.
Admission: Adults $8; reduced admission with combination tickets to selected historic properties.

Built in 1817, representing high-style Greek Revival and Rococo interiors, the Aiken-Rhett House is preserved in a somewhat less formal way than other houses. It's full of atmos-phere, a little worn at the edges. During the fiercest shelling of Charleston in the Civil War, it was the headquarters of Confederate General P. G. T. Beauregard, a purpose for which it was well suited by virtue of its scale, design, and location off the Battery. The intact work yard is a compelling example of African-American urban life.

Audubon Swamp Garden

See "Nature Preserves" in the **Recreation** section.

Boone Hall Plantation

843-884-4371.
www.boonehallplantation.com.
P.O. Box 1554, Mt. Pleasant.
Mon. through Sat. 9–5; Sun. 1–4.
Admission: Adults $12.50; children $6.

Of particular interest are the nine mid-18th–century brick slave cabins (these housed house slaves and skilled craftsmen, not the field hands), the Gin House, used for process-ing cotton, and the magnificent avenue of oaks, which runs three-quarters of a mile.

Congregation Beth Elohim

843-723-1090.
www.kkbe.org
90 Hasell St.
Mon. through Fri. 10–12.

The country's oldest synagogue in continuous use, built in 1840 to replace an earlier building that was destroyed by fire, it is a superb example of Greek Revival architecture.

Cypress Gardens

See "Nature Preserves" in **Recreation** section.

Drayton Hall

843-769-2600.
www.draytonhall.org.
3380 Ashley River Rd. (SC 61, 9 miles NW of Charleston.)
Mar. through Oct., 9:30–4; Nov. through Feb., 9:30–3.

Admission: Adults $12; children $8, free to members of the National Trust for Historic Preservation.

It's a measure of the greatness of this 18th-century Georgian-Palladian dwelling that even as it remains unfurnished, unrestored, unchanged (just stabilized), it exists in a class by itself. Built between 1738 and 1742, and set on a lovely Ashley River site, it is one of the most architecturally significant dwellings in America. House tours start on the hour (written tours in French, German, English, and Spanish available), and you are welcome to take the self-guided walking tours of the grounds. The guides are superior—not to be missed even if it's raining.

Edmondston Alston House

843-722-7171.
www.middletonplace.org.
21 East Battery.
Tues. through Sat. 10–4:30; Sun. & Mon. 1:30–4:30.
Admission: Adults $10; reduced admission with combination tickets to selected historic properties.

First built in 1825 by one wealthy man, later enlarged by another, it reveals—in structure, lavish decoration, documents, family furnishings, silver, and china—the best of what money could buy. You get a sense that this was the life and lifestyle Southerners fought the Civil War, in part, to protect.

Emmanuel A. M. E. Church

843-722-2561.
110 Calhoun St.

The Free African Society, composed of free blacks and slaves, was formed in 1791, and by 1818, under the leadership of Morris Brown, this independent congregation built a small church for their services. Denmark Vesey planned his slave insurrection there; when the rebellion failed, the church was shut for 43 years. Reorganization came after the Civil War; Built in 1891.

Exchange Building/Provost Dungeon
843-727-2165.
www.oldexchange.com.
122 East Bay St.
Daily: 9–5.
Admission: Adults $6; children $3.50.

Before this building was completed in 1771, the site was used for a variety of public purposes in the young colony. Its commanding location, at the foot of Broad Street, defined both an end boundary for the city, and also, from the water, its point of arrival. In terms of sheer geography it looms large. It's the kind of outsized place that was, and still is, used for huge receptions. During the Revolution the British held political and military prisoners in the basement.

French Protestant (Huguenot) Church
843-722-4385.
136 Church St.

French Huguenots fleeing religious persecution worshipped in Charleston as early as 1687. This church, built on the site of earlier ones, dates from 1845.

Heyward-Washington House
843-722-0354.
www.charlestonmuseum.com.
87 Church St.
Mon. through Sat. 10–5; Sun. 1–5. Last tour at 4:30.
Admission: Adults $8; children $4. Discounted admission with combination ticket to other Charleston Museum properties.

Built in 1772 by a rice planter whose son, Thomas Heyward, Jr., signed the Declaration of Independence, this house was also the headquarters of George Washington in 1791. Its furniture collection, including several 18th-century Charleston-made pieces and the magnificent Holmes bookcase, is unmatched.

Joseph Manigault House
843-723-2926.
www.charlestonmuseum.com.
350 Meeting St.
Mon. through Sat. 10–5; Sun. 1–5. Last tour at 4:30.
Admission: Adults $8; children $4. Discounted admission with a combination ticket to other Charleston Museum properties.

The outside of this structure is three stories of brick; the inside is something like shaped light. Designed by native son Gabriel Manigault for his brother and completed in 1803, this house, exuding both formality of plan and spontaneity of gesture, shows the nature of beauty and taste favored by elite planters who may have been, as Gabriel Manigault was, educated in Europe and exposed there to sophisticated design ideas and decorating schemes. The furniture is of the period, English, American, and French.

Magnolia Plantation and Gardens

843-571-1266.
www.magnoliaplantation.com.
3550 Ashley River Rd. (SC 61, 10 miles NW of Charleston).
Daily: 8–5:30; shorter hours in winter.
Admission to the Plantation and Gardens: Adults $13, with additional costs for tours of
the house and rides on the Nature Preserve train.

The current building was floated here by barge in 1873, but the entire tract dates back to
the time of the Barbadian planters who relocated on the Ashley River. The legacy here is
gardens, acres of them, reflecting (in layout and specimen planting) two centuries of hor-
ticulture. The gardens include 250 varieties of Azalea Indica and 900 varieties of Camellia
Japonica; there are bike and walking paths, a petting zoo, a canoe trail, and picnic areas.
You may access an adjacent nature preserve by small train. This is also the site to enter the
Audubon Swamp Garden (see "Nature Preserves" in the **Recreation** section).

Middleton Place

843-556-6020 or 1-800-782-3608.
www.middletonplace.org.
4300 Ashley River Rd. (SC 61, 14 miles NW of Charleston).
Daily: 9–5.
Admission: Adults $15; children $7; House tours always cost an additional $8 per person.

The formal gardens, laid out in 1741 and constructed by 100 slaves over a decade, feature
terraces, camellia allées, butterfly lakes, hillside drifts of azaleas, and acres of landscaped
paths. The site is so grand that it can be appreciated even when little is in bloom: The
geometry of the original plan itself is breathtaking. The adjacent stables and farmyard area
evoke the self-sufficiency of the plantation era
with demonstrations by a potter, weaver, black-
smith, and carpenter. (The animals just hang
around on their own.) The main house was
sacked by Union forces; tours of a remaining
wing honor the Middletons, but the real reason
to come here is what's outside. Nice restaurant
for lunch and dinner.

Nathaniel Russell House

Nathaniel Russell House

843-724-8481.
www.historiccharleston.org.
51 Meeting St.
Mon. through Sat. 10–5; Sun. 2–5.
Admission: $8.

People have no doubt been admiring this brick
townhouse and its garden from the day it was
completed (ca. 1808) and with good reason. It
represents the high point of the Adam style in
the city—its stairway appears to float, a lovely

combination of function and fantasy—and it is one of the most thoroughly conceived and exquisitely executed neoclassical dwellings in the nation. The interpretation (it belongs to the Historic Charleston Foundation) is rich and thorough, from the look of table settings to the lives of slaves who made such a household run smoothly.

St. Michael's Episcopal Church

843-723-0603.
Meeting St. at Broad St.
Daily: 9–4:30.

This church is still the center of many Charlestonians' lives, as it has been since 1761. Research suggests that its stunning white steeple is a close match to the one at St. Martin-in-the-Fields in London, and may have been designed by James Gibbs. It is part of the famous "Four Corners of Law" in downtown Charleston, an intersection that represents, in religious, civic, judicial, and federal buildings, the order imposed on society. There is a tranquil walled graveyard to explore.

St. Philip's Episcopal Church

843-722-7734.
146 Church St.

St. Philip's Episcopal Church

Constructed in 1835–38, facing a central park, and flanked by its graveyard, St. Philip's seems out of the Old World of Europe. The building is sheathed in a mottled, tan, stucco material that reflects the gradual shifting in light over the course of a day. The church is open for services Sundays, Wednesdays, and selected Fridays.

Thomas Elfe Workshop

843-722-2142.
54 Queen St.
Tours Mon. through Fri. 10–12.
Admission: $5.
A meticulously restored Charleston "single house," this dwelling was built before 1760 by the renowned cabinetmaker, who came to Charleston from England in the mid-18th century and left his mark in homes and furniture throughout the city. The carved fretwork that embellishes mahogany tables, chairs, and bookcases makes his work artistically distinctive; his abundant record keeping has enabled historians to understand his life and times. The small house, paneled in cypress, showcases his artistry.

The Confederate Museum, Charleston

Military Sites

The presence of the military—invaders and defenders—has enriched the history of the Lowcountry since the time of the American Revolution, and it is still felt today. You needn't be a veteran, or even a Civil War buff, to enjoy the forts, military museums, and rural sites that are so plentiful in the region. Children—with their innate appreciation of danger and adventure and their love of costume—especially seem to twig these sites and installations.

The Citadel Museum
843-953-6846.
www.citadel.edu.
171 Moultrie St.
Sun. through Fri. 2–5; Sat. 12–5.
Free admission.

Located on the campus of the Military College of South Carolina, founded in 1842, it tells the history of the school and the Corps of Cadets through documents, photographs, and uniforms. Dress parades take place most Fridays at 3:45 during the academic year.

The Confederate Museum
843-723-1541.
188 Meeting St.
Tues. through Sat. 11–3:30.
Adults $5; children $3.
Handicapped accessible.

There's a Gullah expression in the Lowcountry that sums up this museum: When you ask someone on the telephone "Is that you?" the person may reply, in a weary tone laced with irony, "That's what's leff' of me." This may be what's left of the old Confederacy: uniforms, tattered flags, documents, artifacts, and a fragrant sense of the Lost Cause.

Fort Lamar Heritage Preserve

803-734-3893.
(SC Dept. of Natural Resources/Heritage Trust Program).
Fort Lamar Rd., James Island (Take SC 171 to Battery Island Rd. Left for approx. 8 miles to Fort Lamar Rd. Right for approx. 5 miles to small parking lot on left.)
Open: Daily dawn to dusk.
Self-guided tour; maps available on site.

The site of the Battle of Secessionville, waged in the pre-dawn darkness of June 16, 1862, when Federal troops attacked this Confederate earthwork fort. The battle, involving some 1,400 men, was over in three hours. The walking tour directs you across what was an open field rimmed by marsh and woods, around the simple "M" shaped field fortification, by the magazines, dry moat, earthworks, and the likely mass grave of Federal wounded. Off the beaten track: For information call the number listed above which oversees the rustic site.

Fort Moultrie

843-883-3123 (National Park Service local office).
1214 Middle St., Sullivan's Island; 10 miles E. of Charleston.
Daily: 9–5.
Admission: Adults $2; children $1; or $5 per family.

The primary site of Charleston's seacoast defense system, from its first test in the American Revolution, now operated by the National Park Service. The palmetto-log fort that repelled the British fleet is gone, but buildings and earthworks dating from 1809 convey the sense of fragility and isolation the early patriots must have felt. A 20-minute film in the Visitor Center provides an excellent introduction. It is also the burial site of the Seminole warrior Osceola who, meeting under a flag of truce, was imprisoned here in 1838.

Fort Sumter National Monument

843-883-3123.
www.fortsumtertours.com (for boat tour information).
Departures from a new National Park Service interpretative center at 340 Concord St. by the Charleston Aquarium and Patriot's Point.
Trips usually two or three times each day, year-round, but fewer in winter months.
Admission: Adults $12; seniors $11; children (ages 6–11) $6.

A relaxing ferry trip, which offers splendid views of the harbor and peninsula, takes you to the place where the Civil War began. National Park Service rangers are on hand at the Fort to answer your questions; there are gun emplacements to explore, and a museum with artifacts to help you imagine scenes of the siege, which lasted approximately two years and ended in the abandonment of the Fort by Confederate soldiers. The entire tour lasts just over two hours.

H. L. Hunley Exhibit
843-744-2186 (information); 843-448-6539 (to purchase tickets).
www.hunley.org.
Warren Lasch Conservation Center, 1250 Supply St., Bldg. 255, North Charleston.
Open Sat. 10–5, Sun. 12–5.
Admission $10.00.

The *H. L. Hunley* was the forerunner of a modern submarine, most famous for its sinking of the
Housatonic outside Charleston Harbor, during the Civil War. Its last voyage ended in disaster,
all eight men aboard died. The 40-foot submersible, powered by men pedaling a crankshaft, is
undergoing restoration. Tours include a view of the conservation tank and displays of artifacts.

Patriots Point Naval and Maritime Museum
843-884-2727.
www.patriotspoint.org.
40 Patriots Point Rd., Mt. Pleasant.
Daily: 9–6:30, to 7:30 Apr. through Sept.
Admission: Adults $12.50; children $6; seniors and military with ID, $11; free to uni-
formed soldiers.

The big ones are berthed here—the aircraft carrier *Yorktown*, the World War II–sub
Clamagore, the destroyer *Laffey*, and the cutter *Ingham*—and on self-guided tours you can
see their aircraft, guns, and missiles, as well as views of how personnel lived and worked
on board. The view of peninsular Charleston (just over the Cooper River Bridges) from the
platform of the *Yorktown* is unbeatable. Snack bar and gift shop, seating areas for the rest
and air you'll need: There's a lot of walking and close quarters.

Museums
Avery Research Center for African-American History and Culture
843-953-7609.
www.cofc.edu/avery.
125 Bull St.
Tours Mon. through Sat. 12–5.

Housed in one of the first schools dedicated to educating freed slaves, the center is an
archive and library of printed and picture materials and objects related to the heritage of
the region's African-Americans. It was built by the Freedman's Bureau at the end of the
Civil War to meet the needs of 1,000 eager students who had been receiving instruction
from teachers sent by the American Missionary Association and other organizations.
Reading room hours are Mon. through Sat. 12–5.

Charleston Museum
843-722-2996.
www.charlestonmuseum.org.
360 Meeting St.
Mon. through Sat. 9–5; Sun. 1–5.
Admission: Adults $9, children $4; combination tickets to Museum and its historic properties available at a discount.

The museum, founded in 1773, is the oldest in America. This means that both the ideas that gave the collection its intellectual underpinnings and the very objects themselves, many from Charleston's oldest families, reflect more than two centuries of the city's self-consciousness. Exhibits interpreting subjects as diverse as flora and fauna, fashion, the art of silversmithing, Native American life, and plantation life, come together to provide a seamless image of a special place. The section on African-American slavery—texts, artifacts, photographs, charts—is superb.

Charles Towne Landing 1670
843-852-4200.
1500 Old Towne Rd. (SC 171 between I-26 and US 17).
Daily: 8:30–5, to 6 in summer months.
Admission: Adults $6; children $3.
Rental bicycles $2/hour.

Consider this 80-acre park an outdoor museum, where the lives of the Lowcountry's earliest European settlers are interpreted in several ways: in a village setting on a 17th-century replica of a typical coastal trading vessel; and in "wilderness," as found in the Animal Forest, where birds and beasts common to the area in 1670 roam in a secured habitat.

South Carolina Aquarium
843-720-1990.
www.scaquarium.org.
100 Aquarium Wharf.
Daily: 9–5, to 7 in summer months; Nov. through Feb. 10–5.
Admission: Adults $15; seniors $13; children (3–11) $8.

Set on the Cooper River, where its neighbor is a landing for the industrial port of Charleston (a port that sees more than 12 million tons of container cargo pass through each year), the new aquarium provides well-designed displays of the state's aquatic habitat, from the mountain streams of the Upcountry to Lowcountry marshes. More than 10,000 creatures reside here in the 330,000-gallon Ocean Tank, in living habitat exhibits, and in the hands-on water tables. Interpreted dive programs, where you can watch the fish being fed and learn more about them take place at 11, 1, and 3 daily. Kids can spot bottle-nose dolphins for themselves from the expansive deck overlooking the river—and there's always a guide to answer questions. Special exhibits on marine ecosystems around the world also featured.

Music
Charleston has a symphony orchestra and chamber groups that play regularly throughout the year, and, of course, it has **Spoleto**, which brings boys' choirs, operatic soloists, and instrumentalists to the city each May and June. The region is rich in indigenous music, too: blues, jazz, spirituals, gospel. As new audiences for these styles develop, concerts to showcase them are emerging. The **Blues Bash** in February, the **MOJA Arts Festival** in September, and the **Annual Spirituals Concert** in December are some. Often, concerts of gospel music and spirituals take place in conjunction with spring and fall house tours and may be held at a historic site. You should check local newspapers for schedules or, once you arrive in Charleston, contact the organizations below for information.

Charleston Symphony Orchestra (843-723-7528; www.charlestonsymphony.com; 160 E. Bay St.) Performances under the direction of David Stahl in the Gaillard Auditorium (77 Calhoun St.) throughout the year. Concert series might include selections from the classical repertoire, pops, and chamber works.

Lowcountry Blues Society (www.bluesbash.com) The Society's main event—The Lowcountry Blues Bash—runs for about 10 days every February and features performances at sites all over the city, from small clubs to larger theaters. Some concerts are free, others charge a modest cover, usually under $15. The shows are first rate—musicians come from Chicago, North and South Carolina, anywhere the blues are played.

MOJA Arts Festival (843-724-7305; www.mojafestival.com; 133 Church St.) The 16-day festival, whose name is Swahili for "one" or "unity," takes place in the fall and celebrates the African and Caribbean cultural influences on the Lowcountry. It includes many musical performances. Administered by the city's Office of Cultural Affairs.

Nightlife

Nightlife prospers in the Market Area and East Bay St., where there are dance lounges and noisy student spots, but mellow piano bars at the Charleston Grill, the Mills House, and Charleston Chops are reliably rewarding. Farther afield, on the resort-oriented islands, you will discover the land of "shag," the original, stylized South Carolina dance set to beach music. A list of the better-known or easily accessible spots for night owls follows. Cover charges vary widely, depending on the entertainment. Check local newspaper listings when you're in town for special shows.

Charleston Chops (843-937-9300; 188 East Bay St.) Jazz piano bar Tues. through Sat. in this steak-and-seafood restaurant.

Charleston Grill at Charleston Place (843-571-2265; 224 King St.) Jazz trios nightly in a sophisticated, laid-back setting.

Cumberland's (843-577-9469; 26 Cumberland St.) Band music that's live and loud.

Dunleavy's Pub (843-883-9646; 2213 Middle St., Sullivan's Island) A small place on the corner with a half-dozen or so imported beers and ales on tap and music (acoustic, Irish, small bands) on the weekends.

Mills House (843-577-2400; 115 Meeting St.) Two lounges, one with a piano bar where you can relax and visit. Good place to gather for an after-dinner drink. Look for Big Band tunes or jazzy guitar.

Momma's Blues Palace (843-853-2221; 46 John St.) Not a palace, but plenty of blues, acoustic and electric.

Music Farm (843-853-3276; 32 Ann St.) Where the young crowd swarms to dance and mosh.

Spoleto

It is said that the first professional dramatic production in America of a play written here was performed in Charleston in the 18th century by a shipwrecked poet, who was washed ashore, as he put it, "full of lice, shame, poverty, nakedness and hunger."

No such description could conceivably apply to the outstanding performers who come to the city for a cultural festival that has put Charleston on the map, nationally and internationally. For 18 days at the end of spring, a time of budding oleander, fading azalea, and unapologetically fragrant magnolias, Spoleto comes to Charleston and Charleston becomes the city it has long imagined itself to be: an artistic mecca where expressions of high culture find their setting among people who believe they understand the meaning of civilized life.

Spoleto gave Charlestonians a chance to prove their claims of having shucked off their provincial preferences, and prove it they have. Emboldened by the artistic vision of Gian Carlo Menotti (who fell in love with Charleston and organized the first festival in 1977), and egged on by an indefatigable mayor, Joe Riley, Charleston's cultural and business communities have consistently—and with full attention—adapted themselves and their city to the idea that first-class art of many kinds can inhabit, enrich, and be enriched by the lively, unique qualities of this old city. Spoleto instilled new vigor, giving rise to building projects and renovations, new restaurants, and shops: It linked the pride in the Lowcountry's past to confidence in its future. It opened the doors of Charleston to the nation.

Spoleto took its name from the town in Italy where, in the 1950s, Mr. Menotti had organized another festival. Spoleto in Charleston was conceived as the counterpart to that venture, though now it stands on its own artistic direction and traditions. In any one season, it offers more than 100 scheduled events, including premieres of opera and dance as well as dozens of chamber music, choral, jazz, and orchestral performances. Performances take place indoors and out—in parks, plantation gardens, amphitheaters, and auditoriums.

If that's not enough, the regular Spoleto events are augmented by some 600 **Piccolo Spoleto** performances (often free), organized by the city's Office of Cultural Affairs (843-724-7305; 133 Church St., Charleston, SC 29401). These events can include organ, choral, and madrigal recitals in churches; mime shows, outdoor concerts, and numerous theater productions.

There are several ways to purchase tickets to Spoleto. The first thing to do is request, by mail or telephone, the festival ticket brochure and guide, a near-tabloid-size schedule of events with a pre-printed order form. Contact:

Spoleto Festival U.S.A.
P.O. Box 157
Charleston, SC 29402-0157
843-722-2764 / Fax 843-723-6383
www.spoletousa.org

If you want to order a pre-designed "ticket package" which might include a dance performance, a play, an opera, and a chamber music event spread over several days, order the brochure by mid-November or December. If you're not sure of your schedule, you can order tickets to individual events beginning in January. There is a handling charge for ticket orders. The variety and number of events can be overwhelming, but poring over the brochure and making plans offers the same pleasurable anticipation that stirs avid gardeners as they read beautiful seed catalogues. Of course, the earlier you can confirm travel arrangements and lodging, the better.

If April 1st comes and you are without tickets but want to attend to Spoleto, you can still do it. With a basic Spoleto Festival ticket brochure in hand (see above address) you may order tickets by telephone (843-579-3100) and charge them. There's a handling charge levied per ticket.

In person, visit the Spoleto Office at 77 Calhoun St., which is open year-round but extends its hours from April until the festival closes. There are also box offices at all Spoleto venues, which handle tickets for the events held there. They are generally open daily during the festival from 10 AM until thirty minutes after the final performance of the day.

You can even arrive without tickets, and get lucky. Tickets can be purchased up to one hour before curtain time; remaining tickets go on sale at performance sites 30 minutes before curtain. Chairs or standing room for sold-out performances at the Dock Street Theatre and the Garden Theater go on sale at 10 AM on the day of performance.

Theater

By the middle of the 18th century, theatrical performances were well established in the cultural life of Charleston. In the antebellum years, theater was but one jewel in the crown of culture, offset by the brilliant setting provided by a society that lived for pleasure and sought it in balls, concerts, seasonal celebrations, and lavish home entertaining.

In the 20th century, it wasn't until 1927—when DuBose Heyward's novel *Porgy*, the story of a lame Charleston street vendor and his love for Bess, was adapted and performed on the Broadway stage—that drama native to Charleston came alive. Theatrical performances in the Lowcountry still reflect their indigenous stories—they are often showcased during Piccolo Spoleto—but a growing audience also supports new works from nationally known dramatists and selections from the classical repertory. When visiting, call ahead for performance schedules and tickets.

Charleston Stage Company (843-577-5967 or 1-800-454-7093; www.charlestonstage .com; P.O. Box 356) Productions at Dock Street Theatre by a residential theater group that provide special enjoyment for families, plays like *Cheaper By the Dozen* or *A Christmas Carol*; original work, children's theater, and workshops.

Dock Street Theatre (843-720-3968; 135 Church St.) This is a lovely interpretation of a Georgian-style theater, of the sort 18th-century Charlestonians may have patronized. Rebuilt during the depression within the old Planters Hotel (circa 1809) as a project of the Federal Works Progress Administration, the theater's cypress interiors, intimate box seats, and terrific acoustics make it a wonderful place to attend performances. It's the site of the immensely popular Chamber Music Series during Spoleto and festival plays, as well as a stage for roving companies.

Footlight Players (843-722-7521; www.footlightplayers.net; 20 Queen St.) An old, established theater company dedicated to community-theater repertory. Six productions each season, from August through May.

RECREATION

While guessing what a novelist had in mind in his work can be a risky business, perhaps when DuBose Heyward wrote *It is always Sunday on the Sea Islands*, he was thinking that there is, in every day, a piece of Sunday here, a piece of time as yet unscheduled in which to enjoy the best of your surroundings, naturally and simply, with as few complications as possible. This is the definition of recreation in the Lowcountry.

Baseball

Charleston RiverDogs (a Class A affiliate of the Tampa Bay Devil Rays) play April through August at Joe Riley, Jr. Park (843-723-7241; www.riverdogs.com; 360 Fishburne St.) Tickets are $4–$8.

Beach Access

There are hundreds of miles of coastline between Charleston and Savannah and on the barrier islands. At many points the public can reach the coast at designated access sites. Some of these offer changing areas, restrooms, showers, and picnic tables. Others are mere paths in the sand. Some, like the beaches on pristine barrier islands, are accessible only by boat.

The beaches on this coast are flat and wide, without rocks, overlooked by dunes or maritime forest. The surf ranges from placid to roiling (the Washout at Folly Beach is considered a top surfing spot). Lifeguards are not on duty at every beach access point, and swimming may be extremely hazardous: It is not wise to swim in unmonitored areas. Walking on the dunes, picking the sea oats, and driving on the beach are forbidden.

A few suggestions follow for reaching the beach by land or water. For more detailed information about specific access points, contact the chambers of commerce or tourism commissions listed at the end of Chapter Six, *Information.*

Sullivan's Island and **Isle of Palms** are located north of the city on US 17 and SC 703. The beach at Sullivan's is marked by walkways. You may park along the side of streets. **Isle of Palms County Park** (843-886-3863; 1st through 14th Avenue, Palm Blvd.) offers pay parking, restrooms, and changing facilities. Located to the south, off US 17 on SC 171, you can enjoy the fully outfitted **Folly Beach County Park** (843-588-2426; 1010 W. Ashley Ave.), which offers 4,000 feet of oceanfront access, lifeguards, changing rooms, showers, pay parking, and a 1,045 foot fishing pier. A bit farther south off US 17, at the gate to Kiawah Island, is **Beachwalker Park** (843-768-2395; Beachwalker Dr., Johns Island) another well-developed public beach destination with facilities, lifeguards and pay parking.

Shore Refuges

By water, and with advance arrangements, you may visit **Cape Romain National Wildlife Refuge** (843-928-3368; 390 Bull Island Rd., Awendaw, SC 29429) a 64,229-acre site managed by the U.S. Fish and Wildlife Service. The refuge consists of four parts: **Bull Island**, a 5,000-acre barrier island; **Cape Island**, a favorite spot for loggerhead turtles to nest; **Moore's Landing**, the site of ferry services, and an observation pier just right for birders; and **Raccoon Key Island**, a popular spot for shelling.

Coastal Expeditions, Inc. (843-881-4582; ferry information) offers exclusive ferry service to Bull Island, weather permitting. Ticket prices $30 for adults and $15 for children under 12. From Mar. through Nov., the ferry makes two round-trips daily every Tuesday, Thursday, Friday, and Saturday. From Dec. through Feb. there's one trip only, on Saturdays. The company also offers pontoon charters throughout the refuge for larger groups.

Another refuge is **Capers Island**—a classic, undisturbed barrier island managed by the **South Carolina Department of Natural Resources**. Contact them (843-762-5000; P.O. Box 12559, Charleston, SC 29412) for general information regarding public use restrictions, instructions for anchoring and beaching boats, and camping permits. You can get there in a sea kayak (guided tour $85/day) offered by **Coastal Expeditions, Inc.** (843-884-7684;

www.coastalexpeditions.com; 514-B Mill St., Mt. Pleasant, SC 29464); or on a 40-foot boat with **Barrier Island Eco Tours** (843-886-5000; www.nature-tours.com; P.O. Box 343, Isle of Palms, SC 29421). A 3.5-hour day tour led by a naturalist and marine biologist costs adults $32, children $25; a 2 hour sunset cruise costs adults $25, children $20. There are other educational trips, too.

Bird-Watching

The barrier islands mentioned above provide the least-disturbed habitats for birds and wildlife you're likely to find in the Lowcountry; if you're a serious birder, schedule a visit.

But even if you can't make it to the islands, you will not be disappointed in what you can find in more accessible places. Because of its location on the North American flyway and its diverse natural environment, the Lowcountry attracts scores of wading, shore, and songbirds, some of them as unusual as the roseate spoonbill and parasitic jaeger. Woodcocks flock in plowed fields, owls hover in roadside forests, and hawks soar over open grassland. In February, you are likely to see thousands of robins and cedar waxwings swarming in country yards, picking the cherry laurel trees clean.

Local Audubon societies, conducting the annual Christmas count, have reported over 200 types of birds from scrub areas to shorefront. Visitor-friendly sites for birding—where you may find boardwalks, observation areas, and informational slide shows or displays— are listed under "Nature Preserves" later in this chapter.

More informal birding sites recommended by local birders include the following:

Bears Bluff, located southeast of Charleston on Wadmalaw Island, 843-559-2315; www.southeastfws.gov/bearsbluff. This 31-acre fish hatchery offers sensational viewing of common and endangered species in a lovely rural setting that's also good for picnics.

Bear Island W. M. A., located south of Charleston off US 17 at Green Pond, 843-844-8957. Operated by the South Carolina Department of Natural Resources, an extensive habitat characterized by old rice fields, meandering creeks and rivers, marshes, and all sorts of woodlands. Open January 21 through October 31, Monday through Saturday.

I'on Swamp, 15 miles north of Mt. Pleasant off US 17 on U.S. Forest Service Rd. 228. Spring brings warblers—possibly even the shy Bachman's—and also resident upland birds, including red-cockaded woodpeckers, who make their homes here.

Mt. Pleasant, the area leading to the old Pitt St. Bridge. Here sightings of marbled godwits, oystercatchers, grebes, and mergansers have been reported. Activity is best at half tide, especially in fall and winter. A spotting scope is useful.

Sullivan's Island, around the beach behind Fort Moultrie. Here, in fall and winter, you might see peeps or an occasional purple sandpiper.

US 17 by the **Ashepoo** and **Combahee River crossings**. Anhinga, rails, and gallinules nest in the remnant rice fields.

Boating
Jet Skiing
Jet skis (a.k.a. personal watercraft and wave runners) let you navigate in the shallow creeks at a fast, noisy clip. You can rent them by the hour at the following locations. Prices from $50–$75 per hour, depending on whether you take a guided group tour or ride alone.

The City Marina (843-577-7702; www.charlestoncitymarina.com).

Sun & Ski (843-588-0033; Folly Beach).

Tidal Wave Runners (843-886-8456; Isle of Palms).

Sailing
A sailor unfamiliar with Lowcountry coastal waters will encounter dramatic tides and strong currents. If you're interested in renting a sailboat, either for a day's excursion or a sunset cruise, reserve early. It's also wise to check local conditions and discuss your plans with the rental outfitter before you go. (Some boats come with their own skippers if you get nervous.)

Sailboats in a range of sizes are available for hire from the following:

Aqua Safaris (843-886-8133; www.aqua-safaris.com; P.O. Box 309, Isle of Palms, SC 29451).

Bohicket Boat (843-768-7294; Bohicket Marina Village, Seabrook Island, SC 29455).

The City Marina (843-853-4386; 17 Lockwood Dr., Charleston, SC 29401).

Wild Dunes Yacht Harbor (843-886-5100; P.O. Box 527, Isle of Palms, SC 29451).

If you're towing your own boat, there are dozens of landings (19 in Charleston County—most paved and with landing docks, some more rustic) where you can park your trailer and launch. Parking is free, but unmonitored. Contact the following agencies for listings or maps, which show the locations of public boat landings: **Charleston County Parks** (843-795-2628); **South Carolina Marine Resources Division** (843-762-5000; P.O. Box 12559, Charleston, SC 29412); **Lowcountry Resort Islands and Tourism Commission** (843-717-3090 or 1-800-528-6870; 1 Lowcountry Lane, Yemassee, SC 29945).

Bowling
AMF Charleston Lanes (843-766-0241; 1963 Savannah Hwy.).

Ashley Lanes (843-766-9061; 1568 Sam Rittenberg Blvd.).

Camping
In the old days, a camping expedition usually involved sailing or rowing—or being sailed or rowed—in boats loaded like barges to the uninhabited barrier islands. Upon arrival, the party would set up housekeeping at a "fish camp" for several days. These same spots would be revisited year after year, although they might consist of nothing more than driftwood chairs, a palmetto-log windbreak, and a fire pit. The tradition was rustic, the site well off the beaten track, the experience enhanced by the oft-repeated stories it generated.

Today's visitor can be a happy camper, too (but near running water, toilets, a campground store and gnat repellent) at public campgrounds at the following sites:

Buck Hall, Francis Marion National Forest (843-887-3257; Wambaw Ranger District, P.O. Box 106, McClellanville, SC 29458) 15 sites; hiking trails, boat ramp, fishing.

James Island County Park (843-795-7275; 871 Riverland Dr., Charleston, SC 29412) 125 RV sites, 10 three-bedroom cottages on the marsh, primitive camping area; shuttle service to downtown Charleston, paved trails, fishing and crabbing docks, playgrounds and picnic shelters.

Privately operated campgrounds in the area include:

Lake Aire RV Park and Campground (843-571-1271; 4375 SC 162, Hollywood) One hundred sites including full hookups, primitive sites, and camper sites. Seven-acre fishing lake, swimming pool, paddleboat and canoe rental, showers, laundry, recreation area, bike, and foot trails.

Oak Plantation Campground (843-766-5936; 3540 Savannah Hwy.) Full hookups with 15-, 30- and 50-amp. service; 100 tent sites, 150 camper sites, propane, laundry, groceries, bathrooms.

Wood Brothers Campground (843-844-2208 or 8446 Ace Basin Pkwy., 37 miles south of Charleston) Wooded and open sites for RVs, campers, and tents; grocery, propane, showers, fishing pond.

Canoeing and Kayaking

Interest in these activities has exploded. Guides will lead you along miles of creeks and down rivers; adventurous instructors can teach you how to get beyond the breaking waves into the ocean. Here are some popular locations and names of outfitters. The web address for Charleston-area state parks is www.ccprc.com.

The Edisto River, thought to be the nation's longest free-flowing black-water stream, offers calm waters and great bird and wildlife observation. As you meander along, you're likely to see great blue herons wading by the oak-lined riverbank or hummingbirds feeding at wildflowers. The trail follows an ancient waterway used by Native Americans and early settlers. **Colleton State Park** (843-538-8206; Canadys, SC; US 15, 12 miles north of

Kayaks ready to be launched in the shallow creeks

Walterboro, I-95 Exit 68) and **Givhan's Ferry State Park** (843-873-0692; SC 61, 16 miles west of Summerville) are along the route. You can put in there, and also camp and picnic. For more information, contact www.travelsc.com.

To inquire about conditions (canoeing and kayaking are not recommended on the Edisto River when the water level is above 7.5 feet) call 843-538-3659. The **Walterboro-Colleton Chamber of Commerce** (843-549-9595; P.O. Box 426, Walterboro, SC 29488) can assist you in renting canoes or kayaks, or securing a guide at certain times of the year. Their website, www.walterboro.org, is an excellent place to find information and trail guides for paddling in the ACE.

Nearer Charleston, boats are available for rent at **James Island County Park** (843-795-7275; 871 Riverland Dr.), **Magnolia Gardens** (843-571-1266; 3550 Ashley River Rd.), and **Palmetto Islands County Park** (843-884-0832; 444 Needlerush Pkwy., Mt. Pleasant). The following companies offer kayak rentals, tours, and instruction. The price for rentals of kayaks, safety equipment, and basic instruction is about $65–$80 per day; $30 per half day. Tours, depending on their length, cost between $45 and $65.

Bohicket Boat: Adventure & Tour Co. (843-768-7294; www.bohicketboata.com).

Coastal Expeditions (843-884-7684; www.coastalexpeditions.com).

Half-Moon Outfitters (843-881-9472).

Nature Adventures Outfitters (1-800673-0679; www.natureadventuresoutfitters).

Diving

If you want to use that diver's watch you wear for looks—thick black band, fluorescent numbers, rimmed with rings and buttons—contact these outfitters. Lowcountry creeks and rivers tend to be murky with low visibility, but offshore opportunities (and instruction) are available.

Charleston Scuba (843-763-3483; www.charlestonscuba.com).
Trident Charters (843-763-3483).

Family Fun

The Lowcountry's long summer nights, when dusk comes as late as 9 PM, mean there's always extra time for that round of miniature golf or walk on the beach. By day, there are waterslides to offer cooling thrill rides. Here are some activities that adults and kids can enjoy together.

Classic Golf (843-881-3131; 1528 Ben Sawyer Blvd., Mt. Pleasant) Miniature golf land-scaped and lit for night play on two courses

Frankie's Fun Park (843-767-1376; 5000 Ashley Phospate Rd.) Two 18-hole mini golf courses, go-cart tracks, game rooms, batting cages, and bumper boats. Open daily, 10 AM.–midnight. A great reward for kids who have been sightseeing all day.

James Island County Park (843-795-7275; 871 Riverland Dr., James Island) The 50-foot climbing wall and 10-foot bouldering wall would attract older kids, while the little ones enjoy the water park with slides and fountains. Rollerblading on miles of paved trails; canoes, paddleboats, and bikes for rent.

Palmetto Islands County Park (843-884-0832; 444 Needlerush Pkwy., Mt. Pleasant)
Picnic areas and shelters, walking and biking trails, marsh boardwalk and fishing sites.
Bicycles, canoes, and paddleboats are available for rent. Splash Island is a water fun park
with slides, pools and chutes.

Sand Dollar Mini Golf (843-884-0320; 1405 Ben Sawyer Blvd., Mt. Pleasant) Open summer nights until 10 PM.

Fishing

There's always fishing in the Lowcountry, no matter the time of year, and there are as many
styles and venues as there are fishermen. They include: fly fishing in the inland flats, fishing from a pier, fishing with bait from small (15'–26') and large (up to 54') craft, fishing
off an artificial reef, surf casting from the beach, trolling in the Gulf Stream. Many independent guides and charter services have websites to help you match your interest to their
services. Visit them or call for information; there are dozens of options. Reservations and
deposits are almost always required (credit cards accepted); check on cancellation and
inclement weather policies.

Charter fees include equipment, instruction, fuel (sometimes extra), bait, licenses,
and food or drink if applicable. For small craft, the price is generally based on two people, $50 for each additional person (size of party limited by size of boat.) Large craft may
include one or two groups fishing together. Prices for charter boat rentals are from $250
for two passengers for a 4-hour excursion to $300 per person for a long day of Gulf
Stream adventure. If you head out on your own, an unguided powerboat costs from
$30–$80 per hour (capacity is from four to ten people), rental gear extra. You need to
purchase a saltwater fishing license if you fish from a boat; not necessary for shore-based
fishing or recreational harvest of crab and shrimp. Here are some charter services in the
Charleston area:

Bohicket Boat (843-768-7294; www.bohicketboat.com; Bohicket Marina, Seabrook
Island) Large selection of boats from 14–55 feet for inshore bass and trout fishing, jetty
fishing, and offshore fishing for shark, mackerel, tuna, marlin. Full- and half-day trips,
on your own or with a guide.

Captain Ivan's Island Charters (843-762-2020; www.captainivan.com; 805 Deckhawk
Retreat) Captain Ivan Schultz. Thirty-foot, wide beam boat with 21-passenger capacity,
full- and half-day excursions to offshore reefs, trips to the Gulf Stream (12 hours).

Captain Terry's Fishing (843-814-0544; wwwcharlestonexplorers.org.) Inshore family
fishing and crabbing as well as longer trips. By the day or half-day.

Carolina Clipper (843-884-2992; Shem Creek, Mt. Pleasant) Captain Randolph Scott
pilots a large boat with a snack bar and sundeck, and fully outfitted with gear and bait for
Gulf Stream trips. Beginners welcome.

Fitness Facilities

Contemporary vacationers may leave their troubles behind, but few of them forget to pack
their sweats. Though physical fitness hasn't ranked high among Charleston's pastimes
(below hunting, fishing, eating, drinking, visiting, snoozing), the city is accommodating.
Favorite places for runners are a loop that includes King St., the Battery and Meeting St., the

Waterfront Park, and, for the mighty, round trip across the new James Island connector.

Fitness centers have machines and free weights; some offer day-rates for visitors. Your hotel concierge or bed-and-breakfast host may recommend a personal trainer. Resorts and large hotels have their own facilities or spas. Fees vary widely according to service.

Earthling Day Spa (843-722-4737; 245 E. Bay St.).

Lifequest Fitness (843-571-2828; 35 Folly Rd.).

Stella Nova (843-722-9797; 292 King St.)

Studio Phoebe Pember (843-722-4186; www.studiophoebepemberrhouse.com; 297 E. Bay St.) Yoga drop-in.

Golf

The first golf course in America was built in Charleston, and the founding of the nation's first golf club in 1786 followed immediately. Courses here, like the great houses or gardens, are designed with natural beauty in mind, built to accommodate the environmental elements, and intended to offer a variety of surprises that keep you interested. **Charleston Golf, Inc.** (843-805-3067 or 1-800-774-4444; www.charlestongolfguide.com) is a central information and reservation service for tee times, accommodations and discount airfares. Ask for their Golf Guide.

Fees vary according to seasonal categories, sometimes nine in all. Lowest rates are usually Dec. through Feb. Carts are required at peak playing times on many courses. For resort play, golf privileges are sometimes extended to non-resort guests: Check with your concierge or call the resort directly. Club rentals and instruction are available at all courses. Greens fees/cart rentals reflect 2004 prices and do not include tax.

Public and Semiprivate Courses

Charleston Municipal Course (843-795-6517; 2110 Maybank Hwy.) Par 72. 6,400 yards. Greens fees during the week: $12 if you walk, $22 with a cart; on weekends, $15 if you walk, $25 with a cart. Twilight rates (after 3 PM) are $5.

Charleston National (843-884-7799; www.charlestonnationalgolf.com; 1360 National Dr., Mt. Pleasant) Par 72. Range: 5,103-yard forward course to 6,975-yard champion course. Fees vary according to nine separate seasonal categories: $35–$60 (weekdays) and $40–$75 (weekends).

Coosaw Creek Country Club (843-767-9000; www.coosawcreek.com; 8610 Dorchester Rd., North Charleston) Par 71. Range: 5,064-yard forward course to 6,593-yard champion course. Fees: $35–$59 (weekdays) and $50–$65 (weekends).

Crowfield Golf & Country Club (843-764-4618; 300 Hamlet Circle, Goose Creek) Par 72. Range: 5,682-yard forward course to 7,003-yard champion course. Fees: $26–$38 (local residents) and $35–$45 (non-residents).

Dunes West (843-856-9000; www.golfduneswest.com; 3535 Wando Plantation Way, Mt. Pleasant) Par 72. Range: 5,278-yard forward course to 6,871-yard champion course. Fees: $39–$49 (weekdays) and $49–$85 (weekends).

Legend Oaks Plantation (1-888-821-4077; 118 Legend Oaks Way, Summerville) Par 72.

Range: 4,954-yard forward course to 6,974-yard championship course. Fees: $32–$38 (weekdays) and $42–$50 (weekends).

The Links at Stono Ferry (843-763-1817; www.stonoferrygolf.com; 5365 Forest Oaks Dr., Hollywood) Par 72. Range: 4,928-yard forward course to 6,616-yard championship course. Fees: $45–$60.

Patriots Point Links (843-881-0042; www.patriotspointlinks.com; 1 Patriots Pt. Rd., Mt. Pleasant) Par 72. Range: 5,562-yard forward course to 6,856-yard championship course. Fees: $40–$50 (weekdays) and $55–$85 (weekends).

Shadowmoss Plantation Golf Club (843-556-8251 or 1-800-338-4971; www.shadow mossgolf.com; SC 61) Par 72. Range: 2,700-yard forward course to 6,701-yard championship course. Fees: $30–$38 (weekdays) and $40–$50 (weekends).

Courses at Charleston Area Resorts
If you are planning a vacation around golf, you might save yourself travel time by staying in resorts or gated communities where the game is the focus. Accommodations range from deluxe hotel rooms to villas and rental homes; renting through the resort yields savings in greens fees. These resorts also have complete recreational layouts, which include swimming pools, tennis courts, and marinas. Here's a list of some well-known resort golf courses near Charleston and their 2004 fees.

   Kiawah Island (1-800-654-2924 or 843-768-7272; www.kiawahresort.com; 12 Beach Dr., Kiawah) Five championship courses have been carved out of Kiawah's gorgeous Sea Island landscape by the game's top designers: Pete Dye, Jack Nicklaus, Gary Player, Tom Fazio, and Clyde Johnston. **The Ocean Course** (Par 72. Range: 5,327-yard forward course to 7,371 championship course) is probably the best known: The 1991 Ryder Cup was played here, and it was cited by *Golf Digest* as the toughest resort course in the country. **Osprey Point** (Par 72. Range: 5,122-yard forward course to 6,678-yard championship course) is consistently ranked in the country's top 75 courses with a landscape that includes four lakes, a maritime forest, and creeks. **Cougar Point** (Par 72. Range: 4,944-yard forward course to 6,861-yard championship course) and **Turtle Point** (Par 72. Range: 5,285-yard forward course to 6,914-yard championship course) make good use of Kiawah's unique geography—bracketed by the Atlantic and the river. **Oak Point** (Par 72. Range: 4,671 yard forward course to 6,759 championship course) is part of the resort but located on nearby Haulover Creek. Fees for the Ocean Course are $175–$275. For Osprey, Turtle and Cougar, fees are $100–$200. The fees at Oak Point are $50–$100.

   Seabrook Island (843-768-1000 or 1-800-845-2475; www.discoverseabrook.com; 1002 Landfall Way, Seabrook Island) **Crooked Oaks** (Par 72. Range: 5,250-yard forward course to 6,832-yard championship course, designed by Robert Trent Jones, Sr.) and **Ocean Winds** (Par 72. Range: 5,524-yard forward course to 6,805-yard championship course, a Willard Byrd design) won the resort a silver medal commendation from *Golf* magazine. Visiting players must be resort guests. Fees are $90–$150.

   Wild Dunes (1-888-343-7921; www.wilddunes.com; Isle of Palms) Tom Fazio designed both courses: **The Links** (Par 72. Range: 4,849-yard forward course to 6,722-yard championship course) offers oceanfront golf at its best, wind and water hazards notwithstanding. Fees: $100–$190. **The Harbor** (Par 70. Range: 4,774-yard forward course to 6,402-yard championship course) features challenging holes that are, in some cases, an island apart. Fees: $75–$125. Make reservations up to 90 days in advance.

Horseback Riding

The first racecourse in the Lowcountry was built near Charleston in 1735, and the South Carolina Jockey Club was founded there in 1758. Equestrian showmanship, hunting, and riding for pleasure are still popular forms of recreation.

If you want to take a trail ride during your visit, call one of the following stables to make advance arrangements. They may take you from a cypress swamp to the edge of a rice field. The prices start at about $30 per hour.

Middleton Place Outdoor Center (843-556-0500; 4290 Ashley River Rd., Charleston).

Stono Ferry Stables (843-763-0566; 5304 Stono Ferry Course, Hollywood).

Stono River Stable and Farm (843-559-0773; 2962 Hut Rd., John's Island).

Storybook Farm (843-571-2820; 1136 Bee's Ferry Rd.).

Hunting

In the Lowcountry you can hunt a variety of quarry including deer, wild turkey, dove, quail, feral hog, duck, fox, rabbit, woodcock, snipe, and clapper rail. What's more, you can do so during seasons that start as early as late summer (deer) and last through fall and winter until late spring (turkey). The Lowcountry has the longest deer season in the country and is considered the premiere spot on the East Coast to bag marsh hens.

There are six Game Management Areas in the Lowcountry; hunters at work within them are required to have a variety of licenses and permits, to abide by strict size and bag limits, obtain landowners' permission before hunting on private lands, and observe safe and ethical hunting practices in the field. For information, maps, and regulations concerning South Carolina hunting areas, contact the **Wildlife and Marine Resources Dept.** (803-734-3888; P.O. Box 167, Columbia, SC 29202). Outdoor recreation stores that specialize in hunting also provide tips, information, and licenses.

Some of the most popular public hunting grounds in the Charleston area are located in the **Francis Marion National Forest** (843-336-3248; 2421 Witherbee Rd., Cordsville), **Webb Wildlife Management Area** (803-625-3569; www.sctrails.net; SC 1, Box 80, Garnett, SC 29922) and **Palachucola Wildlife Management Area** (843-625-2114; Garnett), and on **Bear Island** (843-844-8957; Green Pond). For hunting licenses call 843-762-5078. Limited hunting is also permitted in the ACE Basin, permits can be downloaded from their website, www.acebasin.swf.gov, or requested at 843-889-3034.

If you prefer a more managed hunt, consider the guiding, cleaning, and transportation services of plantations that specialize in various kinds of game hunting, according to the season. Some offer overnight accommodations. For information, contact the **Lowcountry Tourism Commission** (1-800-528-6870; 1 Lowcountry Lane, Yemassee, SC 29945). **Total Charters** (843-722-2400; www.totalcharters.com) offers fishing and hunting expeditions in the Lowcountry and elsewhere.

The **Southeastern Wildlife Exposition** (www.sewe.com), which takes place every February in Charleston, is the region's most comprehensive gathering of fishermen, hunters, outfitters, and artists who specialize in subjects of interest to sportsmen. Display

sites scattered throughout the Charleston area feature Lowcountry and Western collectibles, crafts, decoys, antiques, and posters. A free shuttle bus service can take you to
them. In addition, there are presentations and demonstrations.

Nature Preserves

Many small islands, swamps, or boggy necks nestled in the creeks and riverways of the
Lowcountry offer natural camouflage and a pristine habitat to the wildlife that live or
migrate there. Some are more developed than others—with boardwalks or marked trails—
but none require strenuous activity or advanced knowledge for enjoyment. If you are
interested in the ecology of the Lowcountry, the life cycle of the marsh, the effects of tidal
flow on vegetation, and the interdependence of plant and animal life, these sites will give
you a feel for the rhythms of the Lowcountry beneath the surface.

ACE Basin National Wildlife Refuge (843-889-3084; www.acebasin.fws.gov; access off
US 17; take SC 174 through Adams Run and follow signs to Headquarters at Grove House,
an old plantation home.) A consortium of private individuals, non-profit organizations,
state, and federal agencies have joined together to preserve some 350,000 acres of diverse
habitat, including several islands, at the center of the Lowcountry. It is one of the largest
undeveloped estuarine sanctuaries on the East Coast. ACE takes its name from the area it
embraces: the lands and waters amidst the Ashepoo, Combahee, and Edisto Rivers on both
sides of St. Helena Sound, a fishery so rich and pristine it accounts for nearly 10 percent of
the state's shellfish harvest. Seventeen endangered species make their home here. Bring
binoculars and cameras. Open year-round, daylight to dusk; you may park and walk in.
Extensive trail maps are available online. **Bohicket Boat** (843-768-7294) and **Cap'n
Richards Ace Basin Tours** (843-766-9664) can take you there by water for $55–$65 per
person.

Audubon Swamp Garden (843-571-1266 or 1-800-367-3517; www.magnoliaplantation
.com; 3550 Ashley River Rd.) Sixty acres of blackwater cypress and tupelo swamp, with trails
and footbridges through virgin pine forests, wild flowers, and exotic plants: This is a place
that impressed John J. Audubon 150 years ago. Self-guided tour. Basic admission $13.

Caw Caw Interpretive Center (843-889-8898; www.ccprc.com; 5200 Savannah Hwy.,
Ravenel, 20 miles south of Charleston. Closed Mon.) You can still see the earth dikes,
floodgates, and rice fields that originally marked this former plantation, now home to
endangered species, songbirds, and migratory birds. There are seven miles of trails, a
swamp boardwalk, and exhibits that highlight the contributions of the African-Americans
who worked here long ago. A good stop if you're heading down the coast to Edisto,
Beaufort, or Savannah.

Cypress Gardens (843-553-2426; 3030 Cypress Gardens Rd., Moncks Corner. I-26 west
to Exit 208, then to SC 52 north) Take a guided tour or paddle a flat-bottom boat yourself
through an old rice plantation reserve, now a protected natural swamp garden. A succession of blooms, from the earliest camellia and narcissus to trumpet vine and azalea,
brightens the shadowy cypress forest. Open 9–5 daily. Adults $9, seniors $8, children $3,
under 5 free.

Francis Biedler Forest in **Four Holes Swamp** (843-462-2150; 336 Sanctuary Rd.,
Harleyville. From I-95 take I-26 east to Exit 177, then south on SC 453 to US 178. Follow

signs east on US 178. From Charleston, take I-26 west to Exit 187, then south on SC 27 to US 78.) The 11,000-acre sanctuary, managed by the National Audubon Society, contains the largest remaining virgin stand of bald cypress and tupelo gum trees in the world. There's a self-guided boardwalk and Visitor Center, but the point here is to walk quietly and observe well, to absorb what you can on your own without the experience being "packaged" in any way. Open 9–5 daily except Mondays. Adults $7, children $4, under 6 free.

Polo

Spectators can pack a tailgate picnic and enjoy Sunday afternoon polo games in September and October, April and May at **Stono Ferry** (843-766-6208; 5365 Forest Oaks Dr., Hollywood). Admission charged for some charity polo events.

Tennis

There are about three dozen public courts in city parks, tennis centers, and county recreation areas, and, of course, manicured layouts at the resorts. Your hotel concierge or bed-and-breakfast host should be able to direct you. Good news for Charleston tennis, the longest-running professional event in women's tennis, the **Family Circle Cup** (1-800-677-2293; www.familycircletenniscenter.com), has moved to a spectacular stadium at Daniel Island. There are 13 clay courts and four hard, all lit and open to the public.

Charleston Tennis Center (843-724-7402; Farmfield Rd., west of Charleston on US 17) has 15 outdoor hard courts, lit for night play. $2.50 per hour per person. Visitors should call ahead to check availability, or may reserve by paying in advance.

Some Lowcountry resorts also offer playing-time for non-resort guests on a space-available basis. Fees vary depending on season and time of day. Reservations are required. Inquire about tennis packages.

Kiawah Island (843-768-2121).

Shadowmoss Plantation (843-556-8251).

Wild Dunes (843-886-6000; Isle of Palms).

Windsurfing

Although the currents and tides make for tricky windsurfing conditions, the Lowcountry's warm water temperature and wide-open spaces have attracted windsurfers for years. Check local forecasts and tides before you go (843-588-2261 for McKevlin's surf report) and surf in well-known areas. Even experienced windsurfers have found themselves thrust well beyond the confines of, say, Charleston Harbor by the outgoing tide, only to find they have to wait until it turns to paddle or sail in.

Many resorts have windsurfers to rent, or provide instruction first on land, then in sheltered creeks or on a quiet stretch of beach. For more information, inquire at sporting goods shops or call some of the following rental/instruction agencies.

Barrier Island Surf Shop (843-588-6666; 32 Center St., Folly Beach).

Folly Windsurfing (843-795-8872; 878 Folly Rd., Charleston).

McKevlin's Surf Shop (843-886-8912; 1101 Ocean Blvd., Isle of Palms; 843-588-2247; 8 Center St., Folly Beach).

SHOPPING

The time has passed since the port of Charleston was small and accessible, since residents had the pleasure of observing dozens of ships along the wharves and wondering what lay in their holds. Yet such pastimes of commercial life were once commonplace. The anticipation of imports—teas, seeds, books, furniture, china, mail—and the reciprocal sending of an export was a satisfying part of life. If the export represented the result of what plantation slavery produced, the import confirmed Charleston's view of itself as a tasteful, cultivated, wealthy society. An ordinary impulse to consume took on meaning as part of a bigger equation.

Today, the impulse is still there, as is the anticipation, but no longer down at the wharves. Now it happens in small places: in glossy boutiques, in shops in old houses, in the open air of a busy corner, in commercial buildings on ballast-stone alleys, under the handsome brick and lattice sheds that line the center of Market St. for several blocks between Meeting St. and East Bay St. The surge in commercial rents due to Charleston's popularity has forced the relocation of several unique and modest stores, the kind of stores that set a tone for a place but don't make a big splash doing so. Seek them out on Queen St., Church St., and especially the upper section of King St. north of Calhoun, which has become popular with stores specializing in home décor and design.

Antiques store down the garden walk

Antiques

The period of poverty that engulfed the Lowcountry after the Civil War called for living by austere means and resourcefulness. It was not a time when renovating and redecorating was considered possible.

Some residents count this as a blessing: A lot of old houses, and all they contained, were spared the wrecker's ball. In the 1920s, many houses caught the eye of northern decorators and curators, who either imitated their look or purchased them, literally, lock, stock, barrel, and window sash. Later, when the families who had lived in the old houses produced a generation with the means to redecorate them, the urge to adorn them in the old style prevailed. Today, antiques stores throughout the Lowcountry retail this classic look, both in original pieces and in excellent reproductions.

While taste, or a good eye, is hard to define, it seems clear that the very experience of living in Charleston has produced antiques dealers who have absorbed its lessons of enduring beauty. They seem to know what fits—whether it's a pair of simple sterling candlesticks or a stunning chest-on-chest.

A short list of some of the more distinctive

antiques shops follows. If you are poking around for something in particular, or a type of thing, ask for it. It's a small world, and dealers should be able to direct you elsewhere.

A'Riga IV Antiques (843-577-3075; 204 King St.) An impressive collection of old scientific instruments and medical kits, some of which can be oddly beautiful as art objects, as well as apothecary jars and ceramic containers that were put to domestic use years ago.

Carolina Antique Maps and Prints (722-4773; 91 Church St.) Deep inventory and a knowledgeable staff: early botanicals, 19th-century maps, woodblocks and hand-colored pieces.

Century House Antiques (843-722-6248; 56-1/2 Queen St.) There's a fineness about this shop and the nature of its stock—English and Chinese export porcelain, botanicals, bird prints. It's the feeling you get from being in the presence of an eye that's appreciated beauty for a long time.

Charleston Antique Mall (843-769-6119; 4 Avondale Ave. at US 17, 10 minutes south of downtown) An interior mall with 20 vendors who sell a mixture of collectibles, antiques, and art. Fun to browse for an hour.

Chicora Antiques (843-723-1711; www.chicoraantiques.com; 102 Church St.) A special eye for decorative art from the Federal and Classical periods makes this an unusual shop— although there's plenty of mahogany and brass, too.

Dailey-Grommé (843-853-2299; www.dailey-gromme.com; 208 King St.) An amazing collection of 20th-century furniture and objects from European Art Deco to Modernist designers. Many unique or studio-made pieces.

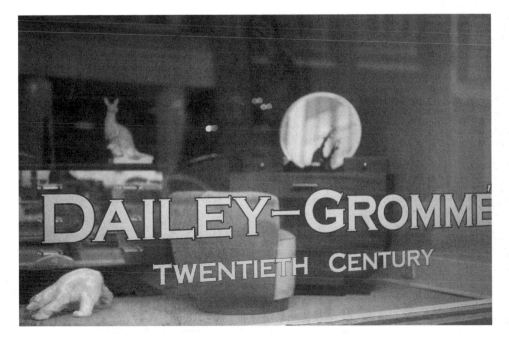

Antiques store on King St.

George C. Birlant & Co. (843-722-3842; 191 King St.) In business for more than 70 years, selling brass, silver, crystal, and small and large English antiques, which they import directly. Big old-fashioned picture windows open onto the street; inside there's lots of room to walk around. Reproductions of Charleston's own cypress-and-iron "Battery Bench" available.

George C. Williams American Antiques (843-377-0290; www.georgecwilliams.com; 155 King St.) A superb collection of American antiques, especially Southern and Charleston pieces, and decorative art accessories mostly dating from before 1830. The best antique store in Charleston.

Historic Charleston Reproductions (843-723-8292; www.historiccharleston.org; 105 Broad St.) Adaptations and reproductions of 18th- and 19th-century furniture, lamps, fabric, brass, wall coverings, and accessories that once graced Charleston homes. High-quality workmanship by companies like Baker Furniture, Scalamandre and Mottahedeh.

Moore House Antiques (843-722-8065; 150 King St.) Fine American pieces where the styles from England show through, as in Sheraton side tables. Shelves of Chinese export porcelain, Oriental rugs.

Ridler Page Rare Maps (843-723-1734; 205 King St.) Antique maps in a variety of sizes, some as old as the 16th century, many hand-colored.

Terrace Oaks Antique Mall (843-795-9689; 2037 Maybank Hwy.) A short drive from Charleston, this well-known establishment houses 20 dealers who sell an amazing assortment of rugs, glassware, silver, large pieces and accessories.

Books

Local independent book dealers know their stock, particularly as it concerns the history, literature, and art of the South, have a good relationship with their customers and their preferences, and thus are a source of suggestions. The national chains, for their part, showcase titles relating to local topics in history, gardening, culture, and photography. There are also several shops for used books and rare and historic volumes.

Audubon Shop (843-723-6171; 99 South Market St.) Field guides galore.

Barnes & Noble (843-572-2322; 7620 Rivers Ave., Charleston); (843-556-6561; 1812 Sam Rittenberg Blvd., Charleston); (843-216-9756; 1716 Town Center Way, Mt. Pleasant) The big book retailer has established itself here with an enormous quantity of books and magazines.

Book Exchange (843-556-5051; 1219 Savannah Hwy.) New and used books and collectible comics.

Boomers' Books (843-722-2666; 420 King St.) Broad selection in fiction, children's, antiques, and architecture.

Charleston Rare Book Co. (843-723-3330; 66 Church St.) Specializing in Charleston and Lowcountry books, including a good nautical section.

Historic Charleston Foundation Museum Shop and Bookstore (843-724-8484; www.historiccharleston.org; 108 Meeting St.) If you want to know more about regional history and the decorative arts, preservation efforts, architecture, and related topics, stop in here. Also many volumes about historic properties here and elsewhere, as well as an excellent children's section.

Millennium Music (843-722-1000; 372 King St.) New and used books as well as CDs, DVDs, and videos.

Pauline Books & Media (843-577-0175; 243 King St.) A religious bookstore with Bibles and a nice selection for younger readers.

Petterson Antiques (843-723-5714; 201 King St.) If the old books and magazines that sit on carts outside the store don't attract your eye, duck in and cast your gaze to the shelves and cases within. It may take time to find a treasure, but after all, you can never get enough of the atmosphere, which is free.

Preservation Society of Charleston (843-722-4360; www.preservationsociety.org; 147 King St.) The Society's headquarters has an unhurried, old-world feeling, with many books on Charleston history, art, architecture, and culture.

Waldenbooks (843-766-5879; 2070 Sam Rittenberg Blvd.) Best-sellers, good history and military section, coffee-table collections of photographs, regional cookbooks.

Clothing

In Charleston, people still wear hats. Not just baseball caps or fedoras, but straw hats, garden-party hats, fishing caps and velvet berets—hats with attitude. They also dress their children, boys and girls, in smockery and suits. Yet among a population that tends to sartorial conservatism, there is usually a fillip of embellishment to be found, accompanied by the natural confidence to pull it off.

Women will be especially fortunate to be shopping for clothes here. There are several comfortable boutiques (low-key, welcoming, with excellent suggestions) that offer unusual suits and separates in linen, silk, and cotton blends, in a range of styles. Given the temperate climate, this is the place to find shawls and patterned sweaters rather than tweeds and down.

The following suggestions do not list clothing stores that are part of a national chain, although those to be found in Charleston include Polo, Laura Ashley, Gap, Victoria's Secret, Saks Fifth Avenue, and Talbot's.

A. J. Davis & Co. (843-577-3088; 296 King St.) Men's clothes, plain and cheerfully sporty, and accessories.

Berlin's (843-722-1665; 114 King St.) Men's and women's clothes in traditional styles and top quality brands. Since 1883.

Bits of Lace (843-577-0999; 302 King St.) Fine lingerie and other little fancy things for women.

Bob Ellis Shoes (843-722-2605; 332 King St.) Vast selection of fine footwear for men and women and a sales staff that keeps bringing out the boxes.

Christian Michi (843-723-0575; 220 King St.) For women, high fashion from top European and American designers. It's as if a small section of SoHo left Manhattan for life in the provinces.

Copper Penny (843-723-2999; 311 King St.) If you saw it in *Vogue* or *InStyle*, it's here, too. Up-to-the-minute fashion and accessories (even if they seem a little too edgy for Charleston).

Cousins (843-937-8002; 161 King St.) Suzy Little has developed a terrific eye in nearly 20 years of selecting women's clothing and accessories and here you can buy anything from a sweater set to a little black dress, to the best work of fresh young designers. Upscale casual.

Ellington (843-722-7999; 82 Society St.) If you're returning to office life after a break and need something unusual and spiffy, or if you don't dress up much but like to wear a finely tailored piece or luscious fabrics when you do, look here for clothes with elegant, modern lines and solid construction. For men, too.

Granny's Goodies (843-577-6200; 301 King St.) Antique and vintage clothes for men, women, and children: poodle skirts, Hawaiian shirts, gloves and gauze, fur-trimmed opera capes, boas. Great selection and guaranteed laughs.

M. Dumas & Sons (843-723-8603; 294 King St.) Even the wallpaper here is riding to hounds. An original source for what has become the "American Country" look.

RTW (843-577-9748; www.rtwcharleston.com; 186 King St.) A boutique for women who delight in gorgeous fabrics, sweaters that tumble with color, one-of-a-kind shirts, hats, scarves, and accessories, and who like to dress with a sense of individuality and esprit. A rare find in any city.

Worthwhile (843-723-4418; www.shopworthwhile.com; 268 King St.) This wonderful, crazy store defies easy categorization: it's ironic (could be a 5&10 for yuppies, lots of small beautiful objects for the house) but sweet (flax and linen clothes for women, goofy baby hats). Cotton sweaters, T-shirts and leggings, nightclothes.

Crafts

The Lowcountry's **sea grass baskets** are a regional specialty, and if you're interested in them, you won't have far to look. The basket weavers are out every day where **Meeting Street** and **King Street** meet **Broad Street** and in the **Market Area**. Prices vary for items as small as keepsake decorations or as large as fanner baskets and hampers. You're welcome to watch the process, which incorporates strips of palmetto frond and pine straw with the pale grass. Other weavers sell their work at stands located north of Charleston on US 17.

American Originals (843-853-5034; www.americanoriginals.cc; 153 East Bay St., second floor) Contemporary crafts by local and national artists whose artistry and high standards shine through in glass, pottery, jewelry, pictures, textiles, and more.

Ceramics Cafe (843-722-7687; 432 King St.) Just behind the Visitors Center, a paint-your-own pottery studio in which you select a piece (from dozens available), paint it with glaze, and get it fired. It's one way to see if Charleston's beauty inspires. Wine and coffee available to stimulate your imagination.

Charleston Crafts (843-723-2938; 87 Hasell St.) Crafts and exhibits by members of this local co-op, who are considered superior in their fields, be they weavers, sculptors, or photographers.

People, Places & Quilts (843-937-9333; 1 Henrietta St.) Folk art, quilts and quilting supplies, patterns, and sewing notions.

Farms and Farmers' Markets

The Lowcountry growing season lasts from February to the first frost in November, with many crops being planted more than once. A visit to the outdoor market at Hutson St. (one block north of Marion Square) on Saturday mornings between April and November may yield anything from fresh basil to watermelon. Farmstands on the Sea Islands have an enormous range of produce, their own and other farmers', as well as jellies, relishes, shrimp, and fruit. Three near Charleston are: **Stono Farm Market** (843-559-9999; 842 Main Rd., John's Island); **Leland Farms** (843-559-1296; 4660 Maybank Hwy., Wadmalaw Island) and **Rosebank Farms** (843-768-9139; 3953 Betsy Kerrison Parkway, John's Island).

The **American Classic Tea Plantation** (843-559-0383; 6617 Maybank Hwy., Wadmalaw Island) is unique in the nation. You may stroll out to the tea fields or watch a video on the harvesting and curing process. Open weekdays from 10–4. (Take US 17 to SC 171. Turn east toward Folly Beach and soon after, turn south on SC 700, Maybank Highway. The plantation is located at nearly the end of this road.)

Gifts

Eighty-Two Church (843-723-7517; 1-1/2 Broad St.) A selection of hand-smocked dresses for girls, sunbonnets, beautiful hand-knit sets for newborns, cotton christening outfits and seersucker playsuits.

ESD (843-577-6272; www.esdcharleston.com; 517 King St.) Elizabeth Stewart has made her store and interior design service a model of the successful blending of old and new, of tried and trendy. She sells books, glassware, funky accessories, furniture, handcrafted jewelry, and antiques—some that are as new as mid-century modern and others that date from 200 years ago.

Gallery Chuma (843-722-7568; 43 John St.) A large gallery with unique gifts representing work by African-Americans in many media, including original paintings, prints, wearable art, and crafts.

Quadrupeds (843-534-1700; 106 Church St.) A tiny shop run by a young designer whose eye, which would make a whole room go bright, is apparent here in a selection of sublime Japanese ceramics, boxes, toile clutches, textiles for the table, and doggie things. But you cannot take the Jack Russell home.

Queen Charlotte Antiques (843-722-9121; www.queencharlotte.com; 61 Queen St.) Quirky pieces for the garden (small enough to carry), old sconces, wooden bowls and little accent pieces that convey the look of old Charleston.

Gourmet and Health Food Stores

Aloha Natural Foods (843-849-5521; 628 Coleman Blvd., Mt. Pleasant) Organic produce and juice bar, books, herbs, face and body products.

Carolina Wine and Cheese (843-577-6144; 54 1/2 Wentworth St.) Fresh German bread, excellent deli meats, coffees and teas, wine, of course, and all the makings for home-brewed beer.

Hoppin' John's (1-800-828-4412; www.hoppinjohns.com) Chef John Martin Taylor's wonderful shop is no more—he's taken it on-line. A marvelous selection of Lowcountry foodstuffs like his signature grits, cornmeal, and corn flour (order early, demand outpaces supply), chow chow, pickles, real hoppin' john for New Year's, and salty Virginia country ham.

Olde Colony Bakery (842-722-2147; www.southerntreats.com; 280 King St.) The source, since 1919, for benne wafers and other regional southern treats.

Raspberry's (843-556-0076; 1331 Ashley River Rd.) Natural, unprocessed foods including grains, herbs, bulk flour, and organic produce. Vitamins and body care items, too.

Uncork (843-577-9303; 333 King St.) Very fine wines and snacks, and lots of ideas for bottles under $10.

Home Furnishings/Kitchenware

Blink (843-577-5688; www.thinkblink .com. 62-B Queen St.) The owner, and the gifted eye behind the wonderful ceramic, glass, metal, and fabric objects in this tiny shop, is Mary Leonard. Nothing in Charleston compares—perhaps nothing south of SoHo.

fred (843-723-5699; 237 King St.) Clean, spare design once limited to black and white and stainless steel, now more color-ful: kitchen basics, cutlery, towels and racks, mechanical wonders. A great local favorite.

Classic ironwork in Charleston

Indigo (843-723-2983; indigohome.com; #4 Vendue Range) Fred and Beth Moore's cre-ative lives, interests, and tastes converge here in a selection of patterned tablecloths and painted mats, iron sculpture, handmade frames, ceramics, little metal animals like crabs and bunnies. A spirited, joyful store.

Le Creuset (843-723-4191; 221 Meeting St.) Famous French enameled cookware at factory prices. (The factory, and another store, is located off I-95 at Yemassee if you're heading south.)

Metropolitan Deluxe (843-722-0436; 164 Market St.) The idea of an old mercantile store, updated. Several large rooms are piled high with household goods, from the opulent (vel-vet upholstery, leather boxes, brass lamps, high-count cotton sheets) to the funky (wire baskets, painted benches, canvas chairs, fresh flowers).

South of Market (843-723-1114; www.southofmarket.biz; 173 King Street) A collection of original and reproduction or remade pieces that are French Country in style but amazingly suited to traditionally Anglophile Charleston, such as iron tables and garden accessories, oversized striped canvas pillows, sturdy bistro plates, and glass chandeliers.

Sporting Goods and Clothing

The Bicycle Shoppe (843-722-8168; 280 Meeting St.) Rent or buy bikes, or choose from cases full of bike hardware and gadgets.

The Charleston Angler (843-571-3899; www.thecharlestonangler.com; 654 St. Andrews Boulevard) Supplies for fly fishing and light tackle, high-end outdoor clothing, and equipment for fishing, shrimping, and crabbing.

The Charleston Bicycle Company (843-571-1211; www.Charlestonbicycleco.com; 1319 Savannah Hwy.) Specialized bikes for all riders and athletic training gear.

Half-Moon Outfitters (843-853-0990; 280 King St.) The most durable and fashionable outdoor wear (like Patagonia) is here, plus coats, tents, packs, camping supplies, and the best advice on local outdoor adventuring to be found in the city.

King Street Skates (843-723-5811; 433 King St.) All the brands of skateboards and the fashion stuff that goes with the sport.

Outdoor Outfitters (843-763-9115; 1662 Savannah Hwy.) A one-stop shop if you're going to be in the woods, the marsh, or on the water.

The Outdoor Shoppe (843-722-0618; 280 Meeting St.) Located next to Charleston's best bicycle shop, it specializes in kayaking equipment and accessories for all skill levels.

Savannah College of Art and Design rehabbed building

3

SAVANNAH

An Old City, A Modern City

It's no secret that the preservation of the great places of the Lowcountry, including the city of Savannah, occurred less as a result of enlightened social policy than from post–Civil War impoverishment. Indeed, the many years of slow growth and stalled expectations treated Savannah as they did Charleston, and to this day the cities share similar assets including vibrant, architecturally intact, downtown historic districts; a heritage that reflects the diverse contributions of generations of residents; and a culture enriched by unique musical, religious, culinary, and artistic contributions.

Yet in subtle ways, Savannah today is a more complex and interesting *modern* city than Charleston. For whatever historic reasons, and they run deep, it seems to have achieved an unusual sense of detachment. For every bold statement claimed about its history or beauty, there will be lurking on the lips of someone nearby a counter-claim, a small sarcasm. (Once upon a time during the cotton boom, Savannah madly envied New York City for its commercial muscle; 165 years later the two cities share a liking for gesture and attitude.)

This trait was evident even during the Civil War. Legend has it that General W. T. Sherman spared Savannah because the city was beautiful, the women were gracious, and the parties were just what he needed at the end of his blazing "March To The Sea" campaign. He took up residence, was indeed feted, and, in a remarkable telegraph of 1864, offered the unmolested city to President Lincoln as a Christmas gift.

Well, Savannah is still beautiful . . . and still partying. (This quality, and the world it describes, is revealed with great skill in the best book on Savannah, John Berendt's 1994 bestseller, *Midnight in the Garden of Good and Evil.*) The blend of reverence and hilarity, of high-mindedness and getting by, gives the city its character. In fact, as time passes, it becomes more palpable. When the local minor-league baseball team renamed itself the Sand Gnats (the top choice in a city-wide poll), it chose for its slogan "Bite Me." The city literally shuts down every St. Patrick's Day to accommodate 24 hours of revelry. There's less standing on ceremony here than in Charleston, for Charleston is an iconic Southern place, a city with such a significant, unique presence in American history that it must meet all sorts of expectations.

By the time national economic and social development did recommend change—after World War II, after a manufacturing and military base undergirded the economy, after federally mandated integration—Savannah residents with the means and interest to do so were faced with reconciling their historic cultural identity, on which they relied so deeply, with a post-war world which placed increasing value on money, mobility, and a celebration

Savannah River

TO:
U.S. 80 W.,
Hwys 17 & 21 N.

TO:
General McIntosh Blvd.

RIVER

ST.

Riverfront Plaza

FACTORS WALK

W. BAY ST.

E. BAY ST.

TO:
U.S. 80 E.,
forts & beach

City
Market

W. BRYAN ST.

E. BRYAN ST.

Franklin
Square

Ellis
Square

W. SAINT
JULIAN ST.

Johnson
Square

Reynolds
Square

Warren
Square

E. SAINT
JULIAN ST.

Washington
Square

W. CONGRESS ST.

E. CONGRESS ST.

W. BROUGHTON ST.

E. BROUGHTON ST.

W. STATE ST.

E. STATE ST.

Liberty
Square

Telfair
Square

W. PRESIDENT
ST.

Wright
Square

Oglethorpe
Square

Columbia
Square

E. PRESIDENT
ST.

Greene
Square

W. YORK ST.

E. YORK ST.

W. OGLETHORPE AVE.

E. OGLETHORPE AVE.

HOUSTON ST.

E. BROAD ST.

(W. BROAD ST.)

W. HULL ST.

E. HULL ST.

Colonial
Park
Cemetery

Elbert
Square

Orleans
Square

W. McDONOUGH
ST.

Chippewa
Square

E. McDONOUGH ST.

Crawford
Square

Visitors
Center

Civic
Center

W. PERRY ST.

E. PERRY ST.

BARNARD ST.

W. LIBERTY ST.

E. LIBERTY ST.

MARTIN LUTHER KING JR. BLVD.

MONTGOMERY ST.

W. HARRIS ST.

E. HARRIS ST.

Pulaski
Square

Madison
Square

Lafayette
Square

Troup
Square

E. MACON ST.

W. CHARLTON ST.

E. CHARLTON ST.

16

JEFFERSON ST.

TATTNALL ST.

W. JONES ST.

WHITAKER ST.

BULL ST.

DRAYTON ST.

ABERCORN ST.

LINCOLN ST.

HABERSHAM ST.

PRICE ST.

E. JONES ST.

16

W. TAYLOR ST.

E. TAYLOR ST.

Chatham
Square

W. WAYNE ST.

Monterey
Square

Calhoun
Square

Whitefield
Square

E. WAYNE ST.

W. GORDON ST.

E. GORDON ST.

W. GASTON ST.

E. GASTON ST.

W. HUNTINGDON ST.

E. HUNTINGDON ST.

Forsyth
Park

N

W. HALL ST.

E. HALL ST.

Victorian
District

W. GWINNET ST.

E. GWINNET ST.

0   0.25 mile

0   0.25 kilometer

W. BOLTON ST.

E. BOLTON ST.

SAVANNAH

© The Countryman Press

The Mercer House

of things modern and new. The time had come to set the ongoing physical and intellectual activities associated with historic preservation, neighborhood renovation, and tourist attraction on a larger and more public stage. This they did, and in the process became what might be called curators of their own collection, a collection whose very display case—the old city—is a work of art.

Originally laid out in an orderly, compact grid, downtown Savannah retains this geography today. It is defined by 21 handsome squares that function as vest-pocket parks. They are embowered and rimmed with native flowering species, and are linked by one-way cross streets along their sides, which, in turn, feed a few broad parkways divided by banks of trees and shrubs. It is the nation's largest registered Urban Historic District, containing some 1,200 buildings of architectural and historic significance. This layout gives Savannah the modern, urban feel of a city—but of course, it isn't a big city and the Historic District is but a section. It includes blocks of magnificent townhouses, many 19th-century places of worship, and several examples of Regency architecture popularized in this country by an Englishman, William Jay. The best way to see them and to feel the roots of American urbanism is on foot or on a carriage or trolley tour.

The restoration and adaptive re-use of private and institutional buildings continues. The Savannah College of Art and Design (SCAD) (www.scad.edu) has itself redone more than 40 sites. Its students are ubiquitous and have brought a feeling of freshness—a sense that things are happening in Savannah. There's no doubt that the presence of SCAD and the publication of *Midnight in the Garden of Good and Evil* (with the Mercer House as a central character) have sparked interest in Savannah, attracted not only young people and visitors, but also offered the opportunity to become modern by believing there is, and always was, more to Savannah than its history and architecture. It is now a place where an old filling station on a main artery has become an upscale market that sells arugula. Perhaps the best case in point is the addition to the Telfair Museum, a Regency-style mansion that serves as the city's art museum. After much back and forth with preservationists, historians, residents, and city government, the architect, Moshe Safdie, has translated into bricks and mortar, so to speak, the idea that bold modern design can relate to the historic city without diminishing its meaning, scale, or intimacy.

Savannah's popularity has led to development in several distinctive sections. **City Market** is a pedestrian streetscape, with shops, galleries, and restaurants. On a sunny afternoon it will be crowded with visitors—and families with young children—eating ice cream and listening to live music. Many carriage tours originate here, and many visitors will be drinking sweet tea in one of the outdoor cafes before or after their ride. On **River Street** 19th-century brick warehouses are filled with commercial and tourist-related attractions. From here, ferries zip across the Savannah River to Hutchinson Island, to the International Trade and Convention Center, and to Westin Savannah Harbor Resort. By night and on weekends, jugglers and street musicians entertain the crowds. **Broughton Street** is once again a vibrant downtown artery, anchored by a luxury hotel, where strolling means window-shopping and, especially in the evening, gourmet dining or entertainment at a renovated theatre. The residential **Victorian District** features large wooden houses faced with decorative moldings, fretwork, and porches, and many gingerbread bungalows. Entrepreneurs in smaller areas, like **Wright Square** and blocks of **Whitaker Street**, have joined together to make their address a destination for design or home and garden shops. More than ever, there are sidewalk cafes where students, locals, and visitors sip lattes and watch the world go by.

Carriages at Savannah's City Market

Renovated cotton factor's offices on River Street

As in Charleston, visitors are given the privilege to feel as residents: Nothing is frozen in amber. There is still motion in and around the most awesome architectural icons: people going to work, to school, home to lunch, to the market, just visiting.

The ways in which Savannah chose to survive have served it well. It has withstood General Sherman and Forrest Gump. Relishing its contradictions as it does, it faces the future with an extraordinary cultural and historic landscape, and a population with the sass and ginger pop to really enjoy it.

GETTING THERE

Savannah/Hilton Head International Airport (www.savannahairport.com) is the gateway, with some 40 stops each day from East Coast and mid-western cities on Air-Tran, American Eagle, Continental Express, Delta, Northwest, United, and US Airways. Flights often stop in Charlotte, NC, or Atlanta, but direct service is expanding. Rental cars from all major agencies are available at the airport, as are courtesy shuttles if you are staying at a big hotel. If you are staying elsewhere, ask the proprietor for advice or select a cab service at the airport. Expect to pay $20–$25 to Savannah. **Greyhound** (912-232-2135 or 1-800-231-2222; www.greyhound.com) serves Savannah regularly with departures and arrivals from around the country at its downtown depot. **Amtrak** (1-800-872-7245; www.amtrak .com) offers regular daily service on the East Coast line, although the station, located between the airport and the Historic District, is a cab ride away from downtown Savannah. By car, I-95 is just 10 miles from the Historic District, with an exit at I-16 that goes directly into town. Savannah is 252 miles from Atlanta, 105 miles from Charleston, 195 miles from Charlotte, 140 miles from Jacksonville, and 467 miles from Knoxville.

LODGING

Savannah and its Sea Island neighbor, Tybee Island, offer a range of accommodations, from upscale inns to funky beach villas. Tybee is closer to Savannah than Charleston's beach areas are to that city (about 20 minutes by car), and unlike Savannah's other nearby resort islands, Tybee is not a gated community.

Like Charleston, Savannah had its tradition of providing guest accommodations in city mansions whose owners had rooms to spare. As more visitors came to the area, "tourist homes" and "guest houses" sprang up to serve the mainly Northern clientele who flocked in springtime to see Savannah's gardens and experience its faded charm.

The only thing you'll find faded in Savannah today is a shirt that's been left out in the sun too long. Splendid inns, some of which are listed below, have emerged as old houses have been renovated and cityscapes renewed.

The caveats invoked in the Chapter Two, *Charleston* hold true here: Reservations are recommended, especially in the "high season" of spring, when a two-night's minimum stay is the usual practice; cancellation policies and room deposits are standard; and smoking takes place outside if it is allowed at all on the property. Access for handicapped persons can be problematic. The larger hotels can be relied on to offer it, but it is not always available in the smaller inns or luxury hotels. Carriage houses with ground-floor access are often a good bet. Don't hesitate to ask about these and other restrictions, including whether or not children are welcome. **B&B Reservation Service** (912-232-7787 or 1-800-729-7787) offers an overview of accommodations and a reservation service for rooms in luxury inns and private homes in the Historic District. The **Savannah Area Convention and Visitors Bureau** (1-877-728-2662; www.savannahvisit.com) provides information and some links to accommodations of all sorts in the city.

The same range of rates applies in Savannah as in other Lowcountry places. They are:

Inexpensive	Up to $60
Moderate	$60 to $120
Expensive	$120 to $200
Very Expensive	$200 and up

These rates do not include room taxes or special service charges that might apply during your stay. Ask about AAA, AARP, and other discounts.

Credit Cards
AE—American Express
DC—Diner's Club
CB—Carte Blanche
MC—MasterCard
D—Discover Card
V—Visa

Hotels and Larger Inns

Days Inn Suites
912-236-4440 or 1-877-542-7666.
www.daysinn.com.
201 W. Bay St., Savannah, GA 31412.
Price: Moderate.
Credit Cards: AE, D, MC, V.
Handicap Access: Yes.

A good budget choice in a renovated building with 253 modestly decorated rooms. It's an easy walk to River Street and City Market, but a bit longer to the heart of downtown.

Hilton Savannah De Soto
912-232-9000 or 1-800-426-8483.
www.desotohilton.com.
15 E. Liberty St., Savannah, GA 31412.
Price: Expensive.
Credit Cards: AE, DC, MC, V.
Handicap Access: Yes.

A wonderful location in the heart of the Historic District, a short walk to the riverfront. Some of the 246 rooms have private balconies, most have great views of Savannah's splendid squares. Pool and health club.

Hyatt Regency Savannah

912-238-1234 or 1-800-233-1234.
2 W. Bay St., Savannah, GA 31412.
Price: Expensive to Very Expensive.
Credit Cards: AE, DC, MC, V.
Handicap Access: Yes.

A 347-room hotel, with the trademark Hyatt atrium lobby and glass elevators, towers over the riverfront with an unparalleled view of the ship, ferry, and tugboat traffic. There's an indoor pool and shopping arcade, and you're steps away from busy River Street. Best location for River Boat excursions, the ferry to Hutchinson Island, or the day-trip ferry to Daufuskie Island and Hilton Head.

The Marshall House

$199

912-644-7896 or 1-800-589-6304.
www.marshallhouse.com.
123 East Broughton St., Savannah, GA 31401.
Price: Expensive to Very Expensive.
Credit Cards: AE, D, MC, V.
Handicap Access: Some rooms.

This thoroughly renovated hotel opened again in 1999, nearly 150 years after it was built in bustling, downtown antebellum Savannah. It's still right downtown, of course, and the Broughton Street area is bustling again with theaters, upscale restaurants, and shopping. Its bar draws a crowd to hear jazz combos Thursday through Saturday nights. There are 68 rooms, some suites among them with separate sleeping areas. It's been modernized with all the amenities, but the heart-pine floors and understated decor make the high-tech assets fit right in.

The Mulberry Inn

912-238-1200 or 1-800-596-3457.
www.savannahlodging.com.

601 East Bay St., Savannah, GA 31401.
Price: Expensive.
Credit Cards: AE, MC, V.
Handicap Access: Yes.

Right across the street from the commercial riverfront, this 145-room inn (including suites with wet bars) blends the close attention found in smaller inns with the full services of a hotel. Informal piano concerts set the tone for afternoon tea, and complimentary hors d'oeuvres are served. There's an outdoor pool and heated rooftop Jacuzzi. Special package rates are often available.

Westin Savannah Harbor Resort

912-201-2000 or 1-800-937-8461.
www.westinsavannah.com.
One Resort Drive, Savannah, GA 31421.
Price: Expensive to Very Expensive.
Credit Cards: AE, D, DC, MC, V.
Handicap Access: Yes.

A full-service luxury resort complex located on Hutchinson Island, 90 seconds by water taxi across the Savannah River from the Historic District or a brief car trip over the Talmadge Bridge. From here the views of Savannah and the river traffic are stunning, especially from the 55 Club Level rooms, some of which feature balconies. It's a huge place (16 stories, 403 guest rooms) with every amenity, from blow dryers to dual-line phones with dataports. Also on the site is the Greenbrier Spa with a menu of treatments to choose from, a fitness center, tennis courts, a par 72 golf course, clubhouse, marina, two pools, bar, grill room, and restaurant.

Luxury Inns

Ballastone Inn

912-236-1484 or 1-800-822-4553.
www.ballastone.com.
14 E. Oglethorpe Ave., Savannah, GA 31401.
Price: Expensive to Very Expensive.
Credit Cards: AE, MC, V.
Handicap Access: Limited.

At Christmas, the Ballastone Inn looks like a scene out of Dickens—holly, magnolia leaves, native mistletoe, and garlands of smilax carry its grand front parlor back in time to 1838 when this townhouse was built and English taste influenced the city. The decor echoes this high-style period in rich colors (like chocolate-toned walls), drapes, and furnishings, but is updated for comfort. There are 17 rooms, including three deluxe suites—many of them with Jacuzzis and fireplaces, and a courtyard you may not want to leave. A handsome full-service bar on the first floor is a wonderful amenity, one of the coziest nooks in the city. A full Southern breakfast is included.

East Bay Inn
912-238-1225 or 1-800-500-1225.
www.eastbayinn.com.
225 East Bay St., Savannah, GA 31401.
Price: Expensive.
Credit Cards: AE, D, DC, MC, V.
Handicap Access: Yes.

Originally a circa-1853 cotton warehouse, there are now 28 guest rooms, each furnished with queen-sized, four-poster beds, reproduction antiques, and coffeemakers. A modestly appointed place, it sits at a great location, across the street from the busy retail and nightlife hub of River Street. Pets and children are welcome: Call ahead for details.

Eliza Thompson House
912-236-3620 or 1-800-348-9378.
www.elizathompsonhouse.com.
5 W. Jones St., Savannah, GA 31401.
Price: Expensive to Very Expensive.
Credit Cards: AE, MC, V.
Handicap Access: Limited.

This 25-room inn gives off a sense of family warmth amidst beautiful old objects. It was one of Savannah's first luxury inns. Its spacious courtyard and fountain, and its wonderful location (on a brick-paved street embowered by oaks and lined with iron-balconied townhouses), still fulfill the expectations of visitors who come in search of the cities of the "Old South." Many extras like breakfast in the courtyard, evening wine, coffee, and desserts.

Forsyth Park Inn
912-233-6800.
www.forsythparkinn.com.
102 W. Hall St., Savannah, GA 31401.
Price: Expensive.
Credit Cards: AE, D, MC, V.

A modest, quiet place with 10 rooms, including a courtyard cottage that can accommodate up to four, this inn might best be used for a romantic weekend getaway for a busy couple. The main house is a Victorian-era mansion with inlaid hardwood floors and furnished with period antiques, reproductions, and four-poster beds. The baby grand piano in the entrance hall seems right in scale with the tall ceilings and long windows.

The Gastonian
Innkeeper: Anne Landers.
912-232-2869 or 1-800-322-6603.
www.gastonian.com.
220 E. Gaston St., Savannah, GA 31401.
Price: Very Expensive.
Credit Cards: AE, D, MC, V.
Handicap Access: Some.

This Regency/Italianate residence complex dating from 1868 has lost little of its imposing feel. Period-appropriate decor and muted colors take a visitor back to the post–Civil War era when "the Old South" was becoming "the New South." Each of the 17 suites has a gas fireplace; many have four-poster beds and some have Jacuzzi tubs. The side garden has been restored to its fragrant, secret self. Local people often reserve months in advance for special occasions. The Carriage House suite, with its own balcony and kitchen, is a favorite for honeymooners. Full Southern breakfast.

Hamilton-Turner Inn

912-233-1833 or 1-888-448-8849.
www.hamilton-turnerinn.com.
330 Abercorn St., Savannah, GA 31401.
Price: Expensive to Very Expensive.
Credit Cards: All major.
Handicap Access: Some.

Home of the eccentric "Mandy" in John
Berendt's book, *Midnight in the Garden of
Good and Evil*, this 10,000 square-foot
house is a must-see for fans of the book.
Even on its own, it's an amazing place, built
in the Second Empire style in 1873, totally
renovated in 1998 by a local family, and
furnished with Empire, Eastlake, and
Renaissance Revival antiques. The four-
story house and carriage house contain 18
rooms and suites, many with private balconies, whirlpools, and fireplaces. Full
breakfast and afternoon tea are served in a
grand dining room.

The Kehoe House

912-232-1020 or 1-800-820-1020.
www.kehoehouse.com.
123 Habersham St., Savannah, GA 31401.
Price: Very Expensive.
Credit Cards: All major.
Handicap Access: Elevator to all rooms.

Fountain, Forsyth Park, Savannah

This restored Victorian mansion has had
several lives: This is its grandest. There are
13 guest rooms (many with private balconies) and several grand public rooms
adorned with huge urns of fresh flowers in
the main building, and three additional
rooms in the townhouse across the courtyard. Everything here is scaled to *fin-de-
siècle* oversize: the ceiling moldings, the
valances, the draperies, the armoires, the
library tables, even the banisters and paneling. Not a corner's been cut in refurbishing
or services. Full breakfast and end-of-the
day wine and hors d'oeuvres define the day.

Magnolia Place Inn

912-236-7674 or 1-800-238-7674.
www.magnoliaplaceinn.com.
503 Whitaker St., Savannah, GA 31401.
Price: Expensive to Very Expensive.
Credit Cards: AE, MC, V.

For many years, praise has been heaped on
this inn from those who enjoy its carefully
appointed décor, including many lovely
Oriental objects and fabrics and because
the rooms are not overstuffed. Housed in a
late-19th century building, it faces Forsyth
Park, which offers a view and sense of rest-
fulness in addition to being a great place to
take a morning run. There are 13 rooms in
the main house, 3 on Magnolia Row. Just
behind the inn are two two-story rowhous-
es, each with two bedrooms upstairs. This
is a good option for couples traveling
together or families with kids.

Bed & Breakfast Accommodations in Homes / Private Suites

Individual homeowners operate B&Bs that
are very nice but not fancy, and services
and brokers list accommodations in homes
or in stand-alone lofts and townhouses in
the Historic District. Credit cards are
accepted for some—but not all—lodgings;
deposits required, usually seven working
days in advance, with penalties or charges

for cancellation. Handicap access is available; some hosts allow pets. Rates are Moderate to Very Expensive. Can be a budget choice, or an option for extended families or friends traveling together. One service is **Coastal Concierge** (912-232-2504 or 1-866-675-6339; www.thecoastalconcierge.com; 201 E. Charlton St.) Here are other ideas:

Colonial Park Inn (912-232-3622 or 1-800-799-3622; www.colonialparkinn.com; 220 E. Liberty St.) offers a carriage house and garden house suite. Children over age 12 welcome.

East Liberty Inn (912-232-8034 or 1-800-989-1232; 202 E. Liberty St.) offers two handicap accessible rooms with off-street parking.

Joan's on Jones Bed and Breakfast (912-234-3863 or 1-888-989-9806; 17 W. Jones St.) Good location on one of Savannah's prettiest streets; two suites; children and some pets welcome.

Resorts and Rentals—Tybee Island

Savannah's beach is Tybee Island, a very informal place, the opposite of a gated resort. It has been for years a retreat from the city where you can take off your shoes and have your neighbors over for a beer, perhaps before lunch. While there are some new luxury homes, it's mostly houses raised up high, with latticed skirts hiding the pilings, and a deck out back. The beach is broad and public, with a pier and plenty of access points. There are shops for beachwear and boogie boards, two excellent restaurants, some fine B&Bs, oceanfront hotels that are not glitzy, and a campground and RV park. It's also the best place to get on the water in a kayak. (See **Recreation.**) Condo complexes and inexpensive motels are typical lodgings but some other options are listed below. Contact the **Tybee Visitors Center** (1-800-868-2322; www.tybeevisit.com) for more ideas.

Dunes Inn and Suites
912-786-4591 or 1-888-678-0763.
www.dunesinn.com.
1409 Butler Ave., Tybee Island, GA 31328.
Price: Expensive.
Credit Cards: AE, D, DC, MC, V.
Handicap Access: Yes.

An upscale version of a chain hotel. Some of the 53 rooms have kitchenettes, some have king-sized beds and Jacuzzis. It's simple, clean, close to the beach, and has a swimming pool.

Fort Screven Inn
912-786-9255.
www.fortscreveninn.com.
24 Van Horn, Tybee Island, GA 31328.
Price: Moderate to Expensive.
Credit Cards: MC, V.

Once part of the Fort Screven infirmary, located one block from the beach on the quieter north end of the island (closer to Savannah) amid live oaks, palmettos, and many places to walk or jog.

Hunter House Inn
912-786-7515.
www.hunterhouseinn.com.
1701 Butler Ave., Tybee Island, GA 31328.
Price: Moderate.
Credit Cards: AE, MC, V.

Four rooms in a circa-1910 house at the beach—sounds like an old-fashioned vacation. It's one block away from the water, 25 minutes from downtown Savannah. Four rooms, including two suites that can accommodate more than just two people. Queen-sized beds and private baths are standard. A fancy restaurant on the premises.

Outdoor Inn
912-786-8732 or 1-888-529-2542.
www.seakayakgeorgia.com.
1018 US 80, Tybee Island, GA 31328.
Price: Inexpensive to Moderate.
Credit Cards: D, MC, V.

Tybee Island Lighthouse

Located next door to Sea Kayak Georgia, which offers instruction, kayak touring, and equipment, this two-story beach house overlooks the marsh and offers beds in a very attractive bunkroom with great views, or two private rooms with a shared bath. Many guests stay here while participating in a Sea Kayak Georgia program or expedition (from beginner to advanced levels) but everyone is welcome. Tybee's two best restaurants are practically next door; it's a short car or bike ride to the beach. The staff is friendly and they know the area's paddling waters better than anyone. Share your stories and tales of the outdoors in a common living room and porch.

Savannah Beach & Racquet Club
912-786-6284 or 1-800-864-7985.
www.sbrctybee.com.
1217 Bay St., Tybee Island, GA 31328.
Price: Moderate to Expensive.
Credit Cards: MC, V.

Modest one- to three-bedroom condo lodgings with pool, tennis, and beach access, available by the night, week, or month. Typical rates in summer (six–eight people) from $900/week; Spring Vacation week (March/April) from $1,100/week.

17th Street Inn
912-786-0607 or 1-888-909-0607.
www.tybeeinn.com.
12 17th St., Tybee Island, GA 31328.
Price: Moderate.
Credit Cards: MC, V.

Eight rooms with private entrances and full kitchens, with a deck for all guests and plenty of room for families. Clean, friendly, funky, less than one block from the beach. Kids accommodated with beds at modest additional cost.

Rental Agents at Tybee Island
Oceanfront Cottage Rentals (912-786-0054 or 1-800-786-5889; www.oceanfront cottage.com; 717 First St., Tybee Island, GA 31328) Listing 30 homes on the ocean or with an ocean view. Many welcome pets, and usually provide boogie boards, bikes, and beach chairs. Some with pools and hot tubs.

Sandy's by the Shore (912-786-0531 or 1-866-512-0531; www.sandysbytheshore .com; 1705 Strand St., Tybee Island, GA 31328) More expensive listings, upscale houses, and high-end villas.

Tybee Island Rentals (912-786-4034 or 1-800-476-0807; www.tybeeislandrentals .com; 203 First St., Tybee Island, GA 31328) Some 120 properties are available for rent by the week or month, with a two-night minimum stay.

Tybee Vacation Rentals (912-786-5853 or 1-866-359-0297; www.tybeevacationrentals .com; 1207 US 80, Tybee Island, GA 31328) Listing 60 houses, cottages, villas, houses with pools. Pet-friendly properties. On-line reservations accepted.

DINING

By the end of the American Revolution, visitors to Savannah were impressed with the abundance and variety of its foods, the sophisticated way they were prepared by slaves, and the splendid manner in which meals arrived at the table. Lavish at-home dining established itself as a mark of social position.

The art and pleasure of dining stayed home-based for many years after that, well into this century. There were few places to dine out and few reasons to do so. The culture centered around home, family, the connections of friends and neighbors, and a convivial shared history. You could conduct your business in a restaurant, but not your social life.

Savannah's many restaurants show how that has changed. Today, the city is filled with plain and fancy places to eat. The local population, including thousands of students, is eager to dine out. They have the means to do so; visitors arrive with high culinary expectations. While there may be fewer no-frills lunch counters and cafeterias, there are plenty of informal cafes, cof-

fee bars, and beachside bistros to take their place. Don't discount Tybee Island (see "Savannah Area") as a dining destination: it's not just fried seafood anymore.

The hours and prices of restaurants have been checked as close to the date of publication as possible, but a call ahead to confirm is always wise. The general price range we list is meant to reflect the cost of a single meal, usually dinner, featuring an appetizer, entrée, dessert, and coffee. Cocktails, beer and wine, gratuity, and tax are not included in the estimated price.

Dining Price Code

Inexpensive	Up to $15
Moderate	$15 to $30
Expensive	$30 to $50
Very Expensive	$50 or more

Credit Cards

AE—American Express
DC—Diner's Club
CB—Carte Blanche
MC—MasterCard
D—Discover Card
V—Visa

Delicatessens, sweet shops, and bakeries are listed below larger restaurants; gourmet and health-food stores are listed under Gourmet Food in the Shopping section of this chapter.

Belford's

912-233-2626.
315 W. St. Julian St.
Open: Daily.
Price: Moderate to Expensive.
Cuisine: Southern.
Serving: L, D, Sun. Brunch.
Credit Cards: AE, D, MC. V.
Reservations recommended.
Handicapped Accessible.

Belford's opens on both sides to City Market, and has patio seating, features which make it very attractive for Sunday brunch and lunch. There's a small corner

Enjoying an outdoor concert at City Market

bar where you can eat in a pinch, but you'd want to be in the main dining area, one side an exposed brick wall, lots of glass windows, seating around an open grill. Steaks and seafood are the best choices, and every waiter and the carriage tour operator outside will remind you that the crab cakes have received an award. They do a great job of Lowcountry staples like greens, shrimp, and crab stew.

Bistro Savannah
912-233-6266.
309 W. Congress St.
Open: Daily.
Price: Moderate to Expensive.
Cuisine: American, Southern.
Serving: D.
Credit Cards: AE, MC, V.
Reservations recommended.
Handicapped Access: Yes.

The Bistro draws a mix of residents and visitors staying at the downtown B&Bs. Repeat customers come for the homemade soups and desserts, house smoked pork, greens,

and hot pepper cornbread—and the casual, upbeat atmosphere. In City Market but somehow away from the noise and bustle, it has a serene atmosphere enhanced by comfortable wicker chairs and soft lighting. The menu is full of fresh market specials featuring organic produce, small piquant salads, and lots of seafood. Extensive wine list, specializing in California vineyards.

City Market Cafe
912-236-7133.
224 W. St. Julian St.
Open: Daily.
Price: Moderate.
Cuisine: American.
Serving: L, D.
Credit Cards: AE, CB, D, MC, V.
Handicapped Access: Yes.

This popular and unpretentious restaurant covers a lot of bases well. The menu includes pasta, sandwiches, chicken, and ribs, many varieties of salad plates. The place itself seems full of fizz: brick walls, a black tin ceiling, starched tablecloths, and indoor and outdoor dining. The staff is unfazed by children and won't blink if you order a hefty grilled sandwich for dinner while your companion has beef tenderloin and fine wine. A good choice for lunch after a day of touring.

Clary's Cafe
912-233-0402.
404 Abercorn St.
Open: Daily.
Price: Inexpensive.
Cuisine: American.
Serving: B, L.
Credit Cards: AE, MC, V.
Wheelchair accessible seating.

A bacon-and-egg sandwich on wheat and coffee is a typical order at Clary's, a downtown eatery where your cup stays refilled and breakfast waffles can set you up for the day. At lunch, the Greek salad is big enough to share, or if you're hungry you might try the chicken potpie, which includes salad and a roll. Top it off with a root beer float. *Midnight in the Garden of Good and Evil* fame sent the crowds here, but the diet-busting food makes it worth the trip.

Crystal Beer Parlor
912-443-9200.
301 W. Jones St.
Closed: Sun.
Price: Inexpensive to Moderate.
Cuisine: Southern.
Serving: L, D.
Credit Cards: D, MC, V.

Located at the end of one of Savannah's prettiest residential streets on the edge of the Historic District, the Crystal is a bar with leather booths and frosted mugs, and has been recently freshened up. It's not a secret—it's been written up many times—but it tends to be forgotten when it shouldn't be. Shrimp salad, fried oysters, burgers, and crab stew are popular.

Elizabeth on 37th
912-236-5547.
www.elizabethon37th.com.
105 E. 37th St.
Open: Daily.
Price: Very Expensive.
Cuisine: American; gourmet Southern.
Serving: D.
Credit Cards: AE, MC. V.
Reservations recommended.

The creation of Elizabeth Terry, chef, author, and James Beard Award winner, this restaurant was one of the first in Savannah to bring seasonal products, signature flavorings, and a sense of creative possibility to mundane Southern staples like grits, grouper, and greens—and to offer them to a larger audience. It was the only place serious foodies took seriously. Elizabeth is gone, but diners can still count on elaborate meals in the sumptuous setting of an old mansion. You'll need to drive or take a cab from downtown. Relax and enjoy the formality and the huge wine list and forget about the price. Favorites include rack of lamb encrusted with herbs, local fish, and seafood soups.

45 South
912-233-1881.
20 E. Broad St.
Closed: Sun.
Price: Very Expensive.
Cuisine: Continental; gourmet Southern.
Serving: D.
Credit Cards: AE, MC, V.

A softly lit place, lots of dark green in the decorating, almost like a row house, with elegant tables situated in three sections and a small bar. The service is here in abundance—a waiter to refill your water glasses; another to grind the pepper. Bread gives way to well-dressed food, especially crab cake and roasted red pepper rémoulade, or scallops of veal with garlic potatoes and spicy mustard. Quiet and romantic.

The Lady & Sons
912-233-2600.
www.ladyandsons.com
102 W. Congress St.
Open: Daily.
Price: Moderate.
Cuisine: Country Southern.
Serving: L, D.
Credit Cards: All major.

The lunch buffet offers the full range of Southern specialties, including fried tomatoes, catfish, ribs, and shrimp grits—a smart choice if you plan to be walking and touring for the rest of the day before a late-evening meal. Paula Deen made her name on food-network television and in cookbooks by making down-home dishes burst with pride and flavor. The crowds at the door would make you think a rock star was eating those greens. Expect a wait, so check in and wander around City Market until your table's ready.

Mrs. Wilkes' Dining Room
912-232-5997.
107 W. Jones St.
Open: Mon.–Fri.
Price: Inexpensive.
Cuisine: Southern.
Serving: L.
Credit Cards: None.
Handicapped Access.

This is homemade cooking served as it would be at home: the diners seated around large tables, with heaping platters of fried chicken, baskets of biscuits, and bowls of slaw, vegetables, red rice, and black-eyed peas or green beans placed before them. If you've ever been grateful for the kindness of strangers, the one who gives you the last pork chop could be your friend for life. It's located in the basement of an old red-brick house, but you'll recognize it by the line forming at mealtime.

The Olde Pink House
912-232-4286.
23 Abercorn St.
Open: Daily.
Price: Expensive.
Cuisine: Southern; Continental.
Serving: D.
Credit Cards: All major.

Located in an elegant 18th-century mansion designated a National Landmark, here the Declaration of Independence was read in Savannah for the first time. There's a quiet dining room upstairs, and a more lively tavern downstairs, with fireplaces roaring in winter, piano music, a welcoming bar, and a full dinner menu. This is one of the most popular places downtown to have a cocktail or relax after dinner—that is, if the diners release their tables. The seafood is recommended (a recent appetizer was sautéed shrimp with country ham and grits cake) but the entrées include fish, veal, steak, and lamb, many with a glazed sauce.

Olympia Cafe
912-233-3131.
5 East River St.
Open: Daily.
Price: Inexpensive to Moderate.
Cuisine: Greek.
Serving: L, D.
Credit Cards: All major.

River Street is not a subtle stretch, with its bars and gift shops and crowds, but it's fun, and this is its best restaurant. Savannah's population of Greek descent, proud of its deep roots and civic contributions, make this a casual, friendly place. There are, of course, Mediterranean appetizers like *tzadiki* and *dolmadakia,* and gyros and kabobs, as well as traditional Greek dishes like lemon chicken and *moussaka*. If you hear servers and diners shouting *opa* it means another order of flaming cheese appetizers was a hit.

Sapphire Grill

912-443-9962.
www.sapphiregrill.com.
110 W. Congress St.
Open: Daily.
Price: Expensive to Very Expensive.
Cuisine: American.
Serving: D.
Credit Cards: AE, MC, V.

A sharp, stylish, restaurant on three floors serving a first-rate dinner and open late for nightcaps. Located in the City Market area, it is modern and sleek—bare hardwood floors, wooden blinds, white tablecloths, and lots of brushed metal. The bar, along one side, can get crowded and create a lot of traffic, and the restaurant tends to be noisy. Nonetheless, it's a special place. There's always an excellent choice of beef or duck, several pan-seared or grilled fish dishes, and foie gras added to any plate. Signature appetizers are shrimp, arugula salad, and fried green tomatoes with chèvre croutons.

Vinnie Van Gogo's

912-233-6394.
317 W. Bryant St.
Open: Daily.
Price: Inexpensive.
Cuisine: Pizza, Italian.
Serving: L (Sat., Sun.); D (from 4 PM)
Credit Cards: None.
Special Features: Delivery by bicycle courier to downtown area.

Calzones and thin-crust pizza by the slice or pie (14" or 18") made from dough prepared on the premises during the day, then rolled and tossed while you watch from the counter. These cooks are having fun. Toppings include healthy vegetables. Large selection of imported beers and a concoction called spodeeodee (cheap red wine, 7-Up, splash of orange soda), which sells by the glass or pitcher as fast as they can mix it up. Eat on the patio—you're surrounded by

art students— and get sense of a new population that has enlivened the old city.

SAVANNAH AREA

The Breakfast Club

912-786-5984.
1500 Butler Ave., Tybee Island.
Open: Daily (6:30 AM–1 PM).
Price: Inexpensive.
Cuisine: Southern.
Serving: B, L.
Credit Cards: MC, V.

Get a feel for the kicked-back life of Tybee here among locals sitting at booths and tables set close together in this small, unpretentious place. You might run into the shrimpers coming in or the early anglers and birders just setting out. If you want to get a jump on the day, or take a quiet walk on a deserted morning beach, this is a great place to start. On weekends, or by midmorning, there will be a line.

Crab Shack at Chimney Creek

912-786-9857.
www.thecrabshack.com.
40 Estill Hammock Rd., Tybee Island (second right past Lazaretto Creek Bridge).

Relaxing in one of Savannah's squares

Open: Daily.
Price: Moderate.
Cuisine: Seafood.
Serving: L, D.
Credit Cards: MC, V.

As informal as your own back porch: wooden tables inside and out, beer in the bottle, sandy feet welcome. The food is strictly off-the-boat: raw-bar selections, fat crab served in cakes or blended with spices and cheese, and Lowcountry boil, a platter including shrimp, corn, potatoes, and sausage.

Located at a bend on the creek, the view is premium Lowcountry, enjoyed from the home-made Tiki Bar or from the deck, where "Crab Shack chandeliers" (made from old baskets) light up the night. Its popularity is threatening its funky state—there will be a wait—but it is what it is and does it well.

Georges'
912-786-9730.
1105 US 80, Tybee Island.
Closed: Mon.
Price: Expensive to Very Expensive.
Cuisine: American Fusion.
Serving: D.
Credit Cards: All major.
Reservations highly recommended.

Georges' is a handsome, mellow restaurant that ranks in Savannah's top three, although it's out of town and by no means in a majestic building. Sometimes the food has Asian influences like wasabi, sesame seasonings, or ginger rice, but not always. The reduction sauces flavored with fig, mango, apricot, or pomegranate are subtle and smooth, encouraging the rack of lamb or seared yellowfin tuna they're paired with.

The standout appetizer is soup made with local crab, corn, leek, and artichoke. Wines average about $30 per bottle from a good and varied list. A tasting menu is available:

Call ahead. If you appreciate a meal that is itself a destination, make time to come here. Dress is upscale casual.

North Beach Grill
912-786-9003.
41-A Meddin Dr. (by the Lighthouse), Tybee Island.
Open: Daily.
Price: Inexpensive to Moderate.
Cuisine: Seafood; Caribbean.
Serving: L, D.
Credit Cards: AE, MC, V.

Take an old beachside snack bar (where you could have rented surf boards and umbrellas and bought a hot dog), screen it in, add island spices and beer, and you're getting close to describing this place. It's very small, informal, and nonchalant, serving jerk chicken and pork, conch fritters, Cuban pot roast, crab with asparagus, and plantains. Success hasn't spoiled it one iota.

Tango
912-786-8264.
tangorestaurantandtropicalbar.com.
1106 US 80, Tybee Island.
Open: Daily.
Price: Expensive.
Cuisine: Seafood; Asian, Caribbean, and Latin touches.
Serving: D; Sun. Brunch.

The menu was inspired by years of cruising the Caribbean and Pacific, and the place looks like it belongs there, too. Several small rooms, upstairs, downstairs, on the porch and on the deck describe the layout; the decor is tropically bright colors offset by a dark wooden bar.

Local people, young enthusiastic staff, upbeat in every way. You could make a meal out of a margarita and cilantro-infused spring roll with pork and shrimp or go for West Indian spiced shellfish with curry, cashews, and coconut. Vegetarian plates, too. Music on the deck.

Food Purveyors

Some of the places listed below should not be overlooked for lunch or brunch, although they are a welcome sight at mid-afternoon, after a day of touring. There are more of these very good, informal places than ever before.

Bakeries/Coffeehouses

Ex Libris (912-525-7550; 228 Martin Luther King, Jr. Blvd.) Three floors of books, art supplies, and overstuffed sofas to sit on and sip your coffee after you browse.

Firefly Cafe (912-234-1971; 321 Habersham St.) Neighborhood spot on Troup Square, walk a few steps down to the dining area or eat outside. Highly recommended Sat./Sun. brunch, although lunch salads and sandwiches are exceptional. Dinner is also served, if you're tired of the formality and simply want a good meal.

Gallery Espresso (912-233-5348; 6 E. Liberty St.) Coffees, rum cakes, outdoor tables, and indoor art exhibits. Longtime favorite of artsy locals.

Gryphon Tea Room (912-525-5880; 337 Bull St.) A real Edwardian-style, overdecorated, high-ceilinged cafe, with tile floors, stained glass, dappled light, and potted palms. Treat yourself to afternoon tea.

Savannah Coffee Roasters Cafe (912-232-5282; 7 E. Congress St.) Pastries and simple snacks, lots of overstuffed chairs, and no one particularly bothered if you're eating, sipping, and reading slowly. On Johnson Square.

Soho South Cafe (912-233-1633; 12 W. Liberty St.) The bakery opens at 8 AM but lunch starts at 11:30, and Sunday brunch at 11 AM. Inside a hip art gallery with good things to see and good people-watching. To-go menu.

Wright Square Cafe (912-238-1150; 21 W. York St.) The wraps at lunch are terrific (the menu also includes panini and salads) and the setting is very European, with indoor and sidewalk dining, racks of fine chocolates and coffees, comfortable chairs, and a serious attention to architectural detail, from floor to ceiling. On a square with several shops for antiques, books, upscale clothing, and home furnishings.

Candy and Ice Cream

Byrd Cookie Co. (1-800-291-2973; www.byrdcookiecompany.com; 6700 Waters Ave.) A local institution since 1924. Delicious cookies and gourmet desserts made on site. Tours available.

Peaches and Cream (912-233-3131; 5 E. River St.) Frozen yogurt and French ice cream on the waterfront.

Savannah's Candy Kitchen (912-233-8411; 225 E. River St.) The largest candy store in the South, where you can see the candies made and have some sent home.

Delis and Faster Food

Brighter Day (912-236-4703; 1102 Bull St.) A family-run health-food store featuring a full line of natural foods and health-care products, as well as excellent sandwiches to go or to eat there, breads, and organic produce.

Savannah carriage tour

Express Cafe and Bakery (912-233-4683; 39 Barnard St.) An upscale Art Deco-style bakery created in the shell of a downtown storefront. Opens early. The breads and desserts are homemade; omelets are light and fresh. Light lunches include soups and sandwiches.

Sushi Zen (912-233-1188; 41 Whitaker St.) An intimate, minimalist setting where you can get sushi, American sandwiches, and creative "lunchbox specials."

Touring in the Historic District and Beyond

There are so many options for tours in Savannah that you might decide whether you want to concentrate on ghosts, the Civil War, "The Book," gardens, old houses; or whether you want to go on foot, by carriage, trolley, air-conditioned bus or van; or by daylight or moonlight. Most tours last between one and two hours.

Some motorized tours allow you to step off the bus and catch up with it at a later stop. Tours that are more specifically nature-oriented, or may require equipment such as a kayak or canoe, are more fully described in the **Recreation** section, below. Prices range from $10–$20 for adults, from $5–$12 for children. Here are some ideas; check the websites for more information:

By Bus or Van:
African-American History Tours (912-231-8900; www. savannahcivilrightsmuseum.com)

Freedom Trail Tours (912-398-2785)

Gray Line Bus and Trolley Tours (912-234-8687 or 1-800-426-2318; www.graylineof savannah.com).

By Carriage

Carriage Tours of Savannah (912-236-6756 ; www.savannah.com).

Historic Savannah Carriage Tours (912-443-9333 or 1-888-837-1011).

Plantation Carriage (912-201-0001).

By Trolley

Old Savannah Tours (912-234-8128 or 1-800-517-9007; www.oldsavtour.com).

Old Town Trolley Tours (912-233-0083; www.trolleytours.com).

By Foot

Explore Savannah (912-507-9144; www.exploresavannah.com).

Ghost Talk, Ghost Walk (912-233-3896 or 1-800-563-3896; www.savannahgeorgia.com).

Savannah Haunted History Tours (912-604-3007; www.savhauntedhistory.com).

Savannah Walks (912-238-9255 or 1-888-728-9255; www.savannahwalks.com).

See Savannah Walking Tours (912-234-3571; www.seesavannah.com).

Tours by BJ (912-233-2335; toursbybj.com).

By Boat

Dolphin Magic Tours (1-800-721-1240; www.reelemn.com).

Lowcountry River Excursions (912- 898-9222).

Old Daufuskie Crab Co./Calibogue Cruises (843-342-8687). Cruises and tours of Daufuskie.

Palmetto Coast Charters (912-786-5403; www.palmettocoast.tybeeisland.com).

Wilderness Southeast (www.wilderness-southeast.org).

CULTURE

Architecture

Appreciating architecture in Savannah is a little like being a parent: You can read about it, you can hear it described fully and well, you can understand why people do it, and you can give it a rational and historic context. But you haven't begun to feel its power until you face it for yourself, four-square, on a lazy walk in the city.

It is not necessary to arrive and hit the ground running. Whether or not you visit every historic house and church, or mentally catalogue its interior detailing, is not that important. You can buy an exquisite book for that (see Chapter Six, **Information** for suggestions, or visit a bookstore listed under **Shopping**). What's special about this region is that you can experience architecture in drifts, in vistas, as a harmonious whole that came into being as a response to the natural conditions of climate and the studied ones of prevailing fashions.

Further, the very settings of these built gems bear appreciation for their scale and for the surviving scale of the environment around them. This you can experience only by being there.

Savannah's architectural inventory includes Federal-period mansions and townhouses; buildings designed by William Jay, the Regency-period architect who delighted in fancy scrollwork and a free-hand imposition of Greek motifs; grand antebellum homes; and a whole district of Victorian homes (made of both wood and masonry). Whatever their specific style, the older buildings downtown share a formal and restrained design that makes a cohesive whole. Their colors come from a muted palette of grays, greens and tans, and the end result is that they resonate with the geometry of Savannah's squares.

A good place to start is the **Savannah Visitors Center** (301 Martin Luther King, Jr. Blvd.; open daily.) where you can join a tour or get an overview of the city's history.

Local people appreciate your interest and are generally welcoming, but since all but a few of the historic homes are privately owned, remember that while photographing is fine, entering gardens or climbing front stairs is not. For such closer looks, visit the house museums where well-briefed and accommodating docents can answer your questions. In addition, there are annual tours of private homes and gardens, sponsored by local preservation organizations or churches. They usually take place in March and October, last all day, and range in price from $15–$40. For information, contact the **Savannah Tour of Homes and Gardens** (912-234-8054; www.savannahtourofhomes.org.) or **The Garden Club of Savannah** (912-351-7178; P.O. Box 13892, Savannah, GA 31416) about its **Annual NOGS** Tour (gardens north of Gaston St.).

Late-afternoon shadows in Savannah

Film

(Also see Theater entries below—several local venues offer both live and film events.)

Carmike Cinemas (912-353-8683; 511 Stephenson Ave.).

Eisenhower Cinemas (912-352-3533; 1100 Eisenhower Dr.).

Galleries

The Savannah College of Art and Design has greatly raised the profile of the city as an arts center. Frequently changing exhibitions of work are on display in college buildings throughout the city. Find schedules at www.scad.edu or call 912-525-4950. A glance at *Connect Savannah* (www.connectsavannah.com) a free weekly, will turn up undiscovered or short-run shows. Here are some places to look at art—it may or may not be for sale.

Beach Institute (912-234-8000; 502 E. Harris St.) Established in 1865 by the American Missionary Association to educate the newly freed slaves of Savannah, the Beach continues to be an African-American cultural center, which features exhibits of arts and crafts. Of special interest is the collection of hand-carved wooden sculptures, including likenesses of Presidents, by acclaimed folk artist and Savannah barber Ulysses Davis. Open Tues. through Sat. 12–5. Admission is $3.50.

Ellis Gallery (912-234-3537 or 1-800-752-4865; www.rayellis.com; 205 W. Congress St.) Paintings, watercolors, bronzes, and prints of golf and traditional maritime scenes by Ray Ellis, perhaps the best-known of Lowcountry artists. Also, books of his work and note-cards.

Jack Leigh Gallery (912-234-6449; 132 E. Oglethorpe St.) Photographs taken for close to three decades of the rural and coastal South, including beautiful photo essays on oystering, shrimping, and boating. By appointment.

John Tucker Fine Arts (912-231-8161; 5 W. Charleton St.). This handsome gallery on Madison Square features several shows each year of established artists whose work sometimes reflects Southern themes.

Pei Ling Chan Garden for the Arts (322 Martin Luther King, Jr. Blvd., at West Harris St.) This walled garden, with individual sections reflecting African-American, English, French, and Asian cultures, is the backdrop for sculpture exhibits. There is a small amphitheater used during theatrical productions. A nice place in the thick of downtown to have a quiet moment.

Sandfly Gallery (912-231-2300; www.sandflygallery.com; 407 Whitaker St.) Located along a stretch of design and art-oriented shops, with an emphasis on fine expressions of Lowcountry scenes, from realistic to abstract, in pottery, photographs, and paintings.

shopSCAD (912-525-5180; 342 Bull St.) A gallery of the Savannah College of Art and Design, featuring work by students, faculty, and occasional guests each month. It has expanded into a terrific shop.

Historic Homes, Gardens & Religious Sites

A distinguishing quality of longtime Lowcountry residents is that they are, to slightly alter the words of the Rolling Stones, "practiced in the art of perception"; that is, they know how to see and how to honor, over the generations, what they see. In Savannah, this means that historic sites—be they mansions, gardens, forts, or houses of worship—are cared for in a personal way. A site is valued not just because it is important and beautiful (though they all are), but because it has given meaning to the community. Structures that could be classified as monuments are familiar touchstones. Such an attitude puts flesh on the bones of historic preservation talk.

And it's not just buildings that are treated well: Savannah's squares and cemeteries are testimonials to public beauty. Observing the years of care that have been lavished on Savannah's historic places—from efficient, Federal-style frame dwellings to vast Romantic Revival warehouses—is one pleasure that will come naturally to every observant visitor.

Andrew Low House

912-233-6854.
www.andrewlowhouse.com.
329 Abercorn St.
Mon. through Wed., Fri. through Sat. 10:30–4; Sun. 12–4; closed Thurs.
Admission: Adults $7; students $4.50.

A city house in the high style, although adapted to the rigors of Savannah's summer heat by means of jalousied rear porches. By 1849, when it was built, Savannah was in its prime: This is how the wealthy cotton merchants lived, and there is a large collection of furniture to tell their story. It was from this house that Juliette Gordon Low founded the Girl Scouts and where she died in 1927.

Domestic ironwork in Savannah

Congregation Mickve Israel Temple

912-233-1547.
20 E. Gordon St.
Mon. through Fri. 10–12 and 2–4.

The Gothic-style synagogue was built in the 1870s, more than 100 years after the congregation was established. The museum and library house the oldest Torah in America, as well as letters, books, and historical documents.

First African Baptist Church

912-233-6597.
23 Montgomery St.
Mon. through Fri. 10–3:30.

Believed to be the oldest continually active church for black worshippers in North America, and the birthplace of the Civil Rights Movement in Savannah. Within the church (circa 1861) is a small museum and archive.

The Gift

To His Excellency President Lincoln, Washington, D.C.: I beg to present you as a Christmas-gift the city of Savannah, with one hundred and fifty heavy guns and plenty of ammunition, also about twenty-five thousand bales of cotton.

—W. T. Sherman, Major-General. From *Savannah*, Dec. 22, 1864.

Green-Meldrim House
912-232-1251.
1 W. Macon St.
Tues., Thurs. through Fri. 10–3:30; Sat. 10–12:30.
Admission: Adults $5; students $3.

Used as headquarters by General W. T. Sherman during his 1864 Christmas occupation of Savannah, this Gothic Revival mansion on Madison Square was the city's most expensive house when it was built in 1850. The exterior ironwork and porches are the best example of the style in the city.

Isaiah Davenport House
912-236-8097.
www.davenportsavga.com.
324 E. State St.
Mon. through Sat. 10–4; Sun. 1–4 (last tour at 3:30).
Admission: $7.

The proposed demolition of this landmark (built circa 1820 by a master-builder from Rhode Island for his family) to salvage the brick and make way for a parking lot galvanized Savannah preservationists. That was 1954, and the effort marked the birth of the Historic Savannah Foundation. Today it's a museum adorned with furnishings and decorative arts of the Federal Period. There's a lovely garden out back and an excellent museum shop.

Juliette Gordon Low National Birthplace
912-233-4501.
10 E. Oglethorpe Ave.
Mon. through Tues. and Thurs. through Sat., 10–4; Sun. 12:30–4:30.
Admission: Adults $7; children $4.

A Regency townhouse decorated in postbellum period style, this building commemorates the childhood of the founder of the Girl Scouts, who was born here in 1860. Gift shop with special things for Scouts.

King-Tisdell Cottage
912-234-8000.
www.kingtisdell.org.
514 E. Huntingdon St.
Tues. through Fri. 12–4:30; Sat. and Sun. 1–4.
Admission: Adults $1.50; children $0.75.

This charming, original Victorian cottage (circa 1896) houses a museum of the black history and culture of Savannah and the Sea Islands. Walking or driving tours on the Negro Heritage Trail, highlighting events and significant sites that pertain to black history, can be arranged in advance. It has been closed for the 2003–04 season; call ahead.

Laurel Grove—South Cemetery

912-651-6772.
At the western end of 37th St.
Daily. Tours by appointment.

The South Cemetery of Laurel Grove was dedicated in 1852 for the burial of "free persons of color" and slaves. Many of the city's most famous African-Americans are buried here.

Owens-Thomas House Museum

912-233-9743.
124 Abercorn St.
Mon. 12–5; Tues. through Sat. 10–5; Sun. 1–5. Last tour at 4:30.
Admission: Adults $8; children (6–12) $2.

Designed in 1816 by Englishman William Jay and considered the best example of an urban villa in his Regency style, this house contains a collection of European and American decorative arts and has a formal garden. The Carriage House is the site of one of the few discovered slave quarters in the Historic District, and its collections offer insight into the lives of urban African-American slaves.

Ralph Mark Gilbert Civil Rights Museum

912-231-8900.
460 Martin Luther King, Jr. Blvd.
Mon. through Sat. 9–5.
Admission: Adults $4; children $2.

Dr. Gilbert, who died in 1956, was a leader in early efforts to gain educational, social, and political equality for African-Americans in Savannah. This museum features state-of-the-art interactive exhibits focusing on the history of the Civil Rights Movement in Savannah.

Roundhouse Railroad Museum

912-651-6823.
www.chsgeorgia.org.
601 W. Harris St.
Daily 9–4.
Admission: Adults $4; students $3.50.

This National Historic Landmark is a collection of structures first built in 1838 and used as a railroad manufacturing and repair facility. Today you can see the roundhouse and turntable, a 125-foot brick smokestack, antique steam engines, diesel locomotives, and rolling stock.

Second African Baptist Church

912-233-6163.
123 Houston St.
Mon. through Fri. 10–2. Tours by appointment.

The church was established in 1802, and was the site of two historic occasions: General W. T. Sherman's reading of the Emancipation Proclamation to the newly freed slaves and, nearly a century later, Dr. Martin Luther King's delivery of his "I Have A Dream" sermon.

Wormsloe Historic Site

912-353-3023.
www.gastateparks.org.
7601 Skidaway Rd., Isle of Hope.
Tues. through Sat. 9–5, Sun. 2–5:30.
Admission: Adults $2.50; children (6–18) $1.50.

The tabby ruins, an avenue of oaks, and artifacts excavated from the site are all that remain of the colonial plantation built by Noble Jones, a physician and carpenter who came with the first settlers on the ship *Anne* and established the Georgia colony. An audio-video presentation and interpreters of colonial life make the period vivid for visitors.

Military Museums & Sites

A strategic upriver location and an abiding sense of history that predates the American Revolution make Savannah rich in military history. The island forts and lighthouses, in particular, recall both the sense of estrangement felt by soldiers stationed there and the effort they made to create a community in an isolated setting.

Fort Jackson

912-232-3945.
1 Fort Jackson Rd., 3 miles from downtown.
Daily 9–5.
Admission: Adults $4; seniors and students $3.

The oldest standing fort in Georgia, Fort Jackson saw action during both the Revolution, when an outbreak of malaria forced its abandonment, and the Civil War, when it was central to the Confederate network of river batteries. A self-guided tour takes you to military exhibits in the fort's casemates. Special military history programs enliven the fort several times each year.

Fort McAllister Historic Park

912-727-2339.
www.gastateparks.org.
3894 Fort McAllister Rd., Richmond Hill (24 miles south of Savannah on I-95).
Tues. through Sat. 9–5; Sun. 2–5.
Admission: Adults $2; children $1.

The fall of Fort McAllister, on the Ogeechee River, signaled the end of Sherman's "March To The Sea." By that time it had already outlasted other forts due to its earthen walls, which, unlike the popular masonry equivalent, could be swiftly repaired after a round of bombardment. There are self-guided tours, rangers on hand, and a good, small museum. Picnicking in the park is popular, but bring insect repellent. Biking trails and canoe/kayak rentals.

Fort Pulaski National Monument
912-786-5787.
www.nps.gov/fopu.
Cockspur Island, US 80 east, about 30 minutes from Savannah.
Daily 9–5; to 7 in summer months.
Admission: Adults $3; ages 16 and under, free.

A young officer named Robert E. Lee had his first military assignment here, soon after the fort was built. It's a masterpiece of engineering, a huge and heavy brick building, surrounded by a moat, sitting on an unstable marsh. And yet during the Civil War, rifled cannons blasted holes in the masonry of such forts, and they became obsolete. Interpretive programs explain life at the fort during the Civil War, and you are free to roam its ramparts. An excellent selection of books is available at the gift shop.

Mighty Eighth Air Force Heritage Museum
912-748-8888.
www.mightyeighth.org.
175 Bourne Ave., Pooler. (Take exit 102 off I-95, then E on US 80, then left on Bourne Ave.).
Daily 9–5.
Admission: Adults $8; children (6–12) $6; under 6 free. Discounts for seniors and military.

Dedicated to the men and women who served in the "Mighty Eighth" Airforce (formed in Savannah in 1942) during World War II. Exhibits also track later engagements, such as Operation Desert Storm, supplemented by photos and film presentations.

Tybee Island Museum and Lighthouse/Fort Screven
912-786-5801.
www.tybeelighthouse.org.
30 Meddin Dr., Tybee Island, 18 miles E of Savannah.
Daily except Tues. 9–5:30.
Admission: Adults $5; children $4.

Located within Fort Screven, which was acquired by the Federal government in 1808 and used as a post through World War II, the Museum and Lighthouse offer visitors a glimpse of life at a beach outpost over the years. The museum has an assortment of objects, Native American and Civil War weaponry, as well as illustrated newspaper accounts of the Civil War and memorabilia. A lighthouse has marked this site since 1736. Today you can climb this 19th-century version (over 150 feet tall) for a wonderful view of the river.

Museums
Oatland Island Education Center
912-897-3773.
www.oatlandisland.org.
711 Sandtown Rd.
Daily 9–4; Sat. 10–4.
Admission: $3.
Children will love walking the nearly two miles of wooded trails in this 175-acre preserve, where they can watch for animals and experience the salt marsh, forest, and wetlands

habitat of the Lowcountry. Sheep, goats, ponies, and swans may cross your path; bald eagles and hawks soar overhead. There is a farmyard, too.

Savannah History Museum

912-238-1779.
303 Martin Luther King, Jr. Blvd.
Mon. through Fri. 8:30–5; Sat. and Sun. 9–5.
Admission: Adults $4; children (6–12) $3.

Audio and video presentations, displays, and objects relating to Savannah's history are housed in the old Central of Georgia railway depot train sheds, in the Visitors Center. The Black Soldier exhibit highlights the 1st South Carolina Volunteers and the 178,895 black men who fought in the Civil War.

Savannah Science Museum

912-355-6705.
4405 Paulsen St.
Tues. through Sat. 10–5; Sun. 2–5.
Admission: Adults $4.50; children $2.50.

If you are weary of house museums and want to see one of the Southeast's largest collections of amphibians and reptiles, living and dead, comprehensive collections of shells, rocks, minerals, and a wonderful pressed herbarium of indigenous plants, spend time here. There's a great planetarium, too.

Ships of the Sea Museum

912-232-1511.
www.shipsofthesea.org.
41 Martin Luther King, Jr. Blvd.
Tues. through Sun. 10–5.
Admission: Adults $7; students, seniors $5.

Telfair Museum of Art

Ship models, a magnificent dollhouse-style construction of a huge 19th-century ship, and ships-in-
bottles tell the exciting story of maritime adventure,
war, commerce, and exploration in the world's
oceans, from the time of the Vikings forward.
Located in the William Scarbrough House, a
Regency jewel with a lovely garden.

Telfair Museum of Art

912-232-1177
121 Barnard St.
Tues. through Sat. 10–5; Sun. 1–5; Mon. 12–5.
Admission: Adults $8; students $2.

Savannah's main art gallery, housed in a Regency-
style mansion, hosts a permanent collection of

American and European Impressionist paintings, and frequent exhibits of modern art. A Moshe Safdie–designed modern addition is under construction.

University of Georgia Marine Extension Service Aquarium
912-598-2496.
30 Ocean Science Circle, Skidaway Island, 14 miles from downtown.
Mon. through Fri. 9–4; Sat. 12–5; Closed: Sun.
Admission: $2.

This is a working research lab and facility, but visitors are welcome to visit the aquarium and exhibits, which depict the underwater marine and plant life of coastal Georgia. Fossils of sharks' teeth and whale skulls are prominently displayed. A self-guided visit takes about an hour. Afterward, you can picnic. From here it's but a short hop to Skidaway Island State Park (912-598-2300; see "Camping") where you can walk through a maritime forest, bird-watch, and observe the teeming life of the marsh.

Music
Savannah Music Festival (912-236-5745; 1-800-868-3378; www.savannahmusicfestival .org.) A terrific jazz, blues, classical, and world music festival that takes place for about two weeks in March and April at churches, halls, clubs, and auditoriums around the city. A mini-Spoleto that draws music aficionados from all over to the city.

Savannah Symphony Orchestra (912-236-9536 or 1-800-537-7894; 225 Abercorn St.) The orchestra presents regularly scheduled symphony performances; chamber music ensembles often play on Sun. afternoons at the Telfair Academy.

Nightlife
Club One Jefferson (912-232-0200; www.clubone-online.com. 1 Jefferson St.) If you're looking for Chablis, who sang and carried on in the book *Midnight in the Garden of Good and Evil*, this is the spot.

Doc's Bar (912-786-5506; 10 16th St., Tybee Island) A funky, fun beach bar.

Jazz'd (912-236-7777; 52 Barnard St.) Located under the GAP store on Broughton St., an unlikely place for live jazz. No cover. Fri. and Sat. nights, with the bonus of a tapas (small plate) bar.

Monkey Bar/Fusion (912-232-0755; 8 E. Broughton St.) Everything from piano bar music to who knows what. Food, too. Closed Sun. and Mon.

O'Connell's Irish Pub (912-231-8499; www.oconnellsirishpub.com; 108 W. Congress St.) Live, folk, and traditional Irish music until 3 AM.)

Theater
City Lights Theatre Company (912-234-9860; 125 E. Broughton St.) Productions in a small 75-seat theater; "Shakespeare-in-the-Park" in Washington Square in spring.

Lucas Theatre (912-232-1696; www.lucastheatre.com; 32 Abercorn St.) An old movie palace, renovated in 1998, features films, musical performances, and theatricals.

Savannah Theater Company (912-233-7764; www.savannahtheatre.com; 222 Bull St.) Seasonal productions of contemporary drama, musicals, and comedy.

SCAD'S Trustee's Theater (912-525-5015; www.trusteestheater.com; 206 E. Broughton St.) A former Art Deco movie house transformed by the Savannah College of Art and Design into a glittering 1,105-seat performance art hall, featuring movies, plays, and dramatic readings.

RECREATION

Baseball
The area's professional farm team is the **Savannah Sand Gnats** (912-351-9150; www .sandgnats.com; Grayson Stadium, 1401 E. Victory Dr.) When at home, they play games weeknights at 7:15, and Sundays at 3 PM. Admission is $5 for adults, $3 for children.

Beach Access
The only beach accessible by car on Georgia's northern coast, Tybee Island lies 18 miles east of Savannah on US 80.

Ossabaw Island is a barrier island 20 miles south of Savannah. There are five campsites, and the minimum stay is two nights for groups of four or more. Transportation and fresh drinking water are available. Contact 912-233-5104 for information and reservations.

Birds in the Savannah Wildlife Refuge

Wassaw Island, located east of Savannah and Skidaway Island, can be reached by private or charter boat arranged through the U.S. Fish and Wildlife Service, Savannah Coastal Refuges Office (912-944-4415; 1000 Business Center Dr., Suite 1, Savannah, GA 31405). Within its 10,000 acres, there are more than 20 miles of inland island trailsand a 7-mile beach to explore.

Bird-Watching
The best spots for birding around Savannah are all part of the **Savannah National Wildlife Refuge System**, a complex of seven coastal parks that provide habitat on the beach and dunes as well as in abandoned rice fields, swamps, creeks, and estuarine systems. Get to **Tybee Island North Beach** by parking at the Tybee Island Museum (see listing above in "Military Museums & Sites"). **Skidaway Island State Park** (912-598-2300; www.gastateparks.org; 52 Diamond Causeway, Savannah, GA 31411) is separated from the Atlantic to the east by

Kayak tour guide ready at the landing on Tybee Island

salt marsh and to the south by Wassaw Island. This unique geography attracts a wide variety of songbirds, as well as large ospreys and bald eagles. To get there take Exit 164 off I-16 west of Savannah and head south. It will become Diamond Causeway. **Harris Neck National Wildlife Refuge** (912-652-4415), an old World War II Army airfield, supports a large colony of wood storks and dozens of nesting wading birds. Take US 17 south to Harris Neck Rd., then travel 6.5 miles to the refuge entrance. Get a map at the Visitor Center and drive along the 4-mile Laurel Hill Wildlife Road for a good introduction to the area, which includes fresh-water marsh, river-bottom hardwood swamp, and tidal rivers and creeks. Contact the Georgia Dept. of Natural Resources (912-994-1438; www.dnr.state.ga.us; 116 Rum Creek Drive, Forsyth, GA 31029-6518) and ask for the pamphlet and map of Georgia's Colonial Coast Birding Trail. **Wilderness Southeast** (912-897-5108; www.wilderness-southeast.org) offers all kinds of weekend birding trips near Savannah and further afield.

Boating
Canoeing and Kayaking
Access points along the Savannah River allow you to travel through tidal creeks leading into the **Savannah National Wildlife Refuge** (912-944-4415). For outing ideas, instruction, guided tours, maps, and expedition opportunities, **Sea Kayak Georgia** is the leader in the field. Day trips are scheduled regularly (call ahead for reservations) and camping expeditions are also offered. In 2004, the price for three-hour kayak lessons started at $85 per person and skills workshops ranged from $85–$150 per person. A typical three-hour guided day trip cost $55 per person. In general, daily kayak rentals started at $20 for a single, $35 for a double. Half-day and full-day canoe trips on the Blackwater River, including shuttle service, cost $35 per canoe.

Alakai Outfitters (912-786-4000; 1213 US 80, Tybee Island, GA 31328).

Isle of Hope Marina (912-354-8187; 50 Bluff Drive, Savannah, GA 31411).

Lands End Beach Rentals (912-786-7865; www.tybeeislandcruises.com; 1712 Butler Ave., Tybee Island, GA 31328).

Ogeechee Park Rentals (912-748-5996; US 80, Eden, GA).

Sea Kayak Georgia (912-786-8732 or 1-888-529-2542; www.seakayakgeorgia.com; P.O. Box 2747, Tybee Island, GA 31328).

Wilderness Southeast (912-897-5108; www.wilderness-southeast.org).

Sailing
For sailors unfamiliar with Lowcountry waters and tides, renting a sailboat or having a lesson is a good way to get acquainted with local conditions. Prices vary according to season, length of sail lesson or charter, and type of boat.

Sail Harbor Academy (912-897-2135; 606 Wilmington Island Rd.).

Savannah Sailing Center (912-231-9996; at Lake Mayer Community Park, Montgomery Crossroad and Sallie Mood Drive) offers lessons for $25 an hour in the calm setting of the 35-acre lake, which may be easier for a beginner to negotiate.

Whitehorse Sailing Charters (912-786-5592 or 1-800-567-3403; Tybee Island).

Bowling
Major League Lanes (912-925-0320; 115 Tibet Ave.).

Victory Lanes (912-354-5710; 2055 E. Victory Dr.).

Camping
River's End Campground and RV Park (912-786-5518 or 1-800-786-1016; www.gocampingamerica.com; 915 Polk St., Tybee Island, GA 31328) 100 sites, full hookups, tent sites, and cabin rentals.

Skidaway Island State Park (912-598-2300; www.gastateparks.org; 52 Diamond Causeway, Savannah, GA 31411). A 533-acre park with 88 tent, trailer, and RV sites; laundry, pool, bathhouse, nature trail, and interpretative walks and programs.

Diving
Diving Locker and Ski Chalet (912-927-6603; 74 W. Montgomery Crossroads).

Gray's Reef Dive (912-398-8470 or 912-786-7865, with USCG Capt. Bruce Carter).

Family Fun
Island Miniature Golf (912-898-3833; 7890 US 80, Whitemarsh Island) On the way to the beaches and boat landings; a good stop on the way home.

Putt-Putt Golf Course (912-355-4795; 202 Mall Blvd.) Three courses, lit for night play, open to midnight.

Fishing
The waters off Savannah provide a variety of fishing experiences. Inshore, there are fish in shallow waters and narrow creeks when the tide is right; offshore, there are bigger game fish in the Gulf Stream. Some guides specialize in the art of saltwater fly-fishing.

A good place to plan a fishing trip is at a marina although some sporting goods stores may have recommendations (see **Shopping**, below). Non-commercial saltwater fishing does not require a license; non-resident freshwater fishing does. Contact the **Wildlife Resources Division's** Savannah office (912-651-2221) for information on licenses and regulations, or talk to your guide. Licenses are available at most sporting-goods stores and bait shops.

A listing of some of the many **Charter Boat Services** available follows. Most boats are fully outfitted with supplies and bait, but check in advance, especially if you have questions about bringing your favorite rod—an option for fly-fishing—or if the length of the trip requires food. Always bring sunscreen, a hat, and a windbreaker. The cost does not include gratuity for the mate(s). The 2004 prices for half-day trips (generally 1–3 passengers for inshore fishing, 4–6 for offshore fishing) started at $250. A 14-hour trip to the Gulf Stream costs about $1,100.

Bull River Marina (912-897-7300; www.bullriver.com; 8005 US 80 East) Located halfway to Tybee, very accessible, and offering Boston Whalers for rent (to fish or crab on your own) or fully outfitted charters.

Coastal River Charters (912-441-9930; www.coastalrivercharters.com) Inshore fishing and sightseeing tours of barrier islands and secluded creeks.

Lazaretto Creek Marina (912-786-5848 or 1-800-242-0166; www.tybeedolphins.com; 1 Old Hwy. 80, Tybee Island) A full-service marina offering everything from inshore trips for 6 people to Gulf Stream expeditions.

Miss Judy Charters (912-897-4921; www.missjudycharters.com; 124 Palmetto Dr., Savannah) Deep-sea fishing and trolling, Gulf Stream trips, and inshore fishing with Captain Judy Helmey.

Reel Em N (1-800-721-1240; www.reelemn.com) Up to 10 anglers fish the artificial reefs or head to the Gulf Stream.

Savannah Light Tackle Fishing Co. (912-238-5582; 1908 E. DeRenne Ave.) Fly-fishing a specialty.

Sundial Fishing and Ecotours (912-786-9470 or 1-866-786-3283; www.sundialcharters .com; Chimney Creek) Deep-sea fishing for snapper, grouper, and shark; inshore for trout, drum, and tarpon. Ask about the naturalist-led outings to Little Tybee and Wassaw Islands.

Tybee Island Charters (912-786-4801; www.fishtybee.com; P.O. Box 1762, Tybee Island) Fish inshore from a 21-foot Carolina skiff, in deeper waters aboard a 30-foot Delta Sport, or take a nature cruise.

Fitness Facilities

Coastal YMCA (912-350-5480; 6400 Habersham Pkwy.) This facility honors YMCA memberships from other parts of the country.

Downtown Athletic Club (912-236-4874; 7 E. Congress) Step training, aerobics, spa facilities, classes, and fitness machines.

Tybee Island YMCA (912-786-9622; 204 E. 5th St., Tybee). A new facility, open daily.

West Broad St. YMCA (912-233-1951; 1110 May St.) Recreation center, gym facilities.

Golf

The most varied opportunities for golf are really at Hilton Head (See Chapter Five, **Hilton Head**), but here are some local options.

Bacon Park Golf Course (912-354-2625; www.baconparkgolf.com; Shorty Cooper Drive) Par 72. 27 holes; 6,700 yards. Lighted driving range; putting green. Fees for 18 holes: $25–$29.

Henderson Golf Course (912-920-4653; www.hendersongolfclub.com; 1 Henderson Drive) Par 71. 18 holes; 6,700 yards. Five sets of tees. Lighted driving range; putting green. Fees: $33–$44. Cart included.

Savannah Inn and Country Club (912-897-1612; 612 Wilmington Island Rd.) Par 72. 18 holes; 6,876 yards. Driving range and putting green. Fees: $35-$50. Cart included.

Southbridge Golf Club (912-651-5455; www.southbridgegolf.com; 415 Southbridge Blvd.) Par 72. Rees Jones–designed 18 holes, 6,990 yards. Driving range, putting green, and a full staff of teaching pros onsite. Fees: $32–$45. Twilight play $29–$35. Cart included.

Horseback Riding

Local stables can accommodate riders of varying skills, and it's best to call in advance to arrange lessons, trail rides, or workouts in the ring. 2004 prices ranged from $30–$50 per person for 90 minutes of riding time, depending on the setting. Here are two places to contact for more information:

Norwood Stables (912-356-1387; 2304 Norwood Ave.).

Triple B Ranch (912-964-6698; 60 Triple B Rd.).

Hunting

As in other regions of the Lowcountry, land quarry in the Savannah area include a variety of waterfowl, turkey, and various sizes of game. Familiarize yourself with specific hunting seasons, license requirements, and bag limits by visiting an outdoor recreation store (see **Shopping**) or contacting the **Game and Fish Division** of the **Georgia Dept. of Natural Resources** (912-727-2112; www.dnr.state.ga.us; 22814 Hwy. 144, Richmond Hill, GA 31324). More useful information can be found at www.savannah.fsw.gov, where you can download hunting and fishing brochures and permits.

Popular public hunting grounds in the greater Savannah area are located in the **Webb Wildlife Management Area** and **Palachucola Management Area** (843-625-3569; Hampton and Jasper Counties), **Turtle Island** and **Victoria Bluff** (843-844-8957; Jasper and Beaufort Counties), and in the **Savannah National Wildlife Refuge** (843-784-6754).

Nature Preserves

Some of the most accessible, and user-friendly preserves in the Lowcountry are located within 30 minutes of Savannah. They include:

The Bamboo Farm and Coastal Gardens (912-921-5460; Canebrake Rd. off US 17) A 46-acre educational and research center (now under the management of the University of Georgia) that started more than 100 years ago when a local bamboo fancier was given three Japanese giant timber bamboo plants and cultivated them on her property. Today there are more than 100 types of plants, flowers, and trees growing here, and more than 200 species of bamboo. Hours are 9–4 Mon. through Fri., and 9–3 Sat. Free.

Harris Neck National Wildlife Refuge (912-652-4415; www.harrisneck.fws.gov; I-95 Exit 67 to US 17 South, and travel approximately one mile to Harris Neck Rd.) The refuge entrance is 6.5 miles on the left, and signs direct you to the driving and biking trails, which wind through this 2,700-acre area of freshwater impoundments, salt marsh, forest, and field.

Pinckney Island National Wildlife Refuge (912-652-4415; US 278 at the foot of Hilton Head bridge) A 4,053-acre complex of small islands and hammocks set in the marsh. Only Pinckney Island, with 14 miles of trails, is open to visitors. A good place to spend an hour walking and birding.

Savannah National Wildlife Refuge (843-784-6751; I-95; Exit 5 to US 17 South; 6 miles south of Hardeeville on SC 170) The refuge consists of 25,608 acres spread across land once used for growing rice. Get a map at the Visitor's Center and drive along the 5-mile Laurel Hill Wildlife road for a good introduction to an area that includes fresh-water marsh, river-bottom hardwood swamp, and tidal rivers and creeks. Hiking trails (39 miles in all) are well marked, many of them following the path of the old rice dikes.

Victoria Bluff Heritage Preserve (Sawmill Creek Rd., off US 278, 3 miles from the Hilton Head bridge) This beautiful parcel of some 1,000 acres on the Colleton River has long been eyed for residential or industrial development, but local residents secured its protection as a passive recreation area.

Tennis
Seven city parks in and around Savannah have a total of 47 courts, and nearly all are lighted for night play. The custom at public parks is first-come, first-served. The locations are: **Bacon Park** (6262 Skidaway Rd.); **Daffin Park** (1001 E. Victory Dr.); **Forsyth Park** (Gaston St. & Drayton St.); **Lake Mayer Park** (Montgomery Crossroad & Sallie Mood Dr.); **Stell Park** (Bush Rd.); **Tybee Memorial Park** (Butler Ave.); **Wilmington Island Community Park** (Lang. St. & Walthour Rd.)

SHOPPING

There's not much you can't buy in Savannah, from collard greens off a truck to a gilded armoire. There are galleries displaying the work of students from the Savannah College of Art and Design; stores with goods to dress up your house; bookstores with rare and current volumes; places to buy old prints, sea charts, and maps; and antiques stores by the dozen. In fact, antiques stores and home-furnishings stores with unusual accessories might be considered the city's specialty. The Lowcountry habit of preservation has meant that English and American antiques and accessories of an earlier day, purchased during the boom years, have remained in the old houses. Today they are trickling out to local dealers. The region's temperate, multi-crop climate means you can buy lettuce, collards, potatoes, tomatoes, watermelons, and peaches most of the year. The man with the bags of boiled peanuts may knock at your door only in summer, but most everyone else can, and does, peddle their goods year round.

There are, too, right in the city and certainly out in the country, stores that are old and vibrant centers of community life, places of shelves that bear small quantities of many things, of dangling fly-paper, squirrel nut candies, pickled eggs, moon pies, single beers, and icees. They are too modest to claim National Register status; they'll never disappear, either. Drop in for a local newspaper and a "Co' Cola."

There's particularly good strolling and shopping along Whitaker Street, Broughton Street, Abercorn St., and Wright Square. Parking downtown can be difficult. Make use of Municipal Parking garages at City Market and Bryan Street (at Abercorn). Discount parking passes are sold at the Visitors Center, at the Bryan Street garage, and at several hotels and inns.

Antebellum Artifacts

Blatner's (912-234-1210; 347 Abercorn St.) Civil War era military items, old bottles, glassware, and silver.

Cobblestone Lane Antiques (912-447-0504; 230 W. Bay St.) A 10,000-square-foot warehouse that is chock-a-block with relics and more.

Pinch of the Past (912-232-5563; 109 W. Broughton St.) Architectural fragments and vintage house parts, including doorframes, columns, mantels, lighting fixtures, and hardware.

Antiques

A Savannah street

There are antiques of probably every period and style in the city—or a dealer will find you what you want. Whether you live in a sleek, minimalist apartment or a farmhouse, you're likely to find a piece that works. A man was quoted in the paper as saying: "We love old things. It makes life easier because you don't have to like the new ones." A good listing can be found at www.savannahexpert.com.

Arthur Smith Antiques (912-236-9701; 402 Bull St.) Four floors of rooms filled with antique tables, rugs, armoires, beds, and side pieces. It helps to know what you want.

E Storia (912-443-0202; 5 W. York St.) Art, divans, tea sets, and textiles—even old cameras.

Francis McNairy Antiques (912-232-6411; 411 Abercorn St.) The loveliest antique shop in Savannah. Fine antiques, many of Southern origin, and many small pieces. If you don't buy one item you can educate yourself here.

J. D. Weed & Company (912-233-0997; 137 Bull St.) An area native who knows just what the old houses used to have in them and has many examples, from tea caddys to dining tables.

Limehouse Plantation (912-232-7212; 124 E. Jones St.) European and 20th-century American furnishings with a good selection of iron and garden ornaments and accessories. Sometimes you find nice old fabric.

Michael V. DeCook Antiques (912-232-7149; 20 W. Hull St.) Furniture like sideboards and bedsteads, and especially lighting devices of all kinds, from the 18th and 19th century.

Portobello (912-651-1056; www.portobellollc.com; 413 E. Liberty St.) A local favorite with many dealers exhibiting glass, linens, silver, and rugs.

V. & J. Duncan (912-232-0338; 12 E. Taylor St.) You could browse through the files and piles of prints, maps, old advertising art, and illustrations here for hours. A comprehensive, well-organized collection of fine antique material.

Books

Savannah has an unusual number of little bookstores, many specializing in certain areas. Don't overlook the small ones.

Barnes and Noble (912-353-7757; 7804 Abercorn St.) As you would expect, a thorough inventory of Savannah books and many coffee-table size volumes on architecture and related subjects.

"The Book" Gift Shop (912-233-3867; www.midnightinsavannah.com; 127 E. Gordon St.) Headquarters for *Midnight in the Garden of Good and Evil* fans, the base for tours, a mini-museum of the book that changed Savannah.

Book Lady (912-233-3628; 17 W. York St.) Used and antique volumes, a longtime city business.

E. Shaver Booksellers (912-234-7257; 326 Bull St.) Right downtown and great for browsing. If some topic of Lowcountry history has captured your interest, you'll find something about it. Rooms of new and rare books, history, fiction, children's section, and excellent art books.

Ex Libris (912-525-7550; 228 Martin Luther King, Jr. Blvd.) This three-story bookstore provides course books and supplies for students at the Savannah College of Art and Design, and it is also full of treasures for the avid reader.

Jacqueline Levine Books (912-233-8519; 107 E. Oglethorpe Ave.) Collectible books with fine bindings, limited and first editions, maritime titles.

Clothing

There is preppy and retro fashion in Savannah, but it's still the South, after all, and there are plenty of small-scale dress shops (selling more dresses these days) that are thriving and up-to-date in their sensibility. Men's styles tend toward the casual and outdoorsy, given the weather.

Gaucho (912-232-7414; 250 Bull St. and 18 E. Broughton St.) Jewelry, leather, flowing scarves, and both rustic and romantic clothes for women, including lines from Eileen Fisher and many from new, smart designers.

Hilton Decker/Nickie Grace (912-236-6632; 11–15 W. York St.) Very up-to-date, European-styled clothes for men and women, from the little black dress to silk and linen suits.

Jezebel (912-236-4333; 25 E. River St.) Light-hearted and good-looking dresses, casual wear for women.

Terra Cotta (912-236-6150; 34 Barnard St.) Elegant, soft cottons for the bed and bath, also simply cut, stylish casual wear.

Crafts/Galleries

If you'd like to see local artists at work, drop by the **City Market Art Center**, a downtown art colony located upstairs (there's elevator access, too) at 308 and 309 West St. Julian St., www.citymarket.com. Other galleries worth checking out include:

Atelier Galerie (912-233-3140; www.agsavannah.com; 150 Abercorn St.) Hand-crafted jewelry by local, regional, and international artisans.

Bella Ferrum (912-233-7956; 2602 Whitaker St.) A studio and gallery of custom ironwork by Michael Sebacher, who makes dog beds, table bases, and garden furniture.

Bull St. Station (912-236-4344; 151 Bull St.) Model-railroad supplies and other accessories, kits, and tools for hobbyists of all kinds.

Elena Madden Studio Gallery (912-341-8662; www.elenamadden.com; 417 Whitaker St.) A painter's working studio in the midst of high-end design shops.

Friedman's Fine Art (912-234-1322; 28 W. State St.) A collection of the region's best representational artists is on exhibit here, but there's also fine art framing and a large selection of antique botanical and maritime prints for sale.

Gallery 209 (912-236-4583; 209 E. River St.) Thirty of the region's finest artists and craftsmen show here. Their works include batik, fiber, glass, pottery, wood, paintings, and sculpture, displayed in a 19th-century cotton warehouse.

MDH Designs (912-644-7833; 41 Habersham St.) Devoted to handmade, original, contemporary, art jewelry like arm cuffs, rings, ear wear and more, in unique or limited-edition castings.

Village Craftsmen (912-236-7280; 223 W. River St.) Original arts and crafts are still being created by members of this 25-year-old co-op gallery. You'll see jewelry, books, quilts, decorative painting, and much more.

Gifts

@home (912-201-0015; 7 W. York St.) New and shabby-chic objects for bedroom, office, and kitchen, and delightful retro-styled baby things.

Cottage Shop (912-233-3820; 2422 Abercorn St.) Linens for bed and table, stationery, lamps, and crystal.

Davenport House Museum Shop (912-236-8097; 324 E. State St.) Gifts with a Savannah theme and a Lowcountry flavor in the first house restored by the Historic Savannah Foundation.

Folk Traditions Store (912-341-8898; www.folktraditionsstore.com; 414 Whitaker St.) Books on Savannah's founding and history, but also an unusual selection of folk instruments like Celtic harps, fifes, wooden flutes, and whistles.

Owens-Thomas House Museum Shop (912-233-8252; 124 Abercorn St.) A superior gift shop in a recently renovated ground-floor space with a great selection of art and architecture books, travel books, small clothing items, and prints.

Gourmet Food

Brownesville (912-321-2345; 40th & Bull St.) Breads, tarts, cakes, cookies, and pies baked here every day.

Cafe Mucha (912-447-0636; 202 E. Broughton St.) Gourmet coffee, bakery, a large wine selection, and gifts for the kitchen.

Hunter Horn Plantation Co. Store (912-355-1812; 7202 White Bluff Rd.) The store specializes in spiral-sliced, honey-glazed hams, but also carries baked chickens for take-out (the best in the city), and sells many varieties of salads and other deli items by the pound.

Parker's Market (912-233-1000; 222 Drayton St.) The hippest recent rehab downtown, a 24-hour market on the site of a 1930s filling station, featuring 350 wines and microbrews, fresh herbs, fresh cookies and pastries daily, custom-blended coffee.

Sophisticated Palate (912-355-6160; 238 Eisenhower Dr.) Gourmet foods including wines, cheeses, canned goods, and coffees; also the tools to make your cooking gourmet, too: pasta machines, coffee grinders, small appliances, and the like.

Home Furnishings/Kitchenware

Two sections of the city have emerged as centers of home furnishing/decoration. One is the **Downtown Design District** (www.downtowndesigndistrict.com), located on Whitaker St. between Charleton St. and Gaston St., and the other is the **Starland Design District**, just south of downtown between 37th and 41st Streets, from Whitaker to Habersham. The furnishings can be sleek and modern, hand painted, antique, or really rustic.

Arcanum (912-236-6000; 405 Whitaker St.) The designers here have a way of mixing the old with the contemporary.

The Gypsy Moth (912-232-61-800; 30 Barnard St.) Folk art, birdhouses, funky wooden medallions and sculpture, Day of the Dead mementos, wooden animals, and rugs.

One Fish Two Fish (912-447-4600; 401 Whitaker St.) Painted chairs, benches, floor cloths, and little household accents, mixed with antiques and elegant objects.

London Flat (912-234-9141; 412-B Whitaker St.) Hip furniture for home or office, body products for men and women, retro and modern styles.

Sporting Goods and Clothing

Most of the following stores not only have athletic equipment and accessories for sale, but they rent equipment, too. Call ahead to check on the availability of rental goods, or to reserve them in advance of your stay.

Bicycle Link (912-233-9401; 22 W. Broughton).

Fleet Feet Sports (912-355-3527; www.fleetfeet.com; 3405 Waters Ave.).

Rec-Arts Outdoor Clothing and Gear (912-201-9393; www.rec-arts.com; 15 E. Broughton St.).

Thompson's Sports Shop (912-920-0977; 8110 White Bluff Rd.).

Wilderness Outfitters (912-927-2071; 105 Montgomery Crossroads).

A tidal creek defines ante-bellum homes in Beaufort's "Point"

4

Beaufort, Edisto & Bluffton

Sea Island Gems

> A place that ever was lived in is like a fire that never goes out. It flares up, it smolders for a time, it is fanned or smothered by circumstance, but its being is intact, forever fluttering within it, the result of some original ignition. Sometimes it gives out glory, sometimes its little light must be sought out to be seen, small and tender as a candle flame, but as certain.
>
> —Eudora Welty, 1944
> (*The Eye of the Story: Selected Essays and Reviews.* Viking International, 1990)

The fields, creeks, sandy roads, and spreading marshes of the rural Lowcountry, the place where Lowcountry history began, have once again become its center of attention. All along the coast, from Charleston to Savannah, there is an increasing awareness of what the culture of the countryside, expressed in a lifetime of habits and rituals, has meant to the two great cities that bookend the region and present themselves, to today's visitor, like magnificent finished products.

Perhaps the shift in emphasis from urban to rural is simply nostalgic, spurred on by a wishful return to the basics. Perhaps it has come because coastal development is accelerating. Typical Lowcountry spaces—fields rimmed by live oaks and stands of pine—are no longer simply evocative "open space:" They are potential building sites. Or maybe the mood has shifted because another shape has emerged from what was a familiar picture—like in those clever drawings, where it is sometimes the vase that appears before your eyes, and then it is the facing profiles.

The Lowcountry's alternative view, the rural view, can be seen most clearly in the areas around Beaufort—Lady's Island, St. Helena Island, and Port Royal—on Edisto Island, and in the little village of Bluffton. Before the Civil War they were as imposing, in their own small incarnations, as Charleston and Savannah: They boasted luxurious houses, profitable plantations, hundreds of slaves. Planters sent their children to be educated abroad. But all that changed one day, the day in 1861 that Federal troops arrived to occupy the Sea Islands. All at once, these self-satisfied and self-conscious towns receded from the foreground view into the rural background.

It took years for them to recover, but recover they have. Furthermore, they seem to have done so with a unique sense of the importance of celebrating both views of themselves—the

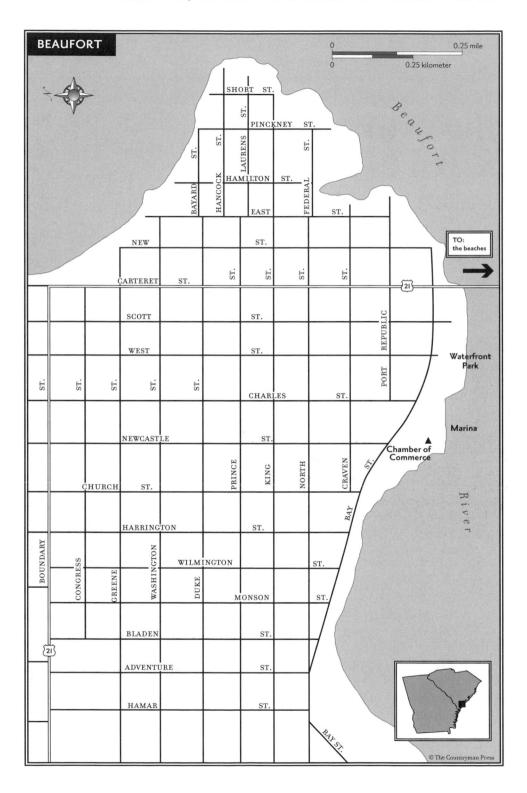

BEAUFORT

0   0.25 mile

0   0.25 kilometer

Beaufort

SHORT ST.

ST.

PINCKNEY ST.

ST.

LAURENS

BAYARD ST.

HANCOCK

HAMILTON ST.

FEDERAL ST.

EAST ST.

NEW ST.

TO:
the beaches

CARTERET ST.

ST.

ST.

ST.

ST.

21

SCOTT ST.

REPUBLIC

WEST ST.

PORT

Waterfront
Park

ST.

ST.

ST.

ST.

ST.

CHARLES ST.

NEWCASTLE ST.

Marina

Chamber of
Commerce

PRINCE

KING

NORTH

CRAVEN

ST.

CHURCH ST.

BAY

River

HARRINGTON ST.

BOUNDARY

CONGRESS

GREENE

WASHINGTON

WILMINGTON

ST.

DUKE

MONSON ST.

BLADEN ST.

21

ADVENTURE ST.

HAMAR ST.

BAY ST.

© The Countryman Press

part of them that was prosperous, worldly, and city-like, and the part of them that strug-
gled for decades to make do with the essentials. It comes as no surprise that they are places
where vistas, boughs, and fields are valued as much as brickwork, eaves, and intersections.

Today, rather than rely simply on one picture of themselves, these places celebrate the less
apparent patterns in their composition: the landscape of "vernacular" homes of farmers and
fishermen; the old market roads; the remains of a wharf; the praise houses and plantation

neighborhoods; the plantation cemeteries; the creek
landings and fishing holes;
the "rabbit-box" stores and
packing houses. The appreciation of what's plain has
brought a proud recognition
of how resourceful country
people were.

To a visitor, this means
that there is more to seek out
and understand, and many
more chances to do so. The
most mundane memories
and the most idealized ones

Praise House, St. Helena Island

are spilling forth from the vault of the past. Their blending is what gives the Lowcountry its
dramatic, cohesive, sense of place, a sense that is felt especially (if it is not immediately
seen) in the rural Sea Islands.

Beaufort

Beaufort has been a small town for a long time. Spanish and French explorers came to the
area 100 years before the Pilgrims landed at Plymouth Rock; they were followed, in due
course, by English and Scottish settlers. The city of Beaufort is itself on Port Royal Island,
one of the 65 islands that make up Beaufort County. It is the county seat. Other islands
include St. Helena, Lady's, Fripp, Hilton Head, Daufuskie, Cat, Harbor, Hunting, Coosaw,
Dataw, Polowana, Parris, Cane, Bray's, Lemon, and Pinckney.

Formally founded in 1711, Beaufort was a frontier settlement and trading center,
attacked at times by Yemassee Indians, beset with illness, and populated by the scrupulous
and unscrupulous, who made the best of the resources they had. The resources, in fact,
were plentiful: Beaufort's outlying lands sustained dense forests, which gave up shipbuild-
ing timber and naval stores; vast tracts of land, suitable for raising cattle and crops like
corn, potatoes, indigo, rice, and cotton; and rich marshes to feed fowl and game. The maze
of waterways provided fish and shellfish in abundance.

Over time, investors spotted Beaufort for what it was and staked their claims. Settlers
drifted in from Charleston and Savannah, a parish system of governance was established,
and, by the time of the Revolution, Beaufort was bustling. The real boom, however, came
immediately after the war. The stability of the newly independent country, the increase in
population (both slave and free), the southward migration of New England merchants and
families, and, perhaps above all, the successful cultivation of highly prized long-staple Sea
Island cotton and the development of the cotton gin lit the fuse. The explosion of wealth
that resulted launched Beaufort's heyday. It was a time of building houses and churches in

town and developing cotton plantations and plantation households on the islands.

A visitor can see the legacies of this period throughout Beaufort. They include Palladian-inspired doorways and windows, and huge, pillared porches; ornate Adam-style carved moldings and delicately scaled gardens; churchyards filled with camellias and azaleas, and towered over by steeples. Standing in Beaufort's Waterfront Park, it is easy to imagine a 19th-century scene come to life as dozens of schooners, bateaux, and cottonbox barges, brimming with crops, timber, mail, cotton bales, animals, passengers, produce, and the latest in English fashion and furniture, load or unload goods. There was a lot of activity, for like many societies made newly rich, Beaufort's had a taste for luxury and indulged it.

That, of course, changed abruptly. In another time and place, the shelling of a Federal fort (in this case Fort Sumter) not all that far away, and the Federal response to it, might have produced a shred of hesitation as to the wisdom of the Secessionist rebellion. Not so in Beaufort: It was apparently with great surprise that on November 7, 1861, white Southerners found themselves in flight—leaving hot food on the table, the story goes—from Yankee troops who had just demolished the Confederate port defenses at Bay Point.

Thus the occupation began. Soon the grand old houses were being used as hospitals and headquarters. The area was under military command. Pickets were posted at the outskirts of town and along creeks and boat landings: Some on guard duty watched the smoke of rebel campfires across the water. Whole plantations were turned over to regiments who appropriated the cows, the liquor, the furniture, the wagons, and the food crops.

By April 1862, the first wave of Northern abolitionists had arrived in town with a mandate to live in and manage the plantations and teach the former slaves to read and write: essentially to "prepare them for freedom." Their enterprise, which was funded by private missionary societies in the North and carried out with the approval of the federal government, came to be called the Port Royal Experiment. In a sense this was an old-time Peace Corps, in which idealistic, mostly young, men and women volunteered to assist a cause they believed in, at some personal risk and under conditions of definite hardship. Their efforts had an impact on the lives of freedmen that resonates today, in particular at Penn Center on St. Helena Island, still an important institution for education and empowerment.

In the years following the Civil War, promises made were usually promises broken. Some former slaves were given land; some bought tracts communally; some worked the old fields under a new owner. A nascent phosphate mining industry provided jobs for a while, but it eventually collapsed. The terrible hurricane of 1893, in which some 5,000 islanders

There is something very sad about these fine deserted houses. Ours has Egyptian marble mantels, gilt cornice and centre-piece in parlor, and bath-room, with several wash-bowls set in different rooms. The force-pump is broken and all the bowls and their marble slabs smashed to get out the plated cocks.... Bureaus, commodes, and wardrobes are smashed in, as well as door panels, to get out the contents of the drawers and lockers, which I suppose contained some wine and ale, judging by the broken bottles lying about. The officers saved a good many pianos and other furniture and stored it in the jail for safe-keeping. But we kindle our fires with chips of polished mahogany, and I am writing on my knee with a piece of flower-stand across them for a table, sitting on my camp bedstead.
—Edward S. Philbrick to his wife in Brookline, MA, Beaufort, March 9, 1862 (from *Letters From Port Royal 1862–1868*, ed. Elizabeth Ware Pearson. Arno Press, 1969)

died, soured Sea Island soil for fine cotton plants. The scourge of boll weevil in the 1920s dimmed the last hope of large-scale cotton production. For most people, living returned to subsistence-level farming and fishing. Photographs from the early 1900s and those taken even as late as 1936 by employees of the Farm Security Administration—Walker Evans and Marion Post Wolcott among them—showed islanders dressed in rags and living in shacks with matted palmetto fronds for roofs. In 1969, Beaufort County was still one of the poorest counties in the United States, the focus of a Hunger Tour by several U.S. Senators. In town, these were the years of unpaved roads and bare feet, when white people were "too poor to paint, too proud to whitewash."

As in many other parts of the South, it took the American entry into World War II to improve the economy. The United States Marines had been a presence in Beaufort since the turn of the century, and at this point their role was expanded. While not exactly prosperous, Beaufort now benefited from slow, steady growth. Commercial farming of tomatoes and other vegetables, and seafood processing, became healthy industries. By the mid-1960s, with the development of resort islands like Hilton Head and Fripp, and with the first wave of retirees flocking to its shores, Beaufort's economic future was assured.

It is hard to believe that today's downtown Beaufort ever suffered reverses. The paint doesn't dare peel. It has become a destination for tourists, a second home to people from the north and west, and a first home for young families who are looking for an ideal, charming, "small town" in which to raise their children. It has been turning up on "Best Small Town" lists for several years. It has even become a character in Hollywood movies: Two of native son Pat Conroy's novels have been filmed here, *The Great Santini* and *The Prince of Tides*, as well as *The Big Chill* and *Daughters of the Dust*. Parts of *Forrest Gump*, *Something to Talk About*, and *The Jungle Book* were shot here, too. Ron and Natalie Daise's acclaimed television series for children, "Gullah Gullah Island," was set in Beaufort and its environs, and featured many local residents in its cast.

It will take a lot more than Hollywood to turn Beaufort's head. The problems associated with regional planning and zoning, improved education, traffic and water service, land preservation, and economic development seem pressing here, as they do on the other Sea Islands. Having spent the better part of the 20th century becoming what it is today, Beaufort, it turns out, is still a work in progress.

GETTING THERE

Beaufort is 65 miles from Charleston, 45 miles from Savannah, and 30 miles from Hilton Head, and each of those locations has an airport. The easiest route by air is via the **Savannah/ Hilton Head International Airport** (www.savannahairport.com), which is served by AirTran, Continental Express, Delta, Northwest, United Express, and US Airways, and all major car rental agencies. From Charleston, access Beaufort from US 17 to US 21; from Savannah (and other points north and south) via well-marked exits on I-95; from Hilton Head, via US 278 to SC 170. **Amtrak** (1-800-872-7245; www.amtrak.org) passes through Yemassee, about 30 miles north of Beaufort. One northbound and one southbound train stop each day. For cab transportation to Beaufort, contact **Yellow Cab** (843-522-1121), **Beaufort Cab** (843-524-4940), **Maude's Cab** (843-524-9096) and **AC Limousine** (843-986-8738). Rates are about $50, and it's best to schedule in advance. **Greyhound** (1-800-231-2222) stops in Beaufort eight times a day. Rental cars are available in Beaufort. For more detailed information, see the Chapter Six, *Information*.

LODGING

The WPA Guide, *South Carolina, A Guide to the Palmetto State,* first published in 1941, indicates the presence of three hotels in Beaufort, and a number of "tourist homes" where guests could stay. Then as now, the preferred season was spring, although beginning in the 1920s, there was an informal "winter colony" of artists, playwrights, and others who found the laid-back town to their liking. Many returned every year for an extended stay in rooms at "Tidalholm," an elegant antebellum house in the neighborhood known as "The Point."

In those days, the comings and goings of visitors were duly reported in the local paper—perhaps an indication of what made news in this sleepy town. Other seasonal arrivals included sportsmen from the north who hunted and fished in several vast private preserves, which by the 1940s claimed up to one-third of the acreage in Beaufort County.

Today, the visitor in the next room might be a painter or a fly-fisherman, a movie director scouting locations, or a honeymooning couple. It's unlikely the newspaper will pay any attention at all. There are at least two luxury inns and several top-notch B&Bs to choose from—quite a selection for a small town—but do ask ahead about their policies regarding children as guests. Smoking is generally permittted on outside porches.

Rates

Inexpensive	Up to $60
Moderate	$60 to $120
Expensive	$120 to $200
Very Expensive	$200 and up

These rates do not include room taxes or special service charges that might apply during your stay.

Credit Cards

AE—American Express
DC—Diner's Club
CB—Carte Blanche
MC—MasterCard
D—Discover Card
V—Visa

Beaufort Inn

Innkeeper: Michael King.
843-521-9000.
www.beaufortinn.com.
809 Port Republic St., Beaufort, SC 29901-1257.
Price: Expensive to Very Expensive.
Credit Cards: AE, D, MC, V.
Handicap Access: Yes; full ramp, some rooms.

Trimmed in vines, and rimmed with trees and flowering shrubbery, this three-story clapboard building with jutting bays and porches owns its busy corner. There's nothing but luxury inside, including an elevator (one of a handful in Beaufort), long hallways covered in plush carpet, chandeliers, and a vivid decorating style characterized by antiques, patterned wallpapers, draperies and soft curtains, and carefully hidden modern amenities. Its restaurant and cozy bar are equally deluxe. There are several adjoining cottages with rooms for rent. Two have two bedrooms, making them ideal for a family or larger groups.

Craven Street Inn

Innkeeper: Geoff Nimmick.
843-522-1668 or 1-888-522-0250.
Fax: 843-522-9975.
www.thecravenstreetinn.com.
1103 Craven St., Beaufort, SC 29902.
Price: Expensive.
Credit Cards: AE, MC, V.

Located right downtown, this inn offers 10 rooms, some with working fireplaces, in the main house, a carriage house wing, and a cottage (two of the rooms share a private porch overlooking a garden). The style is simple, the colors are pale and pastel, and whether you're in the main house or not, there are private entrances for each room. The cottage has a living room, kitchen, and queen-size bed, and is a good choice for a couple taking a long weekend off or traveling with one or two small children.

Cuthbert House Inn
Innkeepers: Gary and Sharon Groves.
843-521-1315 or 1-800-327-9275.
Fax: 843-521-1314.
www.cuthberthouseinn.com.
1203 Bay St., Beaufort, SC 29902.
Price: Expensive to Very Expensive.
Credit Cards: AE, D, MC, V.
Handicap Access: One room.

The Cuthbert House has seen its share of excitement over the last 190 years, and its architecture tells the tale. It was moved from its original site in 1810, embellished with fine Federal-period woodcarving, served as headquarters of Union General Rufus Saxton during the Federal blockade and then enlarged with Victorian additions (sun porches and bays). Accommodations include two one-bedroom suites on the ground level (one is wheelchair accessible) and parlor suites. Its great site on the Beaufort River bluff makes the full Southern breakfast, afternoon tea, evening coffee, or simply lounging, a pleasure. Recently featured in *Coastal Living* magazine.

North Street Inn
Innkeeper: Jo Ann Meares.
843-986-1126.
www.northstreetinn.com.
1411 North St., Beaufort, SC 29902.
Price: Moderate to Expensive.
Credit Cards: MC, V.

Three guest rooms in a restored 1910 Queen Anne home located a block from the Beaufort River in the Historic District. Queen beds with private baths, and a full gourmet breakfast.

Old Point Inn
Innkeepers: Paul and Julie Michau.
843-524-3177.
Fax: 843-525-6544.
www.oldpointinn.com.
212 New St., Beaufort, SC 29902.
Price: Moderate to Expensive.
Credit Cards: AE, MC, V.

There are five guest rooms in this thoroughly renovated turn-of-the-century Victorian, furnished with unique furniture and artifacts collected by the owners from years of living abroad. If you sit on the upstairs porch, you will feel embowered, lofted in the treetops, and very much a resident of Beaufort's "Point," one of its Historic District neighborhoods. Each room has a private bath and cable television; full breakfast is included.

Rhett House Inn
Innkeepers: Steve and Marianne Harrison.
843-524-9030 or 1-888-480-9530.
Fax: 843-524-1310.
www.rhetthouseinn.com.
1009 Craven St., Beaufort, SC 29902.
Price: Expensive to Very Expensive.
Credit Cards: AE, D, MC, V.
Handicap Access: Two rooms.

The Harrisons left their careers in New York's fashion business when they came to Beaufort, but they brought along their taste and a meticulous attention to detail. They've lavished it on their ten-room inn and seven-room annex just a stone's throw away. The inn is simply beautiful, circa 1820, full of sunlight and breezes (only steps from the waterfront), furnished with antiques and comfortable chairs, prints, and vases of fresh flowers, flanked in the back by a garden and on the side by a courtyard fountain. Many of the rooms have fireplaces or Jacuzzi tubs; all have private baths and color televisions with cable service. The porches, upstairs and downstairs, are dreamy places to have afternoon cookies

Beaufort's two-story porches were designed to catch the prevailing breezes

and tea, or read and rest. The rooms in the annex have private porches and entrances, mini-bars, and six have gas fireplaces. Full breakfast, including homemade breads and muffins, is included and picnic baskets can be made up.

Sea Island Inn
(Best Western).
843-522-2090 or 1-800-528-1234.
1015 Bay St., Beaufort, SC 29902.
Price: Moderate.
Credit Cards: AE, CB, D, DC, MC, V.

Conveniently located on Beaufort's main street, the locally owned and operated 43-unit motel has a pool, exercise room, and outdoor patio tables. Continental breakfast is served in the lobby.

TwoSuns Inn
Innkeepers: Henri and Patricia Safran.
843-522-1122 or 1-800-532-4244.
www.twosunsinn.com.

1705 Bay St., Beaufort, SC 29902.
Price: Moderate to Expensive.
Credit Cards: AE, D, DC, MC, V.
Handicap Access: One room.

Facing the Beaufort River at one of its prettiest points, just as it turns the bend and heads away from town, this former residence—now a six-room inn—dates from 1917. The room's decor reflects Victorian, Oriental, and country themes. Rates include a full breakfast.

Farther Afield in the Beaufort Area

Dataw Island (843-838-3838 or 1-800-848-3838; www.discoverdataw.com; One Club Rd., Dataw Island, SC 29920) Dataw is a private, 870-acre residential community with all the expected amenities, about 20 minutes from Beaufort on the way to the beaches. It has limited accommodations, but if you are interested in viewing sales property (homesites or homes) you may call to make arrangements for an overnight or weekend stay.

Fripp Island Resort (843-838-3535 or 1-800-845-4100; One Tarpon Blvd., Fripp Island, SC 29920) Fripp is a private, 3,000-acre island bordered by an ocean beach about 35 minutes by car from downtown Beaufort. It's a residential community with several golf courses, tennis facilities, miles of biking trails, resort shops, pools, a beach club, and marina. Activity programs in the summer keep children busy. Island Realty (843-838-3004) has the best rental listings. In the summer, they range from $1,200 a week for a one-bedroom on the ocean to a three-bedroom, three-bath for $2,450.

Harbor Island Rentals (843-838-4800 or 1-800-553-0251; www.harborisland-sc.com; 2123-B Sea Island Pkwy., Harbor Island, SC 29920) Some 70 units, including villas and homes for rent on Harbor Island, a small private community with pool, tennis courts, and 2.5-mile beach. Oceanfront/ocean-view two-bedroom homes and villas start at $1,225 for a week in high season.

Palm Key (843-726-6468 or 1-800-228-8420. www.palmkey.com; 330 Coosaw Way, Knowles Island, Ridgeland, SC 29936) The idea at Palm Key is to enjoy the outdoor life of the Lowcountry—crabbing, fishing, kayaking, hiking, fossil-hunting, bird-watching—by slowing down and taking notice, either with a guide or on your own. No television or telephones; attractive, fully equipped cottages from $140. Families welcome; pets a possibility.

Royal Frogmore Inn (843-838-5400; 863 Sea Island Pkwy., St. Helena Island, SC, 29920) A modest 50-room inn located midway between Beaufort and the beaches.

National chain motels are also well represented in Beaufort. A list of some of them follows. It's a good idea to make reservations in advance, for they are often booked by family members of the graduating classes (many each year) of "boot camp" recruits from the Parris Island Marine Corps Recruit Depot.

Best Inn (843-524-3322; 2448 Boundary St., Beaufort).

Comfort Inn (843-525-9366; 2227 Boundary St., Beaufort).

Days Inn (843-524-1551; 1660 Ribaut Rd., Beaufort).

Hampton Inn (843-986-0600; 2342 Boundary St., Beaufort).

Sleep Inn (843-522-3361; 2523 Boundary St., Beaufort).

DINING

As Beaufort and the Sea Islands have become popular destinations, restaurants have become more adventurous in tweaking the favorite dishes of a small town for a new audience. Thus, there will be grits and tiny creek shrimp fixed in many ways—with a spicy tasso sauce, with cheese, in soufflés, or served beside fried eggs. The same goes for greens (mustard, collard, kale, and dandelion), crops which are available fresh nearly all year long, and crab, which appears in soft or hard shell, in soups and salads, as a stuffing or a sauce. Tomatoes are a prominent cash crop in late spring and early summer, and are widely featured at that time. (The Sea Islands have a "window" for selling tomatoes on the national market for about three weeks in May, when migrant workers and local people harvest the fields and work in the packing houses well into the night.)

Many other local dishes flourish from late March through May, before the relentless summer heat warms up the creeks and dries out the soil. These include shad roe from the Edisto River, soft shell crabs, strawberries and blueberries, kiwi fruit, and oysters. Game birds, such as dove and marsh hen, and venison, are cooler weather treats.

If you find something you especially like, look for the recipe in *Sea Island Seasons*, a cookbook published by the Beaufort County Open Land Trust, a local non-profit land preservation group. It is available in stores, or by contacting the Trust (P.O. Box 75, Beaufort, SC 29902). Within its covers you'll find out how to make such Lowcountry specialties as Frogmore Stew (sausage, corn-on-the-cob, potatoes, and shrimp in broth); shrimp paste (a spread that retains the delicate, sweet flavor of fresh shrimp); bread-and-butter pickles; and lemon chess pie (the secret ingredient is cornmeal).

The following selections are among the better-known Beaufort restaurants; but don't neglect the smaller spots (listed under Food Purveyors) where a modest job can be done extremely well.

Local produce, St. Helena Island

Dining Price Code

Inexpensive	Up to $15
Moderate	$15 to $30
Expensive	$30 to $50
Very Expensive	$50 or more

Credit Cards
AE—American Express
DC—Diner's Club
CB—Carte Blanche
MC—MasterCard
D—Discover Card
V—Visa

Beaufort Inn and Restaurant
843-521-9000.
809 Port Republic St.
Open: Daily.
Price: Expensive.
Cuisine: American and Continental.
Serving: D; Sunday brunch.
Credit Cards: AE, D, MC, V.

Quiet, white-linen tablecloths, very good looking, low-key. The menu includes the classics (like sirloin steak and delicate veal dishes) and the presentation is routinely beautiful, with drizzled sauces and crisp vegetables arranged on the edge of oversized dinner plates. There's an extensive wine list for dinner and after-dinner drinks. The Grill Room is a little less of a showcase, has a bar menu, and attracts a mix of longtime residents and newly arrived young professionals. Reservations recommended.

Bistro 205
843-524-4994.
205 West St.
Closed: Sun.
Price: Expensive.
Cuisine: American.
Serving: L, D.
Credit Cards: MC, V.

Located on a side street just off the bay, this storefront was recently completely done over, giving it a sleek, sophisticated look that landed it in the pages of *Southern Living* magazine last year. The food is upscale and innovative, with emphasis on local seafood. There is also a wine bar and bar menu for lighter meals.

11th Street Dockside

843-524-7433.
1699 11th St., Port Royal.
Open: Daily.
Price: Moderate.
Cuisine: American; Seafood.
Serving: D.
Credit Cards: AE, D, MC, V.

A casual restaurant, excellent for families, right on Battery Creek, where shrimp boats tie up and the sunsets pour color in the sky. The menu offers fried and broiled seafood specialties, as well as steak and pasta. You can work up your appetite by a visit to the town of Port Royal's marsh boardwalk and observation tower located at "The Sands," a beach to the east of the port terminal at the foot of Paris Avenue. No reservations, so expect a wait.

Emily's Restaurant and Tapas Bar

843-522-1866.
906 Port Republic St.
Closed: Sun.
Price: Moderate to Expensive.
Cuisine: Continental.
Serving: D.
Credit Cards: AE, D, MC, V.

At Emily's you can put together a meal from tapas items—small dishes of hot and cold appetizers, which may have light sauces or seafood stuffing. The small restaurant is dark and cozy, attracting local business people for drinks and boaters cruising through on the Intracoastal Waterway. A good place for a light, late meal: tapas served to 10 PM. Reservations recommended.

Fuji

843-524-2662.
81 Sea Island Pkwy., Lady's Island.
Closed: Sun.
Price: Inexpensive.

Gathering and Corn-Shelling, St. Helena Island

When they go into the field to work, the women tie a bit of string or some vine round their skirts just below the hips, to shorten them, often raising them nearly to the knees; then they walk off with their heavy hoes on their shoulders, as free, strong, and graceful as possible. The prettiest sight is the corn-shelling on Mondays, when the week's allowance, a peck a hand, is given out at the corn-house by the driver. They all assemble with their baskets, which are shallow and without handles, made by themselves of the palmetto and holding from a half peck to a bushel. The corn is given out in the ear, and they sit about or kneel on the ground, shelling it with cleared corn-cobs. Here there are four enormous logs hollowed at one end, which serve as mortars, at which two can stand with their rude pestles, which they strike up and down alternately . . . . They separate the coarse and fine parts after it is ground by shaking the grits in their baskets: the finest they call corn-flour and make hoe-cake of, but their usual food is the grits, the large portion, boiled as hominy and eaten with clabber.
— Harriet Ware (a young abolitionist and teacher from Boston, who lived and taught at Coffin Point Plantation, St. Helena Island) to her parents, May 22, 1862.
(from *Letters From Port Royal 1862–1868*, ed. Elizabeth Ware Pearson. Arno Press, 1969)

Cuisine: Asian.
Serving: L, D.
Credit Cards: AE, MC, V.

Recently doubled in size and enhanced by the addition of a sushi bar, this drop-in favorite has grown up but retains its post-beach, pre-movie informality where a cold Kirin and quick-grilled dishes will get you on your way.

Panini's Cafe

843-770-0071.
Cross Creek Shopping Center, SC 170.
Open: Daily.
Price: Moderate to Expensive.
Cuisine: Italian and Mediterranean.
Serving: L, D.
Credit Cards: AE, MC, V.

A modest location belies an excellent menu of beef, chicken, and veal and pastas with favorite Italian sauces like carbonara and a mild marinara. Brick oven pizzas are a specialty, as well as huge salads and selections that pair Lowcountry seafood and vegetables with spicy sausage and olives. The cafe has become so popular it may be moving, so watch for it closer to town.

Plums

843-525-1946.
904-1/2 Bay St.
Open: Daily.
Price: Moderate to Expensive.
Cuisine: American.
Serving: L, D.
Credit Cards: D, MC, V.

Plums is still the most popular place to eat lunch in Beaufort, good food, very informal. Hot sandwiches like grilled turkey or reubens, excellent chicken salad, and homemade soups are menu favorites; there's peanut butter and jelly for kids. A full bar serves the lively nighttime crowd that spills onto the outdoor porch, now nicely heated in chillier months.

Saltus River Grill

843-379-3474.
www.saltusrivergrill.com.
802 Bay St.
Open: Daily.
Price: Moderate to Expensive.
Cuisine: American.
Serving: D.
Credit Cards: MC, V.

Located on the Waterfront Park with a spacious outdoor deck and comfortable seating, this very attractive, upscale restaurant offers not only a new look for local restaurants (enormous space in a renovated building with a dominant bar and an urban-hip flavor) but new options, such as a full sushi bar and raw bar. Top choices include shrimp and stone-ground grits with bacon gravy or a grilled filet with upstate Clemson Blue cheese. It's definitely the place for locals to see and be seen.

Shrimp Shack

843-838-2962.
1929 Sea Island Parkway, St. Helena Island (about 11 miles south of Beaufort toward the beach).
Closed: Sun.
Price: Inexpensive.
Cuisine: Seafood.
Serving: L, D (until 8 PM).
Credit Cards: None.

Fresh seafood from the family dock—you can see the shrimp boats from the porch—accompanied by slaw, red rice, hush puppies, and beans. Deviled crab and shrimp burgers (ground, seasoned shrimp on a bun) are specialties. You can eat upstairs on the screened-in porch or in an adjacent gazebo. It's laid-back and local, and the hard work of the Upton family keeps the standards high. Lunch only from Nov. through Mar.

Outdoor market, St. Helena Island

Food Purveyors

Bakeries/Coffee Bars

Common Ground (843-524-2326; 102 West St. Ext.) An offbeat place where people in the local arts world hang out. Smoothies, bagels, coffee, magazines, newspapers, comfortable chairs, a view to the water.

Firehouse Books & Espresso Bar (843-522-2665; 706 Craven St.) Coffees, fancy lattes, muffins, and sweets, set amidst a friendly two-story bookshop with an excellent selection of magazines. The wraps are popular at lunch (served until 2:30), especially when eaten on the outdoor patio.

Magnolia Bakery Cafe (843-524-1961; 703 Congress St.) Adjacent to the Visitor's Center, a small restaurant with limited outdoor dining specializing in homemade bread and desserts, snacks, lunch served all day. Beer and wine available.

Candy and Ice Cream

Chocolate Tree (843-524-7980; 507 Carteret St.) A family-owned shop selling many different kinds of chocolates, truffles, and dipped fruits made right on the premises, plus candy-making accessories, gift boxes, jelly beans, cards, and gifts.

Renaissance Fine Chocolates (843-525-1328; 1001 Boundary St. at Newcastle Sq.) Gourmet food items like seasoned nuts and jams, but the best in stock are the handmade chocolates made from Callibaut Belgian chocolate with no paraffin or preservatives.

Southern Sweets Ice Cream Parlor (843-379-0798; 917 Bay St., in the Old Bay Marketplace) Looks like an old-fashioned soda fountain with a long counter and serves Greenwood brand, a rich South Carolina ice cream.

Delis and Fast Food

Alvin Ord's Sandwich Shop (843-524-8222; 1415 Rubaut Rd., Port Royal) Long prized for its home-baked bread (French or whole wheat) and delicious sandwiches. Limited seating and very crowded at lunch, so call ahead to order. Open until 8 PM, Mon. through Fri., until 6 PM on Sat.

Bay Towne Grill (843-522-3880; 310 West St.) If you see a lunch crowd forming at the edge of a parking lot, you're here: a tiny building with outdoor tables and high stools. Burgers, vegetarian sandwiches, salads, subs, and soups. Good food, low prices, lots of character.

Blackstone's Deli & Cafe (843-524-4330; 205 Scott St.) Best breakfast in town, and nice to sit here engrossed in the morning paper. Lunch is also served. Wines and specialty foods for sale, as well as locally produced paintings and furniture.

La Nopalera (843-521-4882; 1220 Ribaut Rd., Port Royal) Authentic Mexican food, with booths and fast, friendly service. Serves lunch and dinner daily and features live music Sunday nights.

Marketplace News (843-470-0188; 917 Bay St. in the Old Bay Marketplace) Stop by for the *New York Times*, grab a quick, inexpensive sandwich and soda and even log on to the Internet.

Maryland Fried Chicken (843-524-8766; 1100 Ribaut Rd.) Chicken and fish by the piece, box, or bucket, as well as side orders like fried okra, mashed potatoes, slaw, and beans. Drive-thru window.

Upper Crust (843-521-1999; 81 Sea Island Pkwy., Lady's Island) Pizza, salads, subs, beer, and wine. A slice of the super-deluxe house pie and sweet tea before a movie (the theater is located across the street) or after a day at the beach goes a long way.

Wine & Provisions (843-524-9463; 403 Carteret St.) A European gourmet market with a great array of cheeses, wines, pâtés and other take-out items. The sandwiches and little pizzas are made to order, inventive, and when paired with a bottle of chilled wine, just the thing for a picnic. Fresh La Brea bread daily. Limited seating.

TOURING IN THE HISTORIC DISTRICT AND BEYOND

Several companies offer narrated tours of Beaufort's Historic District and the Sea Islands. Buggy and walking tours last 45–90 minutes. Guided driving tours may last two hours. Cassettes and CDs that provide information for self-guided tours are available at the **Visitor Center** (843-524-3163; 1106 Carteret St.). More information can be found at the **Chamber of Commerce's** website: www.beaufortsc.org.

By Carriage: Carolina Buggy Tours (843-524-1300) and the cleverly named **Southurn Rose Buggy Tours** (843-524-2900) depart from the Downtown Marina parking lot Mon. through Sat. 9:30–5, Sun. 12–5. Adults $16; children $7.

On Foot: The Spirit of Old Beaufort (843-525-0459) Tours led by costumed guides leave the shop (103 West St. Ext.) Mon. through Sat. at 10:30 and 2:30. Adults $12.50; children $7.50. Reservations required.

By Bus: Beaufort Tour Service (843-525-1300) departs from the Visitor Center and sites downtown Mon. through Sat. 10–3:30. Adults $16; children $7. **Sandlapper Tours** (843-838-0111; 986-6960) depart from the Visitor Center Mon. through Sat. 9:30–4. Adults $16; children $7. Sandlapper also offers tours of Sea Island sites by appointment.

St. Helena Island Tours: "Rev's" Gullah Island Tour (843-838-3185), with Rev. Joseph P. Bryant, is available by appointment. **Gullah-N-Geechie Mahn Tour** (843-838-7516; www .gullahngeechietours.net) runs Mon. through Sat. 9:45 and 1:45. Adults $17; children $15.

If you can tear yourself away from the authentic seductions of "the built environment," you will be rewarded by views of marshes and marine life that exist in such a pristine state in only a few places in the United States. Getting on the water is one such way to do so. For detailed information on tours by boat—small or large—see the **Recreation** section below, specifically listings in "Boat Tours" and "Canoeing and Kayaking."

CULTURE

As Beaufort has grown, so have its cultural activities, both indigenous and imported. The museums and annual house tours have gained a professional thoroughness; bookstores sponsor author's signings; the University of South Carolina at Beaufort has an active exhibition space and chamber music series; there are art galleries and venues for periodic live

Chapel of Ease, St. Helena Island

Old Sheldon Church

theater and dramatic readings. It may be enough to sit and watch the tide go out on a Friday night, but you don't have to in Beaufort anymore.

For information about cultural organizations in town, self-guided tours of artists' studios and galleries, or upcoming events, contact: **The Arts Council of Beaufort County** (843-521-4144; 801 Carteret St., Beaufort, SC, 29902). The *Lowcountry Weekly* (www.lc weekly.com) is a free newspaper with all the current cultural listings. The local newspapers of Hilton Head and Beaufort sponsor an informative website, including cultural listings and events at www.mylowcountry.com. Annual tours of local homes and plantations, in October and March, are sponsored by the **Historic Beaufort Foundation** (843-379-3331; www.historic-beaufort.org) and **St. Helena Episcopal Church Women** (843-524-0363). For a listing of year-round tours, see **Touring in the Historic District and Beyond**, above.

Film
Lady's Island Cinema (843-986-5806; Sea Island Parkway, Lady's Island).

Plaza Theaters (843-524-9468; Beaufort Plaza, SC. 170).

Historic Homes, Gardens and Religious Sites
Baptist Church of Beaufort
843-524-3197.
601 Charles St.

This is an 1844 Greek Revival beauty. The ceiling plasterwork and ornamented cornices seem to match—in their absolute, solid mass of decoration—the abundant self-confidence of the prosperous little town of Beaufort in its heyday.

Chapel of Ease
Land's End Rd., St. Helena Island.

The ruins of this planters' church, built in the 1740s to serve worshippers far from town, are of brick and tabby, a construction material that blends oyster shells with lime, sand, and water. The site is a wonderful place for photographs—spooky in the fog or at dawn, mellow and ageless at dusk.

John Mark Verdier House
843-379-6335.
801 Bay St.
Mon. through Sat. 11–4; last tour at 3:30.
Admission: Adults $5; Children $2.

The showcase property of the Historic Beaufort Foundation (www.historic-beaufort.com), it was built according to the Adam-influenced decoration and floor plans of the day for a local merchant around 1790. It includes a formal parlor and ballroom, ornamental fireplace friezes, carved moldings, and antiques that are original both to the family and to the period of the house.

Penn Center
843-838-2432.
www.penncenter.org.
P.O. Box 126, Martin Luther King, Jr. Drive, St. Helena Island, 29920.
York W. Bailey Museum
Mon. through Sat. 11–4.
Admission: Adults $4; Children $2.

Founded in 1862 by two Pennsylvania women as a school for the newly freed slaves, Penn has remained a vital institution to promote education, self-sufficiency, and cultural expression among native islanders. In the days of segregation, it was one place where blacks and whites could meet together, as they did when the Rev. Dr. Martin Luther King planned his march on Washington. The **York W. Bailey Museum** (843-838-8562) holds a collection of cultural artifacts, African objects, and paintings. Community sings featuring gospel choirs and spirituals, an island tradition to which visitors are welcome, take place in Frissell Hall on the third Sunday of each month from September through May at 7:30 PM. The entire campus is a National Historic Landmark.

Old Sheldon Church Ruins
Secondary Rd. 21, 1.7 miles north of the intersection of US 17 and US 21.

Beautiful brick columns, fragile arches, and sill slabs remain from a church that was burned twice, first by the British in 1779 and then by the Union Army in 1865. It's a little temple in the woods. There's a small shaded picnic area on site.

St. Helena's Episcopal Church
843-522-1712.
507 Newcastle St.
Mon. through Sat. 10–4.

Penn Center, St. Helena Island

This church, built of brick from England in 1724, is adorned inside with graceful columns, upstairs galleries, and tall, multi-paned windows on the deep sills of which rest buckets of blossoming magnolia, daffodils, or narcissi in season. Its shaded, walled churchyard makes for a lovely stroll.

Tabernacle Baptist Church

843-524-0376.
907 Craven St.

A striking, white clapboard building with bell tower; in its churchyard lies the grave—and stands a fine bust—of Robert Smalls, who was born a slave, engineered a daring ship capture during the Civil War, and was later a congressman and significant figure in Beaufort's Reconstruction period.

Military Sites

National Cemetery

1601 Boundary St., Beaufort.

Created by President Lincoln in 1863 for victims of Southern battles, this 29-acre cemetery is the final resting place of some 9,000 Union soldiers and more than 100 Confederates. It is still in service.

Parris Island Museum
843-525-2951.
www.mcrdpi.usnc.mil/.
War Memorial Building, Marine Corps Recruit Depot.
P.O. Box 190001, Parris Island, SC 29905.
Daily 10–4.
Admission: Free.

The museum showcases the history and development of the area on which the famous " boot camp" stands, from its earliest settlement through contemporary recruit training. (Artifacts have been recovered from the Spanish village of Santa Elena, circa 1566; from Charlesfort, a French outpost established by Jean Ribaut in 1562; and from Fort San Marcos, circa 1576. Excavation continues at these sites, located near the depot golf course.) Exhibits of uniforms, personal items, weapons, drawings, and documents trace the history of the Marine Corps in its worldwide engagements. You can also consult *Platoon Books* for listings of Marines. Self-guided driving tour maps are available. If you're interested in observing morning colors or a graduation (held on Fridays), contact the **Visitor Center** (843-525-3650). The Visitor Center is open Mon.–Wed. 8:30–4:30; Thurs. 7:30 AM–7 PM; Fri. 7:30–4:30; Sat., Sun. and holidays 12–4. Bus tours depart the Visitor Center every Thurs. at 9, 10, and 11. You may also picnic in designated areas or have an inexpensive meal at a base restaurant, including the Officer's Club. Parris Island is open to visitors from 6 AM to 6 PM.

Museums
Beaufort Arsenal Museum
843-525-7077.
713 Craven St.
Mon. through Sat. 11–4.
Admission: $3.

The old Beaufort Arsenal, an ochre-colored bastion with a courtyard was rebuilt in 1852. It now houses the museum, overseen by the Historic Beaufort Foundation, which has undergone a thorough renovation of both its building and collection to become a center of local history and culture.

The Lowcountry Estuarium
843-524-6600.
1402 Paris Ave., Port Royal.
www.lowcountryestuarium.com.
Fri. and Sat. 10–5.
Admission: Adults $4; Children $2.

This is a place where tanks and exhibits showcase the natural marine world of the Lowcountry. Creature feedings are at 11:30 and 3.

Music
Hallelujah Singers (806 Elizabeth Lane, Beaufort, SC 29901) The group of singers under the direction of Marlena McGhee Smalls, a superior vocalist who has earned a national reputation for her singing and her acting (she was Bubba's mother in the movie *Forrest*

Gump) performs throughout the year, often in a downtown church at the time of annual house tours; weekly during the summer at various sites. Contact **The Arts Council of Beaufort County** (843-521-4144; 801 Carteret St., Beaufort, SC, 29902) for schedules.

Penn Center Community Sing (843-838-2432; P.O. Box 126, St. Helena Island, SC 29920) Community groups, quartets of senior citizens, gospel choirs, spur-of-the-moment vocalists, and soloists who deacon out lines of spirituals to the audience perform at 7:30 PM on the third Sunday of every month, from September through May, in Frissell Hall on the historic Penn Center campus. The popularity of the sings and the feelings of dignity and fellowship that characterize them are a moving testament to the pride of Sea Islanders in their culture and heritage. Contributions are welcome.

Nightlife

Johnson Creek Tavern (843-838-4166; 2141 Sea Island Pkwy., Harbor Island.) A no-frills beach bar about 25 minutes from town, where you'll find campers from Hunting Island State Park, young couples, and "after-party" groups who come to hear anything from bluegrass to rock.

Kathleen's (843-524-2500; 822 Bay St.) Live entertainment at lunch and dinner, on a patio overlooking the Beaufort River. Beaufort native David Dowling, singer, songwriter, storyteller, performs with his acoustic guitar on Weds. and Thurs.

David Dowling, Beaufort native, songwriter, folksinger

RECREATION

For at least 200 years, Lowcountry people have depended on the reliable bounty of land and sea. They became so accustomed to gathering and returning home with full baskets that the work of it, and the pleasure to be had in it, were easily interchanged. These days the sportsman, the naturalist, and the Sunday painter all take to the outdoors, often with equal results: going in seriousness, returning with, at the very least, a day of pleasure. Such is the natural abundance of the Lowcountry, and the dozens of opportunities to explore it—by power boat, kayak, windsurfer or bicycle; with fishing pole, crab net, paintbrush, or pup tent—that visitors still have this experience today.

Beaufort, in particular, claims the advantage over Charleston and Savannah of having its rural recreational opportunities close at hand. Informally, residents and visitors can fish or throw cast nets for shrimp at bridges off US 21 at **Cowan Creek** from the **Waterfront Park**, among other spots. **Hunting Island State Park** is located off US 21, about a 30-minute drive from town. At the north end of Hunting Island is **Paradise Pier** (843-838-7437), at 1,120 feet, the state's longest. There are dozens of public boat landings within easy reach. Launching is free, and so is parking, but you're on your own—no attendants, telephones, or rest rooms. For locations, or to see about chartering your own boat, inquire at the **Downtown Marina** (843-524-4422; 1010 Bay St.), sporting goods stores, or contact the **Lowcountry Resort Islands and Tourism Commission** (1-800-528-6870; www.southcarolinalowcountry.com; P.O. Box 615, Yemassee, SC 29945). If your recreational pursuits require clothing or equipment you didn't bring with you, see the shops listed in the **Shopping** section under "Sporting Goods and Clothing."

Perhaps the most significant resource for those who love the outdoors and savor its hidden beauty is the **ACE Basin National Wildlife Refuge**—a consolidation of some 350,000 acres of marsh, creek, sound, and forest to the north, east, and west of Beaufort. This crescent of landscape encompasses the forested, inland shore of the Ashepoo, Combahee, and Edisto Rivers and their small tributaries, and the vastness of St. Helena Sound. And not all the activity is on the water, either: From points on dry land, birders have identified more than 250 species of resident and migratory birds. For more information contact the **ACE Basin National Wildlife Refuge** (843-889-3084; www.acebasin.fws.gov; P.O. Box 848, Hollywood, SC 29449). To access the ACE and reach its headquarters, take SC 174 from US 17, about midway between Beaufort and Charleston, continue east through Adams Run and follow the signs to Grove House. It is open year-round from daylight to dark. You may park and walk in; good maps available online. Several options for visiting the ACE Basin are listed under "Boat Tours" below.

Beach Access

Hunting Island State Park (See also entry under "Camping.") Sunrise–sunset; $3 per person. Hunting Island is eroding and as the water reclaims it, it has taken on a beautiful, rather wild aspect, with fallen palmettos and exposed stumps on the beach. Parking is plentiful; there are picnic areas and bathhouses, and still, even before planned beach renourishment, miles to walk at the ocean's edge. The 19th-century **Hunting Island Lighthouse** offers an expansive view of the confluence of the Atlantic Ocean and St. Helena Sound.

Bicycling

Local bicycle enthusiasts have developed cue sheets and maps for enjoyable day trips that can be accessed from your lodgings or by driving a short distance to a trailhead. Their efforts have led to a much greater awareness of the emerging network of linked trails from Hunting Island State Park to the ACE Basin. The trips can be from 25 to 60 miles and wind through scenic, rural areas, by Revolutionary War sites, and movie locations. An online link is at www.beaufortsc.org. Email: dkim2341@davtv.com or Karen56@aol.com.

Low Country Bicycles (843-524-9585; 102 Sea Island Pkwy.) A shop filled with the latest mountain, cruising, high performance, and kid's bikes, maps, and accessories. Owner John Feeser has good touring suggestions, local and longer distance. Bikes for rent by the hour (Adults, $8; children, $5) and day (Adults, $30; children, $18), as well as racks for the car ($15), and helmets, locks, etc. Repairs on-site.

Boating
Boat Tours
ACE Basin Tours (843-521-3099; www.acebasintours.com) will take you on a 3-hour pontoon boat trip in the ACE. The boat leaves from Coosaw Island at 10 AM Weds. and Sats. (Adults, $30; children 6–12, $15.00; under 6 free when accompanied by a parent.) Call for reservations and directions. Tours may be scheduled on other days, with a minimum 8 passengers.

Capt. Dick's Eco/Historic Cruise (843-524-4422) departs from the Downtown Marina (by appointment) and plies the Beaufort River on a 30-foot, canopied pontoon boat with room for six passengers. Rates start at $60 per hour.

Islander Steamship (843-524-4000) is large vessel and a good choice for passengers who might be nervous on the water. Seating, inside and out, for 125. Tours lasting nearly two hours depart from the Downtown Marina most days at 2 PM, but call ahead to confirm or check at the Marina. Adults $20; seniors/military $19; children $12.

Lowcountry Rafting Adventures (843-986-1051; lowcountryraftingadventures.com) offers tours lasting two or four hours aboard a 30-foot Osprey accommodating up to 24 passengers. Daily departures from the Downtown Marina for the shorter cruise: Adults $25; children $20. A unique four-hour tour takes you into the ACE Basin where you board inflatable kayaks and paddle in quiet creeks. No experience necessary, but reservations are required.

Lowcountry Sailing (843-252-7245) offers sailing cruises and instruction by appointment from the Port Royal Marina. Typical custom cruises for four to six passengers include sunset sails or engine cruising with a two-hour minimum start at about $250.

Bowling
Ribaut Lanes (843-524-3111; 1140 S. Ribaut Rd.). Open daily until 10 PM.

Camping
Hunting Island State Park (843-838-2011; www.southcarolinaparks.com; 2555 Sea Island Pkwy., Hunting Island, SC 29920) on US 21, about 30 minutes from Beaufort. 200 sites, 14 cabins, nature trails, picnic sites, showers and dressing rooms, a store, water, and electrical hookups. Some sites can be reserved; some are first come, first served; some cabins are handicapped-accessible. Campsites from about $25 per night; cabins from $600–$900 weekly.

Point South KOA (843-726-5733 or 1-800-562-2948; I-95 at Exit 33).

Tuc In De Wood Campground (843-838-2267; www.tuckinthewood.com; 22 Tuc In De Wood Lane, St. Helena Island, SC 29920) 74 campsites with water, electricity, and cable television connections; 65 sites with full hookups.

Canoeing and Kayaking
Trail guides and other good information about paddling in the ACE Basin and nearby rivers are available online at www.walterboro.org.

Beaufort Kayak Tours (843-525-0810; www.beaufortkayaktours.com.) Two-hour nature tours leave from downtown and include crabbing and shrimping instruction as well as a fine education in the ecology, and a history-focused tour of peninsular Beaufort. Adults $35; children $25. Custom tours by request. Call for reservations.

The Kayak Farm (843-838-2008). Accompanied tours, rentals (either full or half day), or instruction; tours to Hunting Island and nearby creeks; longer trips to ACE Basin sites, tours through lagoon where portions of *GI Jane* and *Forrest Gump* were filmed. Naturalists on staff. Overnight tours by arrangement. Hours amd costs vary.

Outpost Moe's (843-844-2514; www.outpostmoes.com)Located on US 17 between Charleston and Beaufort. Kayak tours through the old rice fields. Customized and arranged by appointment.

Family Fun

A large, partially covered, well-lit **skateboard park** attracts riders to its ramps. It's located in Port Royal on Ribaut Rd., at the entrance to the Naval Hospital.

Beaufort Fun Park, (843-524-2267; www.beaufortfun.com; 591 Robert Smalls Pkwy.) offers miniature golf, go-cart racing, bumper boats, and batting cages.

Fishing

Fishing is so thickly woven into the fabric of local life that it really is a culture of its own. Anthropologists would note its folkways: the way its residents cook, the stories they tell, the skills they wish to pass on, where they live, what kinds of politicians they elect, how they judge character, what their values are for their children. Like the Myth of the Old South and Old Families, the lore of fishing confers a kind of lineage by which people know themselves. And where the Old Families might have Old Houses, people who fish have Old Cars, "fishing cars" as they are widely known—dinged-up rustbuckets that make it to the boat landing (not much farther) with the faithfulness of a hunting hound.

In fact, the opportunities are so numerous, the catches still plentiful, the waterways still generally pristine, the tradition so revered, that a book written in 1856, *Carolina Sport By Land and Water* by William Elliott, can be read as a nearly modern account.

Today's enthusiast can choose freshwater or saltwater sites; fish from piers, bridges, boats, banks, or the beach; or troll an artificial offshore reef. Saltwater fly-fishing is a popular specialty. **Paradise Pier** (843-838-7437) is located on Hunting Island near Beaufort and open 24 hours. The fishing fee is $4. The catch can range from small bream, porgy, and spot—of the family commonly known as "sailor's choice"—to flounder, to big game fish like wahoo, drum, shark, and cobia. In general, the best part of the season extends from April through November, but small panfish remain active beyond those dates. You may also fish in the lagoon on Hunting Island by using light tackle with shrimp and worms for bait.

Licenses are required for freshwater fishing and for saltwater fishing under certain conditions. Most visitors interested in recreational fishing will not need one; they're not necessary for recreational shrimping or crabbing. Licenses are sold in many hardware and hunting stores, K-Mart, and tackle shops. For further information on licenses, and size and catch limits, contact the **South Carolina Wildlife and Marine Resources Dept.** (843-795-6350; P.O. Box 12559, Charleston, SC 29412).

For a comprehensive map indicating recreational fishing facilities in the Lowcountry, including marinas, boat landings, bridges and catwalks, shellfish grounds, and offshore reefs, contact the **Lowcountry Resort Islands and Tourism Commission** (1-800-528-6870; P.O. Box 615, Yemassee, SC 29945).

Find more recreational fishing about 35 minutes north of Beaufort off US 17 (between Beaufort and Edisto) at the **Bear Island Wildlife Management Area** (843-844-8957, for information; 843-762-5078 for licenses).

Sport-Fishing Charters

A sport-fishing charter can take you to the Gulf Stream or to any of the dozen or so artificial reefs offshore. More than 150 years ago, the first artificial reefs used in this area were approximately six feet high, log, hut-like structures that were sunk to attract sheepshead; today's reefs are far more elaborate affairs built of tires, concrete debris, and castoff military machinery that attract dozens of species. Given that much of the sea floor off the coast is sandy, these reefs provide the hard substrate necessary to create a "live bottom" of invertebrates, small fish, coral, crabs, and sponges. They are active feeding stations for the big fish, and experienced guides know them well. Trips of this sort generally take a full day. Trips closer to shore, in smaller boats, can be easily enjoyed by the half-day.

A listing of some of the many **charter boat services** available follows. Rods, reels, bait, and tackle are provided; lunch or snacks are usually available, but you should check in advance; boats are equipped with safety equipment and licenses; all but the smallest have heads. It is wise to bring sunscreen, windbreakers, and a towel.

Many charters will design a trip to suit your particular interest or prepare a boat for a fishing tournament. If stormy weather is forecast, call ahead to confirm that the trip is on. Also check the reservation, deposit, and cancellation policies of each charter. You'll have to plan your trip around the tides, too. The 2004 prices for half-day trips started at about $125 per person, but varied considerably depending on the type of fishing and distance travelled.

Bay Street Outfitters (843-524-5250; www.baystreetoutfitters.com; 815 Bay St.) Visitors who are experienced in the art of fly fishing, as well as those who are rank beginners, can find experienced guides, instruction (Red Fish School one-day seminars, from $150 per person), and a full line of Orvis outfits, accessories, and specialty rods here. In 2003, guided charters, including lunch, cost $300–$475 depending on how many hours were spent on the water. Licenses are not required on the charters; drinks and equipment are provided. Call ahead and see what the season has to offer.

Capt. Eddie Netherland (843-838-3782; www.fishingcapteddie1.com) Offshore and inshore trips by the day and half-day on a 25-foot Grady-White Sailfisher. King mackerel a specialty.

Sea Wolf VI (843-525-1174; www.seawolfcharter.com) Major Wally Phinney Jr. USA, Ret. is your guide. Deep-sea fishing, diving, cruising, by day or half-day aboard 35-foot boat. Call for appointments for half-day, full-day, or Gulf excursions. Trips range from $355 to $1,200.

Fitness Facilities
Omni Health and Fitness Center (843-379-2424; 1505 Salem Rd.) Full range of exercise equipment and programs in a new facility. Day passes cost $10.

Ray's Gym (843-524-8351; SC 170) Complete gym, body-sculpting, Nautilus, weights, fitness machines.

YMCA of Beaufort County (843-522-9622; 1801 Richmond Ave., Port Royal) Pool, gym, classes.

Golf
The Lowcountry probably has more golf courses per person than any other region in the country, and more with holes offering expansive ocean or marsh views, or such scenic diversions as deer, heron, and the occasional alligator. Many are consistently ranked

among the top 100 in the country: Visitors can and do spend every day for a week playing a different one.

Whether you're a duffer or scratch golfer, there's pleasure in being on the links, either early in the morning as the heavy dew dries and the temperature rises, or late in the day as the chuck-will's-widows commence their plaintive call. Lowcountry weather allows for year-round play and (in the summer) late-afternoon starting times. The high-season months are in fall and spring, so it is wise to schedule your playing time well in advance.

On some courses carts are required at peak playing times. Special prices are often posted for midday tee-times in the height of summer. For resort play, it is usually necessary to be an overnight guest. Golf packages that include lodging are numerous, so ask about them. Club rentals and instruction are available at all courses. Greens fees/cart rentals reflect 2003 prices.

Public and Semi-Private Courses

Country Club of Beaufort (843-522-1605; 8 Barnwell Dr., Lady's Island) Russell Breedon design, 18 holes, par 72. Three sets of tees: 4,880 yards, 6,089 yards, and 6,489 yards. Greens fees including cart $40–$60.

Fripp Island (843-838-1576 or 1-800-933-0050; Fripp Island) Set on the rim of the Atlantic and Fripp Inlet, Ocean Point Golf Links, par 72, is a George Cobb course, from 4,951 yards to 6,590 yards. The Ocean Creek Course, the first designed by Davis Love III, is a par 71, winding through the marshes and interior wetlands. Yardage from 4,884 to 6,629. Walking is an option at both courses. Since they lie within a gated community, you must call ahead to reserve tee times and a visitor's pass. Fees are $79–$89 per person.

Gifford's Golf (843-521-9555; 30 Grober Hill Rd., Burton) A friendly, 9-hole course with driving range and pro shop. Fees are $6.50 for 9 holes, $8.50 for 18.

Lady's Island Country Club (843-524-3635; 139 Francis Marion Circle, Lady's Island) Pines Course, par 72, 5,421 yards to 6,811 yards; Marsh Course, par 72, 5,192 yards to 5,929 yards. Greens fees including cart $31–$80.

Legends at Parris Island (843-228-2240; MCRD, Parris Island) Par 72 course redesigned by Clyde Johnston in 2000, now ranked in top 10 military courses. Tees from 5,700 yards to 7,100 yards. Cart or walk $25–$35.

South Carolina National Golf Club (843-524-0300; 8 Waveland Ave., Beaufort) George Cobb's last design, par 71. Four sets of tees: 4,970 yards to 6,625 yards. Greens fees including cart $49–$80. A British-style pub is located in the Clubhouse for lunch.

Horseback Riding

Beaufort Equestrian Center (843-846-4765), **Broomfield Stables** (843-521-1212), **Camelot Farms** (843-838-3938), and **Shalimar Horse Center** (843-521-0419) welcome inquiries from visitors seeking instruction within the ring.

Tennis

Public courts, some of which are lit for night play, are located on Boundary Street across from the National Cemetery; on the corner of Battery Creek Rd. and Southside Blvd. and in the Port Royal Park on Paris Ave. in the village of Port Royal. Free. No reservations required.

Shopping

Antiques
Bellavista Antiques & Interiors (843-521-0687; 206 Carteret St.) Large-scale furniture and vases, stone ornaments, English pine furniture.

Canup Antiques (843-524-8914; 809 Bay St.) American country furniture, tinware, white ironstone.

Der Teufelhund (843-521-9017; 13-B Marina Blvd., near Parris Island) Military books, antique gear, insignias, trunks, and other ephemera of 20th-century warfare.

Michael Rainey Antiques (843-521-4532; 702 Craven St.) A high-end collection, frequently refreshed with new purchases, largely from New England, Pennsylvania, and the south. Baskets, bureaus, benches, and paintings.

Nest (843-521-4965; 314 Charles St.) French and American antiques, fine fabric, small decorative pieces for the garden or mantle.

Beaufort's Bay St. blends the old with the new

Oyster Cay Collection (843-525-6644; 917 Bay St., in the Old Bay Marketplace) Antique furniture and rugs from Indonesia, China, and elsewhere in Asia.

221 Antiques (843-522-3049; 221 Scott's St.) Laid-back and jumbled, with lots of old kitchen items, small furniture, and Victorian and later accessories.

Books/Recordings
Bay St. Trading Co. (843-524-2000; 808 Bay St.) Best-sellers, books-on-tape, excellent children's section, comprehensive local and regional history, and many fine photography books. The staff is very knowledgeable, which makes this store the best place to browse downtown.

Beaufort Bookstore (843-525-1066; Jean Ribaut Sq.) A large selection and wide variety of books, from best-selling fiction and non-fiction to military and Lowcountry favorites.

Firehouse Books and Espresso Bar (843-522-2665; 706 Craven St.) A charming bookstore with an excellent magazine selection; also serving lunch.

McIntosh Book Shoppe (843-524-1119; 919 Bay St.) New and used books on South Carolina you'll find nowhere else. Civil War albums, rare and antique volumes, as well as local writers and local history.

Clothing

Beaufort Clothing Co. (843-524-7118; 723 Bay St.) Everything men and women need for a casual Friday or clean-cut preppy look, featuring cotton sweaters, Hawaiian shirts, pastel polos, and accessories.

Deal's (843-524-4993; 724 Bay St.) Cotton sweaters, khakis, shirts in natural fibers, and imported Irish apparel, all at discounted prices.

Doodlebugs (843-379-3209; 705 Bay St.) Beaufort's only children's store, with charming clothes, gifts, shoes, and little extras.

Jasmine (843-524-6660; 919 Bay St.) A women's boutique with dresses, separates, and colorful accessories.

Lipsitz Department Store (843-524-2330; 825 Bay St.) A family-owned and family-run business for more than 100 years. Everyday wear and shoes in all sizes, superior friendly service. A more modern shoe store is across the street, run by the owners' son.

Plumage (843-522-8807; 104 West St.) Evening clothes with glittering accessories and distinctive casual outfits, including a fine small selection for kids.

Crafts

Carolina Stamper (843-522-9966; 203 Carteret St.) Rubber stamps, supplies, and lots of ideas for making stationery and artwork.

The Craftseller (843-525-6104; 818 Bay St.) Local and regional artists' work, including jewelry, benches made of recycled wood from local buildings, fabric art, handmade paper, wind-chimes.

Sweetgrass Baskets made by local artists can be found on St. Helena Island on US 21, at a roadside stand by the Red Piano Too Gallery and other roadside stands, and in the Gallery itself. The baskets, which incorporate palmetto frond, pine needle, and rush with the pale grass, come in many shapes and sizes, with individual variations inspired by the utilitarian shapes used in the past. They require enormous amounts of labor and skill and are useful as well as beautiful.

Lowcountry shops appeal to a laid-back lifestyle

Galleries

Art & Soul (843-379-9710; 917 Bay St., in the Old Bay Marketplace) Paintings, prints, ceramics, and textiles with a contemporary feel. Art and craft supplies, too.

Bay Street Gallery (843-522-9210; www.baystgallery.com; 719 Bay St.) Original works by Lana Hefner and Sandra Baggette including impressionistic views of marsh and woodland scenes, as well as a fine collection of Sea Island baskets and tiny ornaments.

Beaufort Art Association Gallery (843-379-2222; 905 Port Republic St.) Original works including pottery, prints, jewelry, sculpture, photography, and acrylics by some 75 member artists. New exhibits every six weeks.

Charles Street Gallery (843-521-9054; 914 Charles St.) Original works including bronze sculpture, raku pottery, paintings, and etchings. Full-service framing and regularly scheduled gallery shows.

Crackpots (843-838-0014; 968 Sea Island Pkwy.) A gallery and pottery studio on St. Helena Island that also offers workshops.

Gloria Dalvini Watercolors (843-521-0221; www.dalviniwatercolors.com; 101 Scott's St.) A tiny building by the Waterfront Park houses dozens of watercolors of Lowcountry houses, gardens, and landscapes.

Ibile Indigo House (843-838-3884; www.ibileindigo.com; 27 Penn Center Circle.) The unique studio and shop of Arianne King Comer, a fabric and batik artist whose work is based on West African techniques, including dyeing from the indigo plants she cultivates. Hangings, wearable art, yardage, and smaller art pieces are for sale; custom indigo dyeing by appointment.

Indigo Gallery (843-524-1036; 813 Bay St.) Limited and open editions of many of the best-known Lowcountry artists, as well as serigraphs, original art, and framing.

Red Piano Too Art Gallery, St. Helena Island

Longo Gallery (843-522-8933; 407 Carteret St. and 103 Charles St.) Suzanne and Eric Longo, husband and wife, are proficient and playful artists. Her ideas find expression in clay and concrete sculpture; his in brightly colored, whimsical paintings (sometimes on boards or old roof tin) and found-object constructions.

LyBensons Gallery & Studio (843-525-9006; 711 Charles St.) A large, bright gallery specializing in art from Africa and from African-American artists in a variety of media including verdite stone sculptures; photographs depicting the Gullah culture by Rev. Kenneth Hodges.

The Red Piano Too (843-838-2241; www.redpianotoo.com; 870 Sea Island Parkway, St. Helena Island) Located about 15 minutes from Beaufort, this gallery has an eclectic assortment of folk art and outsider art by individuals from this area and throughout the South, as well as baskets, books, jewelry, African objects, and prints. Fine framing is available.

Rhett Gallery (843-524-3339; 901 Bay St.) Prints and watercolors of the Lowcountry by Nancy Ricker Rhett as well as antique first-edition prints and maps, Civil War and nautical materials, and hand-colored engravings. A companion gallery with work by her sons, also including rugs, furnishings, and hammocks, is on St. Helena Island (847-A Sea Island Pkwy.)

Shipman Art Gallery (843-524-7722; 904 Bay St.) Watercolor artist Barbara Shipman offers some 100 of her paintings in collectible print editions, as well as originals. She captures the Lowcountry in both intimate and grand ways—from one crab or one blossom to an entire coastline scene.

University of South Carolina at Beaufort (843-521-4144; 901 Carteret St.) The University and The Arts Council of Beaufort County sponsor numerous shows throughout the year, from scholarly overviews to the best works of local artists.

Gifts

Beaufort Butterfly Company (843-986-0555; 928-1/2 Bay St.) Everything you'll need to attract, observe, identify, catch, and collect butterflies, as well as books about natural history and tee shirts with nature themes.

For the Birds and Garden (843-322-0277; 902 Boundary St.) Hundreds of birdhouses and feeders designed to attract individual species and garden ornaments to liven up the yard.

Lulu Burgess (843-524-5858; 917 Bay St.) An engaging blend of imaginative gifts such as jewelry, stationery, tableware, totes, and decorative accessories for the home. Opened by a young Beaufort native who has brought her good taste back home.

Rossignol's (843-524-2175; 817 Bay St.) Fine china patterns, silver and gold jewelry, stationery, and expensive stemware—all suitable for wedding gifts—as well as platters, picture frames, and tea towels that would make good house presents.

Sweet Tea Paper and Presents (843-379-7877; 917 Bay St. in the Old Bay Marketplace) Elegant and whimsical stationery as well as cotton pajamas and bath and body products.

Verdier House Gift Shop (843-379-6335; 801 Bay St.) Located in the basement of the historic house museum, it features a collection of books, ornaments, prints, toys, and note cards with sketches of Beaufort's old homes.

Gourmet and Health Food

Cravings By the Bay (843-522-3000 or 1-800-735-3215; cravingsbythebay.com; 928 Bay St.) Savor Lowcountry flavors as well as memories by ordering soups, condiments, sauces, and specialty books by mail. Shrimp, oysters, clams, scallops, and soft-shell crab can be delivered overnight. Drop by for more information.

It's Only Natural (843-986-9595; 95 Factory Creek Court, Lady's Island) Just over the Beaufort bridge, a new store with organic produce, nuts and grains in bulk, and low-carb specialties.

Vita Villa Ltd. (843-522-0583; US 21, Lady's Island Square) Herbs, grains, candies, books, vitamins, local honey, and sugar-free and preservative-free health foods.

Wine & Provisions (843-524-9463; 403 Carteret St.) In addition to serving excellent sandwiches, this market carries a broad range of wine and beer; many kinds of pasta, rice and beans; and sauces and condiments, fresh, frozen or on the shelf.

Home Furnishings/Kitchenware

The Cook's House (843-524-6198; 1101 Boundary St. at Newcastle Sq.) A top-notch showcase for kitchen tools (rice steamers, baguette pans) as well as handsome appliances and tableware.

In High Cotton (843-522-1405; 903 Bay St.) Fine linens and home furnishings.

Le Creuset Manufacturer's Outlet Store (843-589-6650; Yemassee at Exit 38 off I-95) Cast iron cookware, utensils, pottery, and storage pieces from the French maker are available at significant discount from overstock, discontinued, and cosmetically flawed inventory.

Lollygags (843-982-0333; Paris Ave. at 8th St., Port Royal) Striped canvas pillows in the colors of Provence, garden statues, easy chairs, and unique home accessories, located in a 19th-century store in the historic section of Port Royal.

Waterside Place (843-524-0201; 308 Charles St.) Linens and fine furnishings gathered for a custom interior design practice.

Sporting Goods and Clothing

Barefoot Bubba's (843-838-5431; 2135 Sea Island Pkwy, St. Helena Island) The latest in surf wear, surfboards, skimboards, rafts, and toys for the beach.

Bay Street Outfitters (843-524-5250; 815 Bay St.) A full line of high-end sportswear from Orvis and Barbour, as well as fishing gear, reels, binoculars, and books.

Island Outfitters (843-522-9900; 189 Sea Island Pkwy.) Headquarters for serious gun and bow hunters, campers, and fishermen. Rods, coolers, bait, hooks, ammunition, and a big selection of rugged outdoor camouflage and boots. The expert advice is free.

Lowcountry Paddlesports (843-379-5292; 1109 Boundary St.) Kayaks, canoes, big kites, and all the accessories for inland and ocean water activity.

Shrimp boats at Edisto

EDISTO ISLAND

Like the Sea Islands around Charleston and Beaufort, Edisto's history starts with early Native American settlements and agriculture. Later came rice, indigo, and cotton cultivation; slavery; and the occupation of Federal troops. Small farming and fishing operations have remained constant. Unlike the other Sea Islands, Edisto, while lively in the summer season due to the scads of modest rentals on Edisto Beach and Edisto Beach State Park, remains quiet the rest of the time. People from Charleston and other parts of the state love it as a weekend destination for its slow pace, beauty, and chance to get out on the water. Development is accelerating, but local preservation groups have stayed one step ahead of the trend. If you're looking for a few days of peace and quiet, or a family reunion, enlivened by beachcombing, a good meal, a kayak or boat tour, your choice should be Edisto. Recently a sickly loggerhead turtle washed up at Edisto. It was taken to Charleston where it was nursed and healed. When the time came to release it back into the ocean at Edisto Beach, more than 300 people turned up to watch, cheer, and take pictures. They found out by word of mouth. That's Edisto.

The island lies about 45 miles south of Charleston by road, and about 75 miles from Beaufort—of course far less by water. From US 17, take SC 174 (signs alert you to Edisto), the island's main travel route. It is a two-lane road of about 20 miles from the main highway, unlit, embowered by trees. It's a hike to travel from Charleston or Beaufort just for dinner, but fine for a day trip. Cab and car rental services are limited, so it's best to arrive there on your own. A variety of creeks and rivers irregularly indent Edisto, so that today, as in the past, there are roads that cross the marsh or wind through the woods in what seems to be the long way around. Original sections of the King's Highway, laid out in the early 18th century, remain in use today. The main road dead-ends at the Atlantic Ocean.

For a visitor, Edisto is the least immediately knowable of the Sea Islands. What remains of its "Golden Age," the period between the Revolutionary and Civil Wars, is mostly hidden, tucked away along secondary roads that wind through fields and patches of scrub oak, and meander by the North and South Edisto Rivers and their tributaries.

Historic sites that are listed on the National Register of Historic Places (27 so far) do include churches, but consist primarily of private plantation homes and gardens that are not open to the public. A good source of information is the **Edisto Chamber of Commerce** (843-869-3867 or 1-888-333-2781; www.edistochamber.com; P.O. Box 206, Edisto, SC 29438).

For an overview of the island's history, visit the **Edisto Island Historic Preservation Society's Museum** (843-869-1954; wwwedistomuseum.com; SC 174 at Chisolm Plantation Rd. Hours are 1–4 Tues., Thurs., and Sat. Admission $3; free to children 10 and under.) Island artifacts such as baskets, clothing, farm tools, letters and documents, uniforms, and furniture are displayed in several small rooms. There are old photographs and explanatory remarks. The little gift shop sells a variety of natural history items for kids—good to use to explore and collect on their own—as well as a series of excellent reprints of booklets you're not likely to find anywhere else on your travels. They include "Edisto Island in 1808," "Indigo in America," "Gullah," and "She Came To the Island," the Edisto diary of Mary Ames, a Northern abolitionist whose account of teaching and living among the newly freed slaves during the Civil War is among the most poignant of the genre.

Since Edisto's old homes are not open to the public, one way to get inside some of them is by taking a 2.5-hour tour of Edisto's churches, plantations, and other points of historic and natural interest with Edisto natives as your guides. Contact **Island Tours and T'ings** (843-869-1110; www.toursandtings.com) for tour schedule—reservations are required. Adults $20; children $10. **Annual Tours of Edisto** take place the second Saturday in October. Contact the **Edisto Island Historic Preservation Society** (843-869-1954; P.O. Box 393, Edisto Island, SC 29438). Tickets generally cost $25 for adults; $8 ages 6–16.

For an education on the subject of the region's reptile life, visit the **Edisto Island Serpentarium** (843-869-1171; edistoserpentarium.com; 1374 SC 174) where more than 500 reptiles are on display in natural habitats; feeding and educational presentations occur every hour. Open May 1 through Labor Day, Mon through Sat. 10–6.

One of Edisto's best places to eat is the **Old Post Office Restaurant** (843-869-2339; 1442 SC 174) a cozy place that serves lunch and dinner daily in season. This is not fried food cuisine — entrées feature steak, pork, and the best local fish and shellfish available. An affiliated and more informal restaurant is **Sunset Grill** with sunset and water views, located on Docksite Rd., by the Marina. Another is **Po Pigs Bo-B-Q** (843-869-9003; 2410 SC 174) a family-run dining room with a huge buffet and a cheerful atmosphere. It's southern with a twist, offering curried rice with sun-dried fruit as well as country ham. The price is inexpensive to moderate. Open Thurs. through Sat. 11:30–9 PM., and Weds. from May 15–Sept. 15. Call both restaurants to confirm their seasonal and off-season hours. There are also pizza places, and on the docks facing St. Helena Sound, fish markets and informal restaurants.

Shopping on Edisto is limited. **With These Hands** (843-869-3509; 1444 SC 174) is a fine art and crafts gallery; **Fish or Cut Bait Gallery** (843-869-2511; www.fishorcutbait gallery.com; 142 Jungle Rd.) is a regular stop for upscale weekenders. For house and garden furnishings, prints, and fine conversation with owner Leland Vaughn, stop by **The Crab Trap** (843-869-0226; 51 Station Court.)

Continuing across Edisto Island brings you to **Edisto Beach**, the curve of land that faces the Atlantic then turns to embrace the inner marsh and St. Helena Sound. It has been for years the summer destination of South Carolina families—both as day-trippers to the state park or as vacationers who stay for one or more weeks. Families take up residence in the plain, raised, two-story houses that line the boulevards for about three-dozen blocks and spill across adjacent avenues. There's nothing fancy about Edisto Beach: It's informal, full of kids riding bikes (good bike lanes here, and watchful drivers), and minivans parked in the sand. A high point of the day is watching the shrimp boats come in. Plentiful beach access.

Many of these houses rent by the week, and several rental agencies list them. The market is organized by location: beachfront, second row (across the street from the beach usually with an ocean view), beach walk (easy access but on a side street), condos, and homes with docks (deep water, tidal creek, or other access, which may not be near the beach.) It is common for houses to accommodate 10–16 people—part of the charm of Edisto is its family reunion aspect—so the range of prices for a week in the summer can be from $850 to $3,700. Rental specs also include amenities like "fish cleaning sink," "hot and cold outside shower," grills, and cribs. For information contact:

Atwood Vacations (1-800-476-0126; www.atwoodvacations.com).

Edisto Sales and Rentals (843-869-2527 or 1-800-868-5398; www.edistorealty.com).

Kapp/Lyons Co. (1-800-945-9667; wwwkapplyons.com).

A small resort, **Fairfield Ocean Ridge** (843-869-4527; rentals 1-877-296-6335; www.fairfieldvacations.com; 1 King Cotton Rd., Edisto Island, SC 29438) offers rentals. Its 300-acre layout includes non-guest-accessible tennis, golf (Edisto Beach Golf Club 843-869-1111) swimming, a restaurant, and a kid's summer program. The accommodations are more rustic at the 1,255-acre **Edisto Beach State Park** (843-869-2756; www.southcarolinaparks.com; 8377 State Cabin Rd., Edisto Island, SC 29438). There's a 75-site camping area for tents and RVs (some are designated for handicapped visitors) and five two-bedroom cabins. Camping with water and electrical hookups is available, as well as walk-in sites with pads and central water. Restrooms near the sites offer hot showers. The cabins are furnished, heated, air-conditioned, and have access to a dock for crabbing and fishing. For more camping information call 843-869-2156. The park includes 1.5 miles of beachfront, open marsh, a forest with nature trails, a general store, boat launching access to Big Bay Creek, and interpretive programs. The beach is a wonderful place to hunt for fossils and shark's teeth.

Because of its location at the confluence of the North and South Edisto Rivers, the Atlantic, and St. Helena Sound, Edisto Beach offers probably the easiest access to the ACE Basin and all sorts of fishing, boating, and water sports. For maps and information about sightseeing and bird-watching, contact the **ACE Basin National Wildlife Refuge Headquarters** (843-889-3084; 8675 Willtown Rd., Hollywood, SC 29449) or contact the **South Carolina Department of Natural Resources** (843-844-8957; 585 Donnelly Drive, Green Pond, SC 29446).

If you want to tour the ACE Basin by water, stop by **Edisto Watersports & Tackle** (843-869-0663; 3702 Docksite Rd., Edisto Beach, SC 29438). Captain **Ron Elliott's Edisto Island Tours** (843-869-1937) provides boat trips to offshore islands for shelling, island river tours, and inshore fishing. You may also tour by canoe and kayak with him. He is a passionate naturalist and font of Edisto lore. Rent bikes, boats, and kayaks at **Island Bikes and Outfitters** (843-869-4444; 140 Jungle Rd.).

Bluffton

A most common mistake of visitors to Bluffton is that they make too much of the place, fret that they've missed something that was "there." In fact, an hour spent in walking along its quiet streets, looking through the bramble and old fences at some of its 19th-century frame houses, visiting the church on the bluff, browsing in a few shops and art galleries, and doubling back to your parked car about does it for Bluffton.

Why bother? For one thing, the historic Bluffton village is one of the Lowcountry's last, true cul-de-sacs. It's not moving, and it's not bothered by your coming or going, either. There are a couple of "Historic" this-and-that signs nailed up, it is true, but what you thought it ought to have been and whether or not it ever becomes that scrubbed-up, idealized version of itself is of no concern. Tiny Bluffton has all the charm of a wonderful, barefoot kid who is not going to live up to some schoolmarm's idea of "potential."

However, it is also true that in the last two years, Bluffton has annexed so much adjacent land (in an effort to manage development) that the difference between the old, insouciant, square-mile village and the vast sprawl it now controls can be confusing. A restaurant with a Bluffton address may be located in an off-highway commercial park, not the old village. Get directions before you head out!

Visiting Bluffton

From Beaufort (about 35 minutes) follow SC 170 and continue as if you were going to Hilton Head, across the Broad River Bridge. About eight miles ahead, exit right at the sign to Hilton Head and loop around. You are now on US 278 (William Hilton Parkway) the main Hilton Head road. After a couple of miles, you will see SC 46 marked as a right turn. Take it into Bluffton.

Bluffton's mid-19th-century Church of the Cross is a gem of Lowcountry

From Hilton Head (about 30 minutes) follow US 278 across the Gaves Bridge and turn left on SC 46 and follow it to Boundary Street.

Bluffton was a summer community of island planters, and in 1863 it was nearly burned to the ground by Union troops. Ten antebellum buildings remain; another 16 or so houses were built after the Civil War. Taken together, they give a view of classic Lowcountry village life. Far from extravagant, they are nonetheless suffused with a sense of form appropriate to the landscape and to their function as seasonal dwellings belonging to families who had most likely seen better days. It is worth the trip alone to see the **Church of the Cross**

(110 Calhoun St.) an unpainted wooden church (circa 1857) with beautiful interior detailing, original pews, and Gothic-style windows. Docents are on site Mon. through Sat., 11–2.

Start your tour of Bluffton at the town's historic center the **Heyward House** (843-757-6293; www.heywardhouse.org. 52 Boundary St.), an 1840s Carolina farmhouse. It's open Tues. through Fri. from 10–3 and Sat 11–2. Admission $4 adults; $1 students. Then pick up a self-guided walking tour or biking map. Count on about two hours of wandering. Houses are marked by plaques, but not all are visible from the street. One book will help you appreciate them. It is: *No. II A Longer Short History of Bluffton, South Carolina and its Environs* produced by the **Bluffton Historical Preservation Society** (843-757-6293; P.O. Box 742, Bluffton, SC 29910). The price is $9.95. It includes historic essays and descriptions of homes, a map, and wonderful photographs.

If you are biking, Bluffton is well situated for longer treks in rural areas. Local cyclists have created cue sheets and maps for enjoyable day trips from 25–60 miles that take you to historic sites and churches, remote boat landings, and some of the shooting locations for Hollywood movies. Find information online at: www.hiltonheadisland.org or www.beaufortsc.org. or contact bicycling enthusiasts dkim2341@davtv.com or Karen56@aol.org with your bicycle route questions. Two bike shops will rent you equipment: **Jonathon's Bike Shop** (843-706-2453; 30 Plantation Park Dr.) and **Sports Addiction** (843-815-8281; Sheridan Park.)

Recently, Bluffton (Calhoun St. in particular), has emerged as a center for working artists and galleries that show their work. **A Guild of Bluffton Artists** (843-757-5590; 20 Calhoun St.) located in the old Planters Mercantile Building, showcases the best of their fine arts and crafts, from pottery to fiber art, jewelry, and painting. **Pluff Mudd** (843-757-5551; 27 Calhoun St,) features paintings and crafts by local and national artists. **The Society of Bluffton Artists Gallery** (843-757-6586; 48 Boundary St.) includes work of 70 Lowcountry artists in a remodeled gallery space. The working studio of potter **Jacob Preston** (843-757-3084; 10 Church St. between Boundary St. and Calhoun St.)

Art galleries in Bluffton celebrate the eccentric and the traditional

inside a converted church is open Tues. through Sat. 1–6 or by appointment. Off Calhoun St., Leah Lahey is at work at **L. Beaumont Pottery** (843-757-9831; 1132 May River Rd.). **Hummell Studios/Red Stripe Gallery** at 69 Calhoun St. provides self-taught artist Amos Hummel's version of what locals call "the Bluffton state of mind." Outdoor sculpture consisting of remodeled bikes and motorcycles and painted furniture beckon you inside.

A view of the May River, one of the Lowcountry's most pristine waterways

Bluffton's stores are no less unique. **Eggs N' Tricities** (843-757-3446; 71 Calhoun St.), which is located in an old filling station, has funky furniture outside and inside, and sells everything from 1940s era lamps and linens, to contemporary tableware. **The Store** (843-757-3855; 56 Calhoun St.) covers some of the same ground with similar esprit. **Stock Farm Antiques** (843-757-8046; 1263 May River Rd.) offers prints, porcelain, silver, rugs, and furniture—some American, some English—chosen with a sense of what fits in the big new houses at the resorts as well as the real old ones. There are also several consignment shops and thrift stores in the area that offer bargains and maybe a treasure. Ask about them.

Locals take coffee breaks at **The Sippin' Cow Cafe** (843-757-5051; 1230 May River Rd.). By evening, the smells of fresh seafood and maybe even live music drift from **Pepper's Porch** (843-757-2295; 1255 May River Rd.). Back toward "civilization" off US 278 lie a modest Mexican restaurant **Mi Tierra** (843-757-7200; 101 Mellenchamp Rd.) and two fine upscale restaurants: **Cafe at Belfair** (843-815-7818; 1G Sherington Dr.) where lunch and dinner entrées include fancy pastas, duck confit, and grilled seafood; and **Sigler's Rotisserie and Seafood** (843-815-5030; 12 Sheridan Circle) where roast chicken and seared meats are dinner favorites.

Photo courtesy of the Hilton Head Island Visitor & Convention Bureau

5

HILTON HEAD

Courts, Courses, Sails & Sand

The Hilton Head Island that a visitor sees today is a far different place from what it was 40 years ago. It represents a startling change to residents who, in the past, were accustomed to seeing growth in their region come slowly, if it came at all. It is the Lowcountry's boom-town, envied for its tax base, business opportunities, and recreational resources, scruti-nized as an example of the conflict between planned growth and overdevelopment. Its sometimes unenviable popularity caused a recent mayor to remark: "We're just trying to keep from getting run over."

Unlike the rest of the Lowcountry, Hilton Head is a place of condensed pleasure: in one day, a visitor can enjoy a range of activities that might have taken a week's vacation to savor in the past, had even the possibilities existed. The island is twelve miles long and five miles wide, shaped like a boot. It's on the Intracoastal Waterway, so there's river, ocean, and marsh access, with a mild year-round climate. Shops, tennis courts, golf courses, marinas, and restaurants prosper and proliferate. The commercial districts are discreetly screened from view, and even the busiest thoroughfare, US 278 (William Hilton Parkway), lacks neon signs. It's easy to understand why more than 1.8 million visitors come every year. Summer is the busiest time, when the year-round population of about 34,000 sees a turnover of 10,000 visitors a week.

Until 1955, when the first bridge linked Hilton Head to the mainland, the island's his-tory resembled that of its Sea Island neighbors. First settled by planters with slaves who raised rice, indigo, and cotton on about 16 plantations, later occupied during the Civil War by Federal troops, and faced with hard times and isolation after that, the island remained rural and self-sufficient. The African American families who made up most of the island's population farmed and fished; the visitors who came were gentleman hunters from the north. Transportation was supplied by small packet steamers, sailboats, and barges, and more often than not, their market destination was Savannah, for Hilton Head is the south-ernmost area of Beaufort County.

The resort and residential development that began in earnest in the early 1960s led to the "plantation" layout that orders the island's geography today. Most resort activities are based in those original subdivisions, which are accessed by security gates and called pri-vate. They are: Sea Pines Plantation, Shipyard Plantation, Palmetto Dunes, Port Royal Plantation, and Hilton Head Plantation. Within and around them are the dozens of golf courses, tennis courts, and marinas that define island recreation. Stores and restaurants are usually gathered in mall clusters, like Shelter Cove, or in modest shopping pods, like the Village at Wexford or Coligny Plaza. Many smaller residential areas lie scattered across

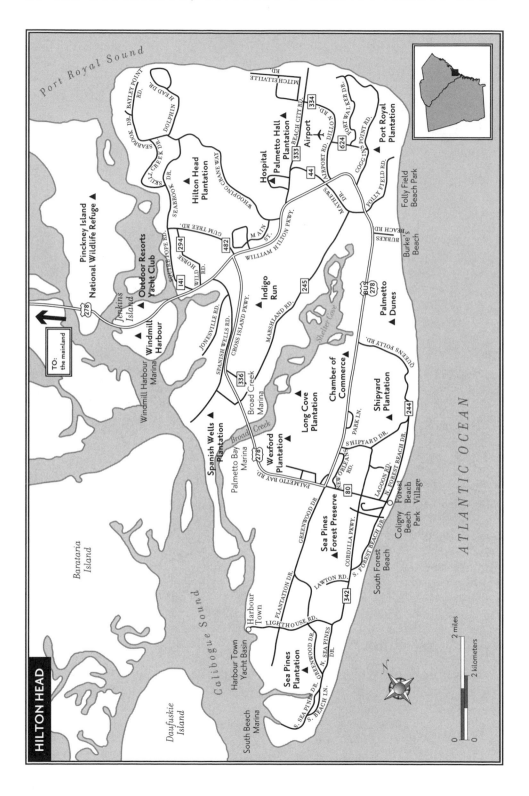

the island, some of them "gated" communities, others not. Because place names tend to sound alike—"cove" this and "water" that—and town regulations limit the size and shape of signs, pick up a free map.

As the island's topography has changed (much of it sculpted into golf courses), so has its population. Census figures categorize residents by race (90 percent white) and by age (some 30 percent over 60 years old). Continuing development has spilled over to adjacent areas that might be called "resort suburbs" in greater Bluffton. The unique character of the Lowcountry has not been blotted out, it's just harder to find it, but you can: vistas of marsh and ocean (where a 9-foot tide makes for a wide beach), flocks of diving pelicans and running sandpipers, loggerhead turtles that lay their eggs in the dark, whistling songbirds, and groves of live oak and pine that shelter deer and dove.

As you plan, you might want to decide what particular quality you'd like your trip to have. If you think you mostly want to play golf or tennis, you might look into options in the **Lodging** section for "stay-and-play" packages. If you're traveling with friends or family, you may want to rent a house or villa (a fully furnished unit in a condominium complex). If you decide upon a resort, you may not need a car—most resort amenities are within walking and biking distance, and you will be provided with airport transportation. For touring without a car, rent a bike and explore island-wide bike trails.

College students on Spring Break

The high season starts in mid-March, when families come on spring vacation, and continues through April, punctuated by the PGA tournament played at Sea Pines **MCI Heritage of Golf** (843-671-2448 or 1-800 234-0017; www.mciheritage.com). May and early June tend to be quiet, before the crowds of summer, as do September and October. When the island is crowded expect congestion and lines everywhere. Inter-island trips can take three times as long, with heavy stop-and-go traffic during morning or evening rush hour. Some of the congestion has been alleviated by the Cross Island Expressway, a new toll road ($1) worth taking.

GETTING TO HILTON HEAD

Savannah/Hilton Head International Airport (www.savannahairport.com) and the smaller, Hilton Head Airport (www.hiltonheadairport.com) are gateways. Flights to Hilton Head usually stop in Charlotte, NC, first; there are many direct flights to Savannah from cities around the country. Rental car service is available at both locations, as are courtesy shuttles if you are staying at a resort. **Yellow Cab** (843-686-6666), **Low Country Adventures** (843-681-8294), and **Angels Limousine** (843-247-0513) serve Hilton Head. Call in advance to check rates and make reservations, especially if you're traveling at high season. By car, take Exit 8 from I-95 to US 278, the link to Hilton Head. **Amtrak** (800-872-7245; www.amtrak.com) serves Savannah twice each day.

Lodging

There are more than 3,000 hotel and motel rooms and 6,000 rental units, including cottages, houses, and villas scattered across the island, from sites on or near the beach to those around golf courses, marinas, lagoons, in residential subdivisions or low-rise housing complexes, even on the main highway. Another 1,000 units are dedicated to "timeshare" arrangements and may be available for rent, too. Your accommodations may be elegant or simple; offer as much or as little privacy as you wish; come with or without kitchens; lie within walking distance, or not, from the beach and recreational amenities.

Rates vary from as little as $60 per night (off-season) for an economy motel room to $6,000 per week for a luxurious oceanfront home with a swimming pool. The range reflects differences in size and location—oceanfront is premium; resort privileges add to the price—and also the time of year: Vacation season here is mid-March through April, and June through mid-August. The shoulder seasons of late April and May, then September and October bring ideal golfing conditions, so prices stay high, though not at the seasonal peak. In the winter months, rates can be half what they are in the high season. Like many resort areas, Hilton Head adds an accommodations tax to lodging bills, and some establishments place a surcharge on credit-card payments. Ask for an estimate of your total bill when you are booking. Whatever accommodation you choose, inquire about special rate packages or coupons offered for restaurants, health clubs, or shops. Many hotels have discounts for golf and tennis; some have family plans, including activities for kids. In larger hotels, children often stay for free. Lodgings that are not located in private resorts often have arrangements to allow you access to some of their recreational facilities.

The easiest way to make reservations in a hotel or motel (listed directly below) is contact by phone or website. To inquire about home and villa rentals, call a property management company (listed under "Vacation Property Rentals"). Central reservation agencies can give you a sense of the whole picture, and they may be especially helpful in designing a package tailored to your specific interests. The **Hilton Head Chamber of Commerce** (www.hilton headchamber.org) is a good place to start. If you're interested in camping, look into the two recreational vehicle parks listed under **Recreation**, later in this chapter. If you're staying on a boat, see "Marinas," also in the **Recreation** listings. Some "vacation ownership" properties that offer weekend packages to attract potential purchasers are: **Disney's Hilton Head Island Resort** (843-341-4100 or 1-800-341-2636) and **Marriott's Vacation Club International** (1-800-527-3490).

The following rates are for one night's stay, per person, double occupancy. They do not include taxes, surcharges, or any special recreation/entertainment discounts. Prices quoted are for high season accommodations. Note that the rates for Luxury Accommodations are at least in the "Very Expensive" category: they can easily run to $260 per night. Villa and home rentals generally run from Saturday to Saturday during peak season. Two kennels provide places for your cat or dog to stay: **Brooke's Bed & Biscuit** (843-757-7387; www.abka.com/brookesbedandbiscuit) and **Evergreen Pet Lodge** (843-681-8354 or 1-866-680-8354; www.abka.com/evergreen); both allow you to pick up your pet during the day, while also providing boarding, care, and grooming.

Rates

Inexpensive	Up to $60
Moderate	$60 to $120
Expensive	$120 to $200
Very Expensive	$200 and up

Credit Cards

AE—American Express
DC—Diner's Club
CB—Carte Blanche
MC—MasterCard
D—Discover Card
V—Visa

Luxury Hotels and Inns

Crowne Plaza Resort

843-842-2400 or 1-800-334-1881.
www.cphiltonhead.com.
130 Shipyard Dr., Shipyard Plantation.
Price: Very Expensive.
Credit Cards: All major cards.
Handicap Access: Yes.

A 340-room oceanfront luxury hotel with full concierge service, two restaurants, and a popular lounge for evening entertainment. Pools, 27 holes of golf and a putting green, tennis courts, a 24-hour health center, sailing, and water sports all on site.

Daufuskie Island Resort

843-842-2000 or 1-800-648-6778.
www.daufuskieresort.com.
On Daufuskie Island.
Price: Very Expensive.
Credit Cards: All major cards.
Handicap Access: Yes.

Though not on Hilton Head, the Daufuskie Island resort is modeled on its neighbor's plan: a well-groomed private plantation (two golf courses, a tennis complex, beach and water sports) with access by ferry. Accommodations are in a main inn and in several cottages of two and four bedrooms. It's not spoiled by over-development (no traffic, no crowds) and appeals to corporate clients and group retreats. The island is 5 miles long by 2.5 miles wide, easy to see on an island tour.

Hilton Oceanfront Resort

843-842-8000 or 1-800-845-8001.
www.hiltonheadhilton.com.

23 Ocean Lane, Palmetto Dunes.
Price: Very Expensive.
Credit Cards: All major cards.
Handicap Access: Yes.

A luxury, 295-room hotel that claims the largest rooms on the island—560 sq. ft. each—with private balconies and kitchenettes. At the oceanfront setting there's an adults-only pool and a family pool, whirlpools, a fitness center, 25 tennis courts and five golf courses. Activities for kids (4–16) can be arranged for an additional charge—even at night. Restaurants and nightclubs within the complex.

Inn at Harbour Town

843-363-8100 or 1-888-843-4136.
www.seapines.com.
1 Lighthouse Lane, Sea Pines Plantation.
Price: Very Expensive.
Credit Cards: All major.
Handicap Access: Yes.

This 60-room inn is the newest addition to the Harbour Town complex, at its core a Mediterranean-style marina village whose lighthouse is probably the best-recognized symbol of Hilton Head. The inn is situated just off the water, in a quieter location by the golf courses. It's more thoughtfully designed than the functional fun-and-sun architecture, or the low-slung Tahiti-roof look of Sea Pines, and its provision of service (butlers on each floor, glorious bathrooms) and serenity (a quiet library and elegant-but-casual furniture and decorations) seem to suggest another way to enjoy the resort experience: to be in it, perhaps, but not of it.

Main Street Inn

843-681-3001 or 1-800-471-3001.
www.mainstreetinn.com.
2200 Main St.
Price: Expensive to Very Expensive.
Credit Cards: All major cards.
Handicap Access: Two rooms.

Hilton Head's Main Street Inn features European-style luxury and private, decorated courtyards over beachfront location

Unique on Hilton Head in that it offers the privacy of a lovely home and the services of a small European hotel. There are 33 luxury rooms, an outdoor lap-pool and hot tub, lounge areas with fireplaces, and a fine restaurant where a full breakfast is included and dinner is usually sought after. The spa offers deep-cleansing facials, skin-care and hydrotherapy treatments, yoga classes, and massage. Outdoors, the Charleston-style, vest-pocket urban garden enhances the feeling of an oasis. Club, AARP, and AAA discounts are honored.

Marriott Beach and Golf Resort
843-686-8400.
www.hiltonheadmarriott.com.
1 Hyatt Circle, Palmetto Dunes.
Price: Very Expensive.
Credit Cards: All major cards.
Handicap Access: Yes.

The largest hotel on the island, with 512 rooms, indoor pool, Olympic-sized outdoor pool, and children's pool. Health club, tennis courts, three golf courses, sailboat and bicycle rentals, and lots of beachfront. Three restaurants and a piano bar offer both formal and casual poolside dining. Children's program (additional fee) available weekends year-round; daily in summer.

Westin Resort
843-681-4000 or 1-800-937-8461.
www.westinhiltonhead.com.
2 Grasslawn Ave., Port Royal Plantation.
Price: Very Expensive.
Credit Cards: All major cards.
Handicapped Access: Yes.

Usually considered the most luxurious of the island's oceanfront resort hotels, with 412 rooms and 30 suites, plus 100 villas. The Westin is praised for its Sunday brunch and upscale grill menu, the elegant decorations, rooms with balconies, and good children's program. Guests may play on three Port Royal courses and on grass, hard, and clay courts. Indoor and outdoor pools.

Smaller Hotels
Best Western Ocean Resort
843-842-3100 or 1-800-528-1234.
www.bestwestern.com.
36 S. Forest Beach Dr.
Price: Expensive.
Credit Cards: All major cards.
Handicapped Access: Yes.

A 140-room hotel featuring rooms with kitchenettes, mini-refrigerators, and cable television. Complimentary Continental breakfast, two pools, and beach access directly across the street.

Holiday Inn Oceanfront
843-785-5126 or 1-800-423-9897.
www.hihiltonhead.com.
1 S. Forest Beach Dr.
Price: Expensive.

Credit Cards: All major cards.
Handicapped Facilities: Yes.

A popular public-access beach is at your doorstep, featuring a playground and guaranteeing people-watching from the beachside snack bar. Kids, who stay free, will enjoy nearby Coligny Plaza with its shops, informal restaurants, and movie theatre.

Marriott Residence Inn

877-247-3431.
www.residenceinnhhi.com.
12 Park Lane, in Central Park.
Price: Expensive to Very Expensive.
Credit Cards: All major cards.
Handicapped Facilities: Yes.

Suites, with rooms larger than average, feature a fully equipped kitchen; some have wood-burning fireplaces. A recreation area includes basketball, volleyball and tennis courts, pool, Jacuzzi hot tub, jogging trails, and a playground. Free shuttle to the beach.

South Beach Marina Inn

843-671-6498 or 1-800-367-3909.
www.southbeachvillage.com.
In Sea Pines Plantation.
Price: Expensive to Very Expensive.
Credit Cards: AE, D, MC, V.

Located in a New England-style marina village in Sea Pines Plantation, this 17-room inn sits above waterfront shops and restaurants. The rooms are condominium suites with living and dining rooms and kitchenettes, overlooking the courtyard or marina. The inn has a Cape Cod feeling: throw rugs, brass beds, and hardwood floors. Tennis, water sports, restaurants, and the beach close by.

Budget Choices

Each of these national chain motels of approximately 100 rooms has a swimming pool and is close to inexpensive restaurants or shopping areas.

Comfort Inn (843-842-6662 or 1-800-522-3224; www.comfortinnhiltonhead .com; 2 Tanglewood Dr.).

Hampton Inn (843-681-7900; www.hilton headhamptoninn.com; One Dillon Rd.).

Holiday Inn Express (843-842-8888 or 1-888-843-4136; www.hiltonheadexpress .com; 40 Waterside Dr.).

Quality Inn (843-681-3655; US 278 at Main Street Village).

Red Roof Inn (843-686-6808 or 1-800-843-7663; 5 Regency Parkway).

Vacation Property Rentals

Most vacation rental properties are concentrated on the south end of the island in Sea Pines Plantation, Shipyard Plantation, South Forest Beach, and Palmetto Dunes Resort. Several villa rental complexes are located mid-island on or near Folly Field Beach. The northern half of the island is geared mainly to permanent residents; the island's other private communities do not generally permit short-term rental programs.

Villas and homes usually rent by the week, but nightly rates are available. The least expensive summer rates are about $900 per week, which can buy you a small villa outside a plantation more than one-half mile from the beach. In 2004, about $5,500 per week in the summer would secure an oceanfront home with pool. From November to February, rates drop substantially.

Most rental companies manage properties in a variety of sizes, shapes, and locations. A desirable vacation rental would offer free swimming, free or discounted tennis, discounts on golf, and should be within walking distance of the beach. Some offer dining and shopping discounts, too. Before you make your final decision, you might consider where you want to be and what it is you wish to do. You need not pay

Hilton Head's broad beach is a 12-mile recreation area

premium oceanfront prices if you're going to be on the links all day.

Before you sign a rental agreement, make sure you understand policies regarding deposits, refunds in the event of cancellation, times of arrival and departure, and charges, if any, for cleaning services. If you have special needs such as handicap-accessible rooms, or will be renting cots, cribs, bicycles, or beach chairs, alert the agent from the start. The agencies listed below are just some of many.

Adventure Inn Resort and Rentals (1-800-845-9500; www.advinn.com) Oceanfront accommodations in efficiencies or one-, two-, and three-bedroom villas.

Beach Properties of Hilton Head (1-800-671-5155; www.beach-property.com) A variety of deluxe and non-oceanfront properties and villas, many available by the night with a four-night minimum.

Harbour Town Resorts (843-671-1400 or 1-800-541-7375; harbourtownresorts.com) Villa and condo rental in the marina village at Sea Pines.

Hilton Head Oceanfront Rentals (843-785-8161 or 1-800-845-6132; www.oceanfrontrentals.com) A selection of more that 200 homes and villas in the major plantations, and on the north end of the island. Golf and tennis packages available.

Palmetto Dunes Resort (843-785-1161 or 1-800-826-1649; www.palmettodunesresort.com) Manages more than 400 villas and homes throughout Palmetto Dunes, including Shelter Cove Marina condominiums.

Resort Rentals of Hilton Head Island (843-686-6008 or 1-800-845-7017; www.hhivacations.com) More than 300 properties in Sea Pines and South Forest Beach.

Resort Quest Vacation Rentals (1-800-448-3408; www.resortquesthiltonhead.com) Representing some of Hilton Head's high-end properties, as well as the best in the moderate range, in five island communities.

Sea Pines Resort (1-800-732-7463; www.seapines.com) One- to six-bedroom accommodations in private homes and villas in the island's most exclusive and well-known resort.

Shoreline Rental Co. (843-842-3006 or 1-800-334-5012; www.shorelinerentals.com) More than 200 villas and homes, mostly ocean-oriented except for those at Sea Pines' Harbour Town.

Recreational Vehicle Parks/Camping

Outdoor Resort Motor Coach Resort (843-785-7699 or 1-800-722-2365; 19 Arrow Rd.) Full hookups, 401 sites, six tennis courts, pool, man-made lake, shuffleboard, horseshoes, basketball, playground, laundry, bathrooms with tubs and saunas.

Outdoor Resort RV Resort and Yacht Club (843-681-3256; 1-800-845-9560; www.outdoor-rv.com) Jenkins Rd., north end of Hilton Head) Full hookups, 200 RV sites, bath houses, two pools, three tennis courts, laundry, exercise room, sauna, and whirlpool.

Stoney Crest Plantation (843-757-3249; 419 May River Rd. Bluffton) Ten miles from Hilton Head, this park has 30 RV sites with full hookups as well as ten campsites.

Reservation Services

The following services can assist you with making reservations in advance of your trip:

Hilton Head Accommodations and Golf Hotline (843-686-6662 or 1-800-444-4772; www.hiltonheadusa.com).

Hilton Head Condo Hotline (843-785-2939 or 1-800-451-3695; www.hhcondohotline.com).

Island Visitor Center (843-341-9184; 1-888-741-7666; www.islandvisitorcenter.com).

DINING AND NIGHTLIFE

The restaurants included in the listing below are just some of the 250 places to eat or relax and listen to music. There are selections in every price category. Where you go may depend on whether you're traveling with children or not (if you're at a resort, ask the concierge about baby-sitting services), your preference in music and late hours, where on the island you're staying, and your budget. Recommendations for spots you can go to after a day at the beach are also included. Fast food and moderately priced chain restaurants are well represented on Hilton Head, too.

The price categories are the same described elsewhere in the guide, and represent per person expenses estimated without tax, tip, or bar beverages. In general, dining out is more expensive on Hilton Head than in similar restaurants elsewhere, although there are savings to be found in eating before the crowd (early-bird specials) or on a particular evening when the restaurant has an advertised special.

Rates

Inexpensive	Up to $15
Moderate	$15 to $30
Expensive	$30 to $50
Very Expensive	Over $50

Credit Cards
    AE—American Express
    DC—Diner's Club
    CB—Carte Blanche
    MC—MasterCard
    D—Discover Card
    V—Visa

Cafe at Wexford
843-785-6300.
Village at Wexford.
Open: Daily.
Price: Expensive to Very Expensive.
Cuisine: Country French.
Serving: L, D.
Credit Cards: All major.

A charming place that feels like Provence: interior brick walls, open kitchen and grill, accents of dried herbs and flowers. Country French specialties include veal and duck. There's a small alcove for al fresco dining. Very popular for lunch.

Charlie's L'étoile Verte
843-785-9277.
8 New Orleans Rd.
Open Tues. through Sat.
Price: Expensive to Very Expensive.
Cuisine: Continental.
Serving: L, D.
Credit Cards: All major.

Charlie Golson, a Savannah native, never went to cooking school and spent vacations in quiet Bluffton, but his years abroad with friends and French chefs fed his talent. His restaurant is often called the best on Hilton Head and his patrons are loyal and sophisticated. He rewrites (by hand) the menu every day, so that dinner may feature the best of what's available daily, including perhaps a dozen fish dishes, soups from stock he makes up, appetizers from the freshest local ingredients. The new location features a bar so informal it seems like a beautiful sun porch, and two dining rooms that could be in the French countryside. His wife, Nancy, who owns Eggs N' Tricities in Bluffton, managed the decoration: Quimper and bistro plates mounted on peach-colored walls, chandeliers, a warm ambiance. You might share the Cobb salad at lunch; you'll probably have to share a homemade dessert. Reservations recommended.

A table for two at Charlie's L'étoile Verte on Hilton Head

Dosido's
843-842-3674.
Island Crossing at Sea Pines Circle.
Open: Daily.
Price: Inexpensive to Moderate.
Cuisine: American.
Serving: L, D.
Credit Cards: AE, D, MC, V.

Fundamentally an upscale sports bar with high ceilings, lots of comfortable booths, a back room with televisions, a pool table, live music, and a dance floor when they can make room. Lunch is mostly burgers and salads. People go for the ribs, the pulled pork, and meal-size appetizers like one pound of wings.

Hilton Head Diner
843-686-2400.
Open: Daily, 24 hours.
Price: Inexpensive.

Cuisine: American.
Serving: B, L, D.
Credit Cards: All major.

An update on the classic American roadside
eatery. Breakfast is served all the time—but
there are big sandwiches, dinner entrées
(with potato, salad, and vegetable) and beer
and wine available, too. Coffee refills, and
desserts from the cold case.

Hudson's Seafood

843-681-2772.
Squire Pope Rd.
Open: Daily.
Price: Moderate.
Cuisine: Seafood.
Serving: L, D.
Credit Cards: AE, DC, MC, V.

Large, informal family restaurant, one of
the first on the island, in a rustic setting
overlooking the Intracoastal Waterway on
the docks at Skull Creek, known for its sunsets. Lunch is served in the Oyster Bar.
Entrées include fresh local seafood like
crab or shrimp (fried, sautéed, boiled) and
blackened or stuffed specials. No reservations—go early on a summer night or risk
waiting two hours to be served.

Julep's

843-842-5857.
14 Greenwood Dr., at the Gallery of Shops.
Open: Daily.
Price: Expensive to Very Expensive.
Cuisine: Upscale Southern.
Serving: D.
Credit Cards: AE, MC, V.

A trend made popular by New South young
professionals, where local foodstuffs (catfish, flounder) are tweaked and glorified,
but not to an unrecognizable (or unpro-
nounceable) state. There's always a light
pasta, sauced veal, beef, or fish. Formal
setting with white tablecloths and fresh
flowers. Reservations recommended.

Just Pasta

843-686-3900.
One Coligny Plaza.
Open: Daily.
Price: Inexpensive to Moderate.
Cuisine: Creative pastas.
Serving: L, D.
Credit Cards: AE, D, MC, V.

Tiny, made cozy by hand-painted murals,
and tucked away at one end of the bustling
Coligny Plaza, this is the place for an excellent meal based on a dozen kinds of pasta,
sauces, and additions. Specials include egg-
plant, shrimp scampi, and sautéed crab
cakes with asparagus, sun-dried tomatoes,
and pesto hollandaise over fettucine. A
short walk from the beach, which makes it a
nice, pre-sunset stop.

Market Street

843-686-4976.
1 N. Forest Beach Dr.
Open: Daily.
Price: Inexpensive.
Cuisine: Mediterranean.
Serving: L, D.
Credit Cards: AE, MC, V.

If on a starry summer night you've decided
to walk the beach near the Coligny Beach
access point and hear Greek music, you
must be nearby. Come back after your walk
to enjoy informal grill food—gyros, pita
wraps—or Greek specialties like *moussaka*,
dolmati, and *spanakopita*.

Michael Anthony's

843-785-6272.
37 New Orleans Rd.
Closed: Sun.
Price: Expensive.
Cuisine: Italian.
Serving: D.

Chef Michael Cirafesi elaborates on northern Italian classics like homemade gnocchi,
osso bucco, and veal tenderloin. Seasonal

additions include game in the fall and specialty mushrooms and truffles when available. Local design firm J. Banks has made an elegant room, divided lengthwise by a curving, granite bar illuminated by pinpoint lights on one side, and a dining area accented by walls the color of terra cotta and pale wood furnishings. The chef is also the pastry chef—many diners come for after-dinner drinks and dessert, often taken at the few booths in the bar. Reservations suggested.

Mi Tierra
843-342-3409.
Fairfield Sq.
Open: Daily.
Price: Inexpensive to Moderate.
Cuisine: Mexican.
Serving: D.
Credit Cards: AE, MC, V.

Located on Hilton Head's north end on US 278, this unpretentious Mexican restaurant attracts locals, workers, and commuters heading for home in Beaufort or Bluffton. The parking lot can be full by 5:00. It's as unassuming as can be: tile floor, wooden booths and tables, linens and walls in festive colors, and mostly Spanish-speaking wait staff. The food is good, the atmosphere welcoming, the portions enormous.

Sage Room
843-785-5352.
13 Heritage Plaza.
Open: Daily; closed Sun. in winter.
Price: Expensive.
Cuisine: American with fusion accents.
Serving: D.
Credit Cards: AE, MC, V.

An open kitchen and chef's "bar" (where you can sit and eat) are the first things you see; dining areas to the right and left, decorated in beadboard, quiet greens, and local paintings. Sage is small and comfortable, smart but not flashy. Professionals from Beaufort and Bluffton like its unpreten-

tiousness and excellent entrées: two cuts only of steak, corn-fed from Nebraska; at least four kinds of fish, some encrusted with nuts; shrimp and pasta; classic salad of greens with vinaigrette. A good choice before or after the movies at Coligny Plaza, just down the road.

Signe's Heaven Bound Bakery & Cafe
843-785-9118.
93 Arrow Rd.
Closed: Sunday.
Price: Inexpensive.
Cuisine: American.
Serving: B, L.
Credit Cards: MC, V.

Founded in 1972 by an enterprising cook, nationally recognized many times since, and a regular stop for returning visitors and for residents who appreciate fresh, healthy, food. Here are sandwiches on whole grain bread (which you can also buy by the loaf), soups, many kinds of coffee cakes and muffins, fabulous pastries, and desserts. The French toast is probably an inch thick; the brownies and blondies even thicker. The cafe and porch are modest—it's the bakery display cases that aren't. Fruit, vegetable, and pasta salads are great for picnics.

Truffles Cafe
843-671-6136.
www.trufflescafe.com.
Sea Pines Center.
Open: Daily.
Price: Inexpensive to Moderate.
Cuisine: American; Continental.
Serving: L, D.
Credit Cards: All major.

Casual atmosphere, homemade soups, huge salads, French-bread sandwiches and wraps, quiche, fresh vegetables, and grilled entrées. Light meals like Cuban pannini or potpie are inexpensive, and you can order them at any time. A couple of dozen wines by the glass. The market is full of gourmet items and take-out is available. It's a cross between a fern bar and a wine bar, with a bistro menu.

Two Eleven Park Wine Bar & Bistro
843-686-5212.
211 Park Plaza.
Closed: Sun.
Price: Expensive.
Cuisine: American/Southern fusion.
Serving: D.
Credit Cards: AE, D, MC, V.

A handsome checkered-floor bistro, with a mural out of Edward Hopper and decor out of Paris in the Twenties. Dozens of wines by the glass and a list two hundred deep for the table. The place may bustle at its capacity, but it feels intimate even when buzzing. A unique feature is the choice of "petite" entrée portions and a big choice of appetizers, in bistro style, but with twists like "tuna tuna tuna," a sushi offering. Rack of lamb, veal chops, and a different pasta every night.

Nightlife

The beat goes on and on at Hilton Head, especially in summer when crowds jam the dance floor or couples find quieter music in lounges or late-night eateries. Check ahead for cover charges or drink minimums. The legal drinking age is 21.

Big Bamboo (843-686-3443; Upstairs at Coligny Plaza) Late-night music and dancing from 10:30 PM every night except Tues. Expect rock, beach music, reggae, all of it loud.

Eugene's Oyster Bar (843-785-9666; Palmetto Bay Marina) The bar and lounge of this marina restaurant fill up quickly, especially when Jim Harper plays acoustic guitar weekend nights. Plates of fresh-shucked oysters (and oysters with specialty toppings) and steamed shrimp are available as early as 5 PM and last well past the sunset over Broad Creek.

Jazz Corner (843-842-8620; www.the jazzcorner.com; Village at Wexford) National and regional jazz artists perform here nightly. Check the schedule to find your favorites: Big Band, Swing, Rhythm and Blues, and Classic jazz. Shows start at 7:30.

Jenny's Ristorante Italiano (843-842-5011; 55 New Orleans Rd.) A restaurant wrapped around a piano bar, with additional seating overlooking a dance floor. Cheryl Christine plays and sings, sometimes with jazzy back up, Thurs. through Sat. from 8:45 until after midnight. Good spot for a nightcap.

Kingfisher (843-842-6400; Shelter Cove Harbour) Live music and dancing begins at 6 PM nightly except Sun. and Wed., including Big Bands, jazz combos, and laid-back keyboardist Jim Eshleman. Bar menu or full meals (steak, pasta, seafood) served.

Quarterdeck (843-671-2222; Harbour Town) Laid-back waterfront lounge, island classic since 1970. Late-afternoon beach music, folk-rock, steel drums outside (4–8 PM); after sunset the music rocks harder and moves inside until 12:30 AM.

TOURING

Here are some suggestions for exploring more of Hilton Head and the surrounding area. The towns of Bluffton and Beaufort are easy day trips. (For detailed information on these destinations, see Chapter Four, *Beaufort, Edisto & Bluffton*.) Each has a historic area of old houses, as well as shops and restaurants. Daufuskie Island is served by tour boat operators who offer cookouts and on-shore touring options. Savannah is about an hour away, and in a day you could tour the historic district, shop, have at least one meal, and be back in time for sunset over the marsh. A trip to Charleston requires a bit more time and planning, including approximately four hours by car round trip. For additional information on canoeing, kayaking, and eco tours, which may include dolphin-watching, see the **Recreation** section below.

Airstream Aviation (843-785-7770; airstream01@aol.com; Hilton Head Airport) Private charters and tours of the island, the Lowcountry, or Savannah, from $60 per person, two person minimum.

Camelot Limousine and Tours (843-842-7777; www.camelothhi.com) On and off-island transportation, personalized tours, maximum of six people per vehicle.

Gullah Heritage Trail Tours (843-681-7066) Two-hour tours through 10 neighborhoods and to sites prominent in the island's African American culture.

Low Country Adventures (843-681-8212; lowcountryadventures.com) Island and off-island tours in a tour van or bus, including day trips with a guide to the historic areas of Charleston, Savannah, and Beaufort (from $35 per person).

Red Trolley (843-689-6767; The Museum of Hilton Head Island; US 278.) Departing Tues., Wed., Thurs., from the museum at 1:30, returning at 4:00, and offering an overview of the island, shopping, and a glimpse of Harbour Town.

Spirit of Harbour Town (843-842-7179; www.vagabondcruise.com; Harbour Town Marina, Sea Pines). Two high-powered vessels take you to Savannah's River Street or Daufuskie Island and pick you up after sightseeing is done. Prices vary, from $25 adults; $17 kids.

CULTURE

As Hilton Head has grown, so has its arts community. Check the Arts & Entertainment section of the daily newspaper, *The Island Packet* (www.www.islandpacket.com), for listings. The largest venue for performances is the **Arts Center of Coastal Carolina** (14 Shelter Cove Lane; 843-842-2787; www.artscenter-hhi.org), which features nationally touring performers, regional orchestras, dance and theatre, children's theatre, and gallery space. It is active all year long, and its high-quality talent attracts residents and visitors. Check its schedule for performances celebrating Gullah heritage in the Sea Islands by local gospel choirs, the **Hallelujah Singers** and **Ron and Natalie Daise,** stars of the television program *Gullah Gullah Island.*

Art

Hilton Head Art League (843-681-5060; Suite 207, Pineland Station) has shows by local artists nearly every month. (See "Galleries" entry under **Shopping** for more art information. Also see **Bluffton** in Chapter Four, *Beaufort, Edisto & Bluffton.*

Walter Greer Gallery (843-842-2787) Part of the Arts Center, the 2,000 sq. ft. space hosts a variety of local and national visual artists in monthly shows.

Cinema

Coligny Theatre (843-686-3500; Coligny Plaza).

Main Street Theatre (843-689-6246; 3000 Main St.).

Northridge Ten Cinemas (843-342-3800; 435 Wm. Hilton Pkwy.).

Park Plaza Cinemas (843-785-5001; Park Plaza).

Historic Sites

Several sites dating as far back as the time of Native American settlements and covering the period of the Civil War are accessible to visitors. For more information and location maps, contact **Coastal Discovery Museum** (see address and hours below). **The Heritage Library Foundation** (843-686-6560; www.heritagelib.org; 32 Office Park Rd., Suite 300, Courtyard Building) offers a unique opportunity to research families, not just sites. A microfiche database and an 80-volume African American research collection places special emphasis on African-American genealogy. Open Mon. and Thurs. through Sat. 9–2, but call to confirm.

Baynard Ruins (Sea Pines; 843- 363-4530; www.seapines.com) The remains of a plantation house and outbuildings first constructed circa 1800 can be seen on a short, self-guided walk or on tours offered Mondays at 10:00. The ruins are made of tabby, a popular homemade Lowcountry building material that resulted from burning oyster shells (to make lime), which were then mixed with whole shells, sand, and water. This is one of few sites where you can still see it.

Coastal Discovery Museum on Hilton Head Island (843-689-6767; www.coastaldiscovery .org; 100 William Hilton Parkway, Hilton Head Island, SC 29925) Located at the north end of the island, near the bridge, Coastal Discovery is an addition to a place where so much is new. Archaeological digs have yielded a collection of artifacts relating to the island's history and culture that are on display, sharing exhibition space with models, dioramas, and explanatory panels on Sea Island biodiversity. Efforts to record island life through oral history interviews are ongoing; solid scholarship produced a fine four-part videotape (which is shown at the museum) documenting early habitation, the years of slavery, Reconstruction and the decades of small farming, and the fishing, oystering, and timbering industries. The gift shop offers an excellent selection of books on the Lowcountry as well as maps, field guides, and activity kits for kids. Call for reservations for walking tours of the marsh, the beach, and other natural areas including historic sites; marine study cruises; bird-watching; and science and nature study for children (fees vary; reservations suggested). Museum hours are Mon. through Sat. 9–5; Sun. 10–3. Donation $2.

Fish Haul Plantation (off Beach City Rd.) Only the chimneys of slave dwellings remain of what was once a thriving Sea Island cotton plantation. Federal troops camped here from the time of Union occupation in November 1861.

Fort Howell (Beach City Rd.) A large earthwork built by the Union troops in 1864 to strengthen the defense of Mitchelville.

Fort Mitchel (Hilton Head Plantation) An earthwork fortification circa 1862, constructed as part of the island's defense system. Coastal Discovery tours given Tuesdays at 2 PM last 90 minutes. Meet by the Old Fort Pub restaurant. Adults $10; children $5.

Indian Shell Ring (Sea Pines Forest Preserve; www.seapines.com) Native Americans occupied Hilton Head and other Sea Islands some 4,000 years ago, and left their mark in huge rings and shell middens. It is thought that this site represents the refuse of oyster shells piled behind each of many huts that stood in a small circle.

Zion Chapel of Ease (William Hilton Pkwy. at Mathews Dr.) A small chapel, built circa 1786 for the convenience of worshippers who lived too far from the Episcopal Church at Beaufort, once occupied this site. The Baynard Mausoleum, circa 1846, within its cemetery is the largest ante-bellum structure extant on the island.

Music

Hilton Head Choral Society (843-341-3339; www.hiltonheadchoralsociety.org.) Often joined by professional soloists and members of the Hilton Head Orchestra, the choral group performs three concerts each year, usually at Christmas and in the spring.

Hilton Head Jazz Society (843-842-4457; www.hhjs.org) The group sponsors formal and informal performances at various island sites on the first Sunday of each month.

Hilton Head Orchestra (843-842-2055; hhorchestra.org) Performances of symphonic and popular music throughout the year, held in the First Presbyterian Church, 540 William Hilton Pkwy.

Theatre

South Carolina Repertory Company (843-681-5194; www.hiltonheadtheatre.com; 136 Beach City Rd., near the airport) The company features a diverse troupe and often collabo- rates with other regional companies to produce professional-quality plays, mostly for the spring season.

RECREATION

Hilton Head's reputation as a place to pursue golf, tennis, fishing, water sports and tour- ing, and to enjoy the beach is well deserved. The following listings offer some sense of the range of activities the island has to offer. As the town has grown, it has gone a long way to develop public beach access and 30 miles of pathways for bikers, in-line skaters, and run- ners.

Beach Access

Twelve miles of gently sloping beaches define the island's ocean edge. They can be as wide as 600 feet at low tide, providing a hard surface for fat-tired bicycles. (For tidal informa- tion, tune into island cable television or check *The Island Packet*.) Although many entry points to the beach are restricted—behind private resort plantation gates—there are several public beach access points. The most popular are **Coligny Beach Park** (located at the end of Pope Ave.), **Folly Field Beach Park** (off Folly Field Rd.), **Dreissen Beach Park** (off Bradley Beach Rd.), and **Alder Lane** (off S. Forest Beach Dr.) All offer metered parking spaces ($.50 to $1 per hour) and Coligny and Dreissen have long-term lots. Within the plantation resorts, the beaches are accessible by marked footpaths.

On some nights (May through October), it is possible to watch the amazing loggerhead turtle, an endangered species, crawl ashore and lay its eggs in nests it digs on the beach; or to see hundreds of loggerhead hatchlings make their way back to the ocean. Volunteer groups monitor the beach and sometimes move the eggs to higher ground or protected

Late afternoon brings a pick-up game of beach volleyball

sites, away from tides and hungry raccoons. The turtles are slow moving and docile, but chary: do not disturb them with light, or touch the nests. Just seeing these huge creatures is magical.

Dogs are not permitted on the beach from 10 AM to 5 PM from the beginning of Memorial Day weekend through Labor Day weekend. Motor vehicles, alcohol, glass containers, and nudity are not allowed. Fishing, boating, surfing, ball-playing, and similar activities are prohibited in designated swimming areas. The beaches are patrolled by sheriff's deputies; lifeguard stations are posted.

Beach Activities

If you haven't brought your beach equipment with you, you can stock up at the **Coligny Flag and Kite Company** (843-785-5483; Coligny Plaza) or rent larger items such as boogie boards, chairs, umbrellas, and floats on the beach.

Coastal Discovery (see entry in the **Culture** section, above) offers guided walks several days per week on the island's beaches, and, on some evenings, a turtle tour to see the loggerheads nesting or hatching. Each tour lasts about 90 minutes and explains the island's ecology, flora, and fauna. Children will like learning about shells and hunting hermit crabs. Call in advance to purchase tickets. Adults $10; children $5.

Bicycling

Bikes are easy to come by and you can expect island-wide pick-up and delivery. If you're traveling with youngsters, you'll be able to get baby-carriers, helmets, bikes with training wheels, baby "trailers" that hook on the back of bikes, and jogging strollers. Ask about in-line skate rentals, too. Local enthusiasts have created maps and cue sheets for rides from 22–60 miles that thread through rural areas. An online link is at www.hiltonhead island.org.

Rental bikes ready to go

Public bike paths extend from the tip of North Forest Beach to the end of South Forest Beach, along Pope Ave., and up William Hilton Pkwy. to Squire Pope Rd., and take detours to the beach and marsh. Bike paths also thread through the plantations. At low tide, ride on the beach. Rental charges for bicycles start at about $15 per day and $30–$40 per week. Check the following outlets:

All American Bikes (843-842-4386).

Bubba's Bike Rentals (843-785-3971).

Hilton Head Bicycle Company (843-686-6888).

Pedals (843-842-5522).

Sea Pines Bike Rentals (843-363-4527).

Bird-Watching

Hilton Head still has some very quiet places for birds to nest and feed. According to the island's Audubon Society chapter, some 200 species of birds regularly visit, and in the last 10 years, more than 350 species have been sighted. Among the most distinctive "frequent flyers" are the snowy egret, great blue heron, white ibis, and osprey. Catch a glimpse of them for yourself during daylight hours at the following sites:

Audubon Newhall Preserve (Palmetto Bay Rd., 3/4 mile from Sea Pines Circle) A 50-acre sanctuary open daily from dawn to dusk that preserves the Lowcountry environment for plants and animals. Trees and plants are labeled for self-guided walks on woodland trails and lists of bird sightings are posted on a bulletin board at the entrance. Interpretative walks are offered in the spring and fall. To arrange a group tour call 843-842-9246.

Coastal Discovery (843-689-6767) offers guided walks in the Sea Pines Forest Preserve and has a birding exhibit on display at its headquarters in the Museum on Hilton Head Island (100 William Hilton Pkwy.). For nearby, off-island sites, see "Nature Preserves" in Chapter Three, *Savannah* and in Chapter Four, ***Beaufort, Edisto & Bluffton***.

Sea Pines Forest Preserve (843-363-4350; www.seapines.com; enter at Greenwood Dr. and Lawton Dr. in Sea Pines Plantation; admission fee to enter Sea Pines Plantation) This 400-acre site with a shell ring and old rice field offers a self-guided walking tour, which takes 1–2 hours; guided tours Tues., Thurs., and Sat. at 10 AM.

Whooping Crane Conservancy (Hilton Head Plantation) features a boardwalk and self-guided nature trail.

Boating and Water Sports

For sailboat charters and bare-boat rentals, contact the companies listed below and also check the "Marina" section. If you want to nurture a wilder streak, look into waterskiing or kneeboarding, floating with a parasail, riding a wave-runner, or "sledding" on a rubber tube. Some companies have special lessons/day programs for kids, so ask. Parasailing costs between $45 and $85 per person; waterskiing (5 people maximum) is about $200 for 2 hours; hourly waverunner rental costs $70–$80. Make reservations in advance.

Action Watersports (843-785-7368; Palmetto Bay Marina) Waverunners, motor boats (17 feet to 19 feet), and pontoon boats for rent.

Commander Zodiac (843-671-3344; South Beach Marina) Visit the dolphins or Daufuskie Island in engine-powered rubber rafts. Small sailboats for rent, private lessons, and rides.

H2O Sports Center (843-671-4386; www.h2osportsonline.com; Harbour Town Marina, Sea Pines) Rentals for, and instruction in, parasailing, waverunning, kneeboarding, hydrosliding, waterskiing.

Intercoastal Watersports (843-681-4111; 43-A Jenkins Rd.) Rent kayaks, skiffs for crabbing and fishing, larger fishing boats or jet skis.

Island Parasail (843-686-2359; Shelter Cove Marina) Soar up to 1,500 feet. It looks safer than bungee jumping.

Island Watersports (843-671-7007; South Beach Marina; 843-689-6800) Power and sail boats for as many as 14 passengers, by the hour, half-day, or day. Guided private cruises, sailing lessons, sunset sails, parasailing. Wave-runners and skis for rent.

Coastal marinas are home to recreational and live-aboard boaters.

Jarvis Creek Water Sports (843-681-9260; 104A Wm. Hilton Pkwy.) The hydro-bikes look like sleek bicycle assemblies mounted on even sleeker rowing shells, pedal-powered by one or two people.

Canoeing and Kayaking

It's ironic that Hilton Head, with all of its constructed, managed, and expensive recreational sites has, in its own backyard, superior low-tech, low-impact recreational options that are just now being fully appreciated. They are found in the creek.

Today you can explore miles of Lowcountry waterways in a canoe or kayak, on your own or with a guided tour, by the half-day, the day, at sunset, by moonlight, on an overnight expedition. No experience is necessary; all safety equipment and basic instruction is provided; kids are welcome. You may end up paddling out to a sandbar, fishing, taking a birding tour, or threading through the web of coastal marshlands, pristine rivers, and nature preserves. Some outfitters offer extended programs for teens. For paddlers who feel comfortable going out on their own, day rate rental charges start at $45 for a single, $55 for a double, and kayaks may be rented for as long as six days. Two-hour guided tours of local waters like Broad Creek, where you are likely to see lots of birds and fish in action, start at $35 per person; $17.50 for kids 12 and under; from $40 for 3-hour tours. Longer tours run about $125 per person, depending on the arrangements. Customized trips and overnight camping/biking expeditions are available, just ask. Reservations suggested for tours.

Here are some outfitters who can help to get you in the water.

Awesome Expeditions Kayak (843-842-9763; www.hhtimeonthewater.com) Naturalist guided tours in singles and doubles depart from Shelter Cove Marina.

Cool Breeze Kayaking (843-683-4040 or 1-877-286-5154; www.coolbreezekayaking.com) Two-hour dolphin-sighting tours that embark from the Pinckney Island Wildlife Refuge or from Broad Creek.

Native Guide Tours (843-757-5411; www.nativeguidetours.com) For serious paddlers, no children under age 13. Tours include the ACE Basin, May River, Colleton River, and sites off Hilton Head.

Outside Hilton Head (843-686-6996 or 1-800-686-6996; www.outsidehiltonhead.com) This long-time island business and outfitter offers clinics, teen camps, weekend retreats, and lessons as well as tours. Trips vary in length and season but always include two-hour and daylong excursions. Ask about special Daufuskie Island tours.

Water-Dog Outfitters (843-686-3554; www.waterdogoutfitter.com) Paddling in Broad Creek is easy enough for families and Pinckney Island challenging enough for intermediates. Bike/kayak excursions are also offered.

Cruises

Adventure Cruises (843-785-4558; Shelter Cove Harbour) Dolphin watch nature cruises last nearly two hours, evening shark trips, and sunset cruises. Adults $19; children $9.

Dolphin Adventure & Nature Cruise (843-681-2522; www.dolphin-watch.net; Broad Creek Marina) Narrated environmental tours (90 minutes) aboard the 20-passenger *SS Pelican*, a restored Navy Motor Whaler with canopy. Adults $15; children $9.

Dolphin Seafari (843-298-0661; hiltonheadisland.com/dolphinseafari; Palmetto Bay Marina) Cruises throughout the day, every day, that last 90 minutes aboard a 24-passenger covered pontoon boat. Safe for even young kids who will enjoy casting for crabs and pulling crab pots. Adults $20; children $15.

Flying Circus **and** *Pau Hana* (843-686-2582; www.hiltonheadisland.com/sailing; Palmetto Bay Marina) *Flying Circus* is a fast-moving catamaran offering 2-hour daylight and sunset cruises for a maximum of six passengers. Tickets are $25. *Pau Hana*, a larger catamaran, can carry 49 passengers. Adults $18–$20; children $13–$15.

Let's Go Shrimping (843-384-7833; Hudson's Seafood dock) A great experience for children to board a trawler and see first hand the power and pull of 40-foot nets and experience a day in the life of a shrimper. During shrimping season, June through November. $30 per person, one child free with two adults.

Lowcountry Nature Tours (843-683-0187; lowcountrynaturetours.com) Another good option for children to see the dolphins and birds up close for two hours. Maximum six passengers. Call for reservations.

Spirit of Harbour Town (843-842-7179; www.vagabondcruise.com; Harbour Town) Narrated cruises, an enclosed dining room, air conditioning—a deluxe way to spend a sunset dinner buffet, a commute to Savannah or evening fireworks. Reservations required. Adults: $45–$49; children $15–$20.

Stars & Stripes (843-842-7933; Harbour Town) A chance to sail on the original 12-meter America's Cup yacht, 65 feet long and powered by the wind in 2,000 square feet of sail. Call for reservations and sailing times; prices vary according to trip.

Family Fun

If you're coming with children, there are simple pleasures at hand: beachcombing, bike-riding, flying a kite, sunset concerts, weekly fireworks displays. Playgrounds are located at **Harbour Town** (in Sea Pines; $5 admission), **Shelter Cove Harbour,** and the **Island Recreation Center** (20 Wilborn Rd. at the north end of the island). **Bristol Sports Arena Skate Park** is located off Arrow Rd., on the island's south end. The **Rec Center** features a handicapped-accessible area with a swing for wheelchairs. Check *The Island Packet* to confirm schedules or find special family-oriented events. Some of the following listings may be of help on a rainy day, or for older kids who might prefer arcades.

Adventure Cove Family Fun Center (843-842-9990; www.adventurecove.com. Folly Field Rd. and US 278) Mini-golf, batting cage, arcade, laser tag, driving range, bumper cars, and more.

Island Recreation Center (843-681-7273; 20 Wilborn Rd.) A year-round activity center with camps, clinics, and sports programs organized by the day, week, and month for children, teens, and adults. Check to see if events like bike races, fishing tournaments, rollerblading races, water carnivals, or craft classes (among others) might coincide with your visit. Call ahead: registration may be required.

Summer Concerts: In the evening, family entertainers gather large audiences for free concerts and shows. Check the local paper for listings, and plan to arrive early to secure parking. In Sea Pines Plantation (under the Liberty Oak at Harbour Town; Sea Pines gate pass $5) singers and guitarists perform nightly from 8:00–10:00 except Saturday. The audience sits on benches and kids are encouraged to participate. Family sing-alongs also take place Monday through Friday at Shelter Cove Harbour and Tuesday nights there are fireworks. Various musicians, puppeteers, and clowns also turn up at Coligny Plaza (off Pope Ave.) each night to entertain families. At South Beach Marina (Sea Pines Plantation) you can enjoy music while the sun sets over the docks.

Waterfun Park (843-842-8108; 6 Tanglewood Dr.) Putt-putt golf course, three water-slides, arcade games, and a toddler's pool.

Fishing

Fishing is easy to do, but have in mind the kind of experience you're looking for. There are many options: size of the boat, length of the day, level of challenge, location, number of anglers, type of catch, and, of course, the probability of success. (All but the last can be provided.) Fly fishing is also available. Boats are fully equipped with tackle, etc., and depart from several marinas for inshore waters, flats, artificial reefs, and the Gulf Stream. Potential catches include tarpon, marlin, and sailfish in the Gulf Stream; amberjack, shark, king mackerel, and bluefish closer to shore; and flounder, red drum, sea trout, and sheepshead in the coastal flats. Prices for four to six passengers for a half-day of fishing cost from about $290 to $525. A Gulf Stream expedition (about 14 hours) starts at about $1,600 for six passengers. Here are some suggestions.

Atlantic Fishing Charters (843-671-4534; www.harbourtown.com; Harbour Town Yacht Basin) Four boats (23 feet to 40 feet long) rigged with fish-finding equipment; fish at night for shark.

Blue Water Charters (843-671-3060; 232 S. Sea Pines Dr., South Beach Marina) Trophy fishing and taxidermy services.

Bonanza Sportfishing (843-689-5873; Skull Creek) Captains Bill Schilling and John DeLoach, longtime professional guides, take you inshore or offshore to their favorite spots.

Capt. Hook (843-785-1700; Shelter Cove Harbour) A good family choice for fishing: 70-foot boat with enclosed cabin and restrooms, food on board. The Tuesday night shark-fishing trip includes a fireworks show; at $40 for adults, a relative bargain.

Lowcountry Outfitters (843-837-6100; 1533 Fording Island Rd. at Moss Creek Village, just off-island) Serious hunters and fisherman often gather and trade stories here. Guided fly-fishing and light tackle expeditions for one or two passengers on an open 18-foot boat are available. Equipment provided (or you can bring your own). Late-October through late-April you're looking for redfish and speckled trout; other times, ladyfish, spanish mackerel, jack crevalle, and bluefish. Prices for a half-day start at about $275.

Palmetto Bay Marina's Fishing Fleet (843-785-7131; Palmetto Bay Marina) Five boats and five captains can take you offshore fishing, to the Gulf Stream, or inshore to the flats. Boats' capacity from four to six passengers.

Fitness Centers/Spas

All About Me (843-785-2558; allaboutmehhi.com; 32 Palmetto Bay Rd.) A day spa offering full facial, body, hair, nail, and massage services. Good idea to book in advance.

Body Pilates (843-842-5562; 55 New Orleans Rd.).

Breakthrough Fitness Center (843-341-2166; 130 Arrow Rd.).

The European Spa (843-842-9355; www.european-spa.com; Sea Pines Circle) Two locations serving men and women, featuring aromatherapy massage, and packages that run from $155–$525, for two- to seven-hour treatments.

Gold's Gym (843-837-4653; Moss Creek Village).

Hilton Head Health Institute (843-785-3919 or 1-800-292-2440; www.hhhealth.com; 14 Valencia Rd.) A full-service spa where you can also go for extended visits to embark on a personalized program of fitness, diet, and healthier lifestyle.

The Sanctuary (843-842-5999; www.thesanctuaryeurospa.com; 216 Park Plaza) A full-service spa for men and women where you can spend an hour or a day.

Golf

Since the first course was built in Sea Pines Plantation in 1961, golf culture has touched every corner of life on Hilton Head; indeed it has shaped life here. Today there are some 30 courses in the Hilton Head area (on and just off the island) and more than half of them are available for public play. The remainder are for resort guests or members, located within private communities like Sea Pines and Shipyard Plantations, Palmetto Dunes Resort, and Port Royal Plantation. Golf is expensive and Hilton Head is no different—anywhere from $80 and up a round at a resort course (less with a package), and from $35–$50 at the public courses. Prices include greens and cart fees unless mentioned otherwise. (Walking is permitted on several courses—check ahead for caddie help.) Reduced rates are available for resort guests. During the low season—winter months—prices can drop by 40 percent. Rates are lower for afternoon or twilight play. For courses in and around Beaufort—within an hour's drive from Hilton Head—check Chapter Four, *Beaufort, Edisto & Bluffton.* For information and central reservations, call 1-888-465-3475; www.golfisland.com.; 866-400-7931; golfersguide.com.

Reservations to secure tee times are essential—some courses accept reservations from non-resort guests up to 90 days in advance, others just 30 to 60 days in advance. (It gets crowded—800,000 rounds of golf are played annually at Hilton Head.) Check websites for advance reservation rules. Unless noted, all courses are 18 holes. Appropriate dress calls for shirts with collars for men and no blue jeans, gym shorts, or jogging shorts. At Sea Pines, non-metal spikes are required.

If you're looking to improve you game, inquire about clinics, private instruction, and programs from one-half day to three days from **Hilton Head School of Golf** (843-681-1785 or 1-800-348-5078; Port Royal and Shipyard courses); **Keith Marks, Sr. Director of Instruction** (843-683-9505); and **Palmetto Dunes/Palmetto Hall Golf Schools** (843-785-1138; palmettodunes.com).

Hilton Head Plantation

Country Club of Hilton Head (843-681-4653; www.hiltonheadclub.com) Par 72. Range: 5,373-yard ladies course to 6,919-yard champion course. Design: Rees Jones.

Oyster Reef Golf Club (843-681-1745; www.hiltonheadgolf.net) Par: 72. Range: 5,288 forward course to 7,023 champion course. Design: Rees Jones.

Indigo Run
Golden Bear Golf Club (843-689-2200; www.goldenbear-indigorun.com) Par 72. Range: 4,974-yard course to 7,014-yard championship course. Design: Nicklaus. Fodor's *Golf Digest* four stars.

Palmetto Dunes Resort
Arthur Hills Course (843-785-1138; www.palmettodunes.com) Par 72. Range: 4,999-yard forward course to 6,651-yard champion course. Design: Arthur Hills. Fodor's *Golf Digest* four-star plus rating.

George Fazio Course (843-785-1138; www.palmettodunes.com) Named one of Fodor's *Golf Digest's* 100 top American courses. Par 70. Range: 5,273-yard ladies course to 6,873-yard champion course. Design: George Fazio.

Robert Trent Jones (843-785-1136) Named South Carolina's Golf Course of the year in 2003, fully renovated in 2002. Permanent junior tees allow young golfers to play a classic course. Par 72. Range: 2,625 junior to 7,005-yard champion course. Design: Robert Trent Jones/Roger Rulewich.

Palmetto Hall Plantation
Arthur Hills Course (843-689-4100; www.palmettodunes.com) Par 72. Range: 4,956-yard forward course to 6,918 champion course. Design: Arthur Hills. Fodor's four-star rating.

Robert Cupp Course (843-689-4100; www.palmettodunes.com) Par 72. Range: 5,220-yard forward course to 7,079-yard tour course. Design: Robert Cupp.

Port Royal Plantation
Barony Course (1-800-234-6318; www.hiltonheadgolf.net) Par 72. Range: 5,183-yard forward course to 6,543-yard champion course. Design: George Cobb.

Planter's Row Course (1-800-234-6318; www.hiltonheadgolf.net) Par 72. Range: 5,119-yard forward course to 6,625-yard champion course. Design: Willard Byrd.

Robber's Row Course (1-800-234-6318; www.hiltonheadgolf.net) A Pete Dye renovation of a George Cobb course near what was Fort Walker, a Civil War camp. Par 72. Range: 4,902-yard forward course to 6,675-yard champion course. Design: Cobb/Dye.

Sea Pines Plantation
Harbour Town Golf Links (1-800-955-8337; www.seapines.com) The MCI Heritage is played on this course every April, rated among the top 75 in the world, among the top 50 in the U.S. Par 71. Range: 5,208-yard green course to 6,973-yard "Heritage" course. Design: Nicklaus and Dye.

Ocean Course (1-800-955-8337; www.seapines.com) First course on the island, redesigned in 1995 by Mark McCumber to remain challenging but still conveying an original beauty that earned it a designation as an "Audubon Cooperative Sanctuary." Par 72. Range: 5,325-yard green course to 6,906-yard "McCumber" course.

Sea Marsh Course (1-800-955-8337; www.seapines.com) Par 72. Range: 5,054-yard ladies course to 6,515-yard champion course. Design: George Cobb; redesign Clyde Johnston.

Shipyard Plantation

Shipyard Golf Club (1-800-234-6318; www.hiltonheadgolf.net) Par 72, 27 holes. A favorite of the senior PGA Tour. Range: 5,240-yard forward course to 6,830 champion course. Design: George Cobb/Willard Byrd.

Off-Island

Crescent Pointe Golf Club (843-706-2600 or 1-888-292-7778; www.crescentpointegolf.com; US 278, Bluffton) Designed for Arnie's "army." Par 71. Four tees from 5,219 yards to 6,772 yards. Design: Arnold Palmer.

Daufuskie Island Resort (1-800-648-6778; Daufuskie Island) Two par 72 courses available to non-resort guests, accessible by private ferry. Reservations necessary, up to 60 days in advance. Bloody Point, with tees from 5,220 yards to 6,900 yards, designed by Tom Weiskopf/Jay Morrish; Melrose, with tees from 5,575 yards to 7,081 yards was designed by Jack Nicklaus.

Eagle's Pointe Golf Club (843-757-5900 or 1-888-325-1833; www.eaglespointegolf.com; US 278 seven miles west of Hilton Head) Designed by a five-time Heritage Classic winner. Par 71. Range: 5,210 yards to 6,782 yards. Advance reservations up to four months. Design: Davis Love III.

Executive Golf Club (843-837-6400; US 278, Bluffton, at entrance to Hilton Head National) Nine holes, par 30, lit for night play. Range: 2,360 yards to 3,330 yards. Casual dress code, beginners welcome, inexpensive.

Hidden Cypress Golf Club (843-705-4653; www.suncityhiltonheadgolf.com; Sun City/Hilton Head, Hwy. 170) Par: 72. Five tees, from 4,984 yards to 6,946 yards. Design: Mark McCumber.

Hilton Head National (843-842-5900 or 1-888-955-1234; www.scratch-golf.com; US 278, Bluffton) Par 72, 27 holes. Range: 4,649-yard course to 6,779-yard champion course. Advance reservations up to one year. Design: Gary Player/ Bobby Weed.

Island West Golf Club (843-689-6660; www.islandgolfwest.net; US 278, Bluffton) Par 72. Range: 4,948-yard ladies course to 6,803-yard champion course. Design: Fuzzy Zoeller/Clyde Johnston.

Old Carolina Golf Club (843-785-6363 or 1-888-785-7274; www.oldcarolinagolf.com; US 278, Bluffton) Par 71/72. Range: 4,725-yard ladies course to 6,805-yard champion course. Design: Clyde Johnston.

Old South Golf Links (843-785-5353 or 1-800-257-8997; www.oldsouthgolf.com; US 278, Bluffton) Par 71/72. Range: 4,776-yard ladies course to 6,772-yard champion course. Design: Clyde Johnston.

Rose Hill Golf Club (843-842-3740; www.rosehillgolf.com; Rose Hill Plantation, US 278, Bluffton) Par 36. Renovations have reconfigured the course to three 9-hole options. Range: 2,512 to 3,583-yard tees. A good value.

Okatie Creek Golf Club (843-705-4653 or 1-866-705-4653; www.suncityhiltonheadgolf .com; Sun City Hilton Head, Hwy. 170). Par 72. The first of the courses at this resort designed for the over-55 crowd. Five sets of tees per hole accommodate the skilled and less-skilled golfer. Range: 4,763-yard to 6,734-yard tees. Design: Mark McCumber.

Horseback Riding

Call ahead for reservations. Small groups and families are welcome; all equipment is provided.

Happy Trails Stables (843-842-7433; Bluffton, behind Old South Golf Links) Rides in and around the golf course and forest preserve start at $25 for adults; $20 for ages 12 and under. Reservations suggested.

Lawton Stables (843-671-2586; 190 Greenwood Dr., Sea Pines) Seventy-minute walking trail rides for adults and kids. Some riding experience required on trips through the 600-acre Sea Pines Forest Preserve. Prices start at $30 per person; pony rides for the younger set. Lessons (all levels) start at $35 per half-hour and include preparation of the horse.

Sandy Creek Stables (843-342-2771; 102 Jonesville Rd.) Boarding, lessons, and trail rides along the edge of the marsh and in the woods.

Sea Horse Farms (843-681-7746; 34 Mitchelville Rd.) Unique, one-hour beach rides leave four times per day except Sunday. Riders must be seven years old or older. $35 per person.

Marinas

The Hilton Head area has eight public marinas that offer boat rentals, transient berths, fishing charters, and services, such as dry-dock storage, launching ramps, fuel, showering facilities, ship's stores, and repair shops. Rates for berthing vary, from $1.00 per foot, or by week/month. Charter fishing boats, small powerboats, sailboats, and yachts as long as 150 feet are berthed side by side, offering a striking example of the many ways residents and visitors choose to enjoy the water.

Broad Creek Marina (843-681-3625; 18 Simmons Rd.) Slips accommodating boats up to 100 feet. Ship's store with boat cleaning supplies and equipment. Charters and sightseeing, sailing instruction, and kayaking available. Low tide draft: 15 feet.

Freeport Marina (843-785-8242; Daufuskie Island) The gateway to Daufuskie for large tour boats and the island touring headquarters. Golf-cart rental for transportation; restaurant, cookouts, gift shop, and marina store. Low tide draft: 15 feet.

Harbour Town Yacht Basin (843-671-2704; Sea Pines Plantation) 85 slips accommodating boats up to 150 feet. Marina store, various types of boats for rent; tours, instruction, and cruises available. Low tide draft: 8 feet.

Outdoor RV Resort (843-681-3256; Jenkins Island at northern tip of Hilton Head) 101 slips, maximum boat length 70 feet. Amenities of Outdoor Resorts RV Park (see **Lodging**) as well as charters, waterski rentals and instruction, ship's store. Low tide approach depth: 8 feet; 20 feet at dockside.

Palmetto Bay Marina (843-785-3910; 164 Palmetto Bay Rd.) 140 slips, maximum length 85 feet. Marina store, boat repair, fishing and sailing charters, parasailing, and youth sailing program. Low tide draft: 20 feet.

Shelter Cove Harbour (843-842-7001; Palmetto Dunes Resort) 170 slips, maximum length 155 feet. Fish and tackle store, charters, cruises, rentals; rod and reel rental. In village-like area of shops and restaurants. Low tide draft: 9 feet.

Skull Creek Marina (843-681-8436; Hilton Head Plantation) 180 slips, maximum length 200 feet. Sailing charters and night fishing, restaurant and lounge, courtesy bike and van transportation. Low tide draft: 10 feet.

South Beach Marina (843-671-6699; Sea Pines Plantation) 100 wet slips, 20 dry slips, maximum length 35 feet. Tackle and bait shop, boat and motor repair, rentals, cruises, instruction, and junior sailing school. Restaurants and shops at the marina village. Approach depth at low tide: 3 feet.

Miniature Golf
A half-dozen courses (par 40 to par 65), featuring water-hazards, dog legs, and sand traps laid out in realistic settings. A great way to spend two hours. Most lit for night play. From $5.95 per adult.

Adventure Cove (843-842-9990; William Hilton Parkway at Folly Field Rd.).

Legendary Golf (Two locations: 843-686-3399; 900 William Hilton Pkwy. and 843-785-9214; 80 Pope Ave.).

Pirate's Island Adventure Golf (843-686-4001; William Hilton Parkway and Marina Side Dr.).

Waterfun Park and Mini Golf (843-842-8108; 6 Tanglewood Dr.).

Tennis
There are more than 300 tennis courts, hard, clay, and grass surfaces, on Hilton Head, spread through 19 clubs. Seven of them are open for public play: they are listed below. Call ahead for reservations—the staff may even be able to set you up with a game. Pros on site offer lessons, daily stroke clinics, and intensive camps year round; fully stocked shops provide stringing services and sales of equipment, clothing, and accessories. Court rental fees range from $15 to $22 per hour—usually with discounts for resort guests or visitors renting villas within the plantation. Many places offer reduced walk-on rates for midday play (12–4). Free exhibitions take place at 5:30 PM Mon. through Thurs. and Sun. afternoons, at different clubs, on a rotating basis. Call to confirm.

Hilton Head Island Beach and Tennis Resort (843-842-0079; 40 Folly Field Rd.) 10 hard, lighted courts.

Palmetto Dunes Tennis Center (843-785-1152; Palmetto Dunes Resort) 23 clay, 2 hard courts. Hard courts and six clay courts are lighted for night play.

Port Royal Racquet Club (843-686-8803; Port Royal Resort) 10 clay, 4 hard, 2 natural grass courts. Night play available on six courts.

Sea Pines Racquet Club (843-363-4495; Sea Pines Plantation) 24 clay, 5 hard courts.

South Beach Racquet Club (843-671-2215; Sea Pines Plantation) 11 clay courts, 2 lighted.

Van der Meer Tennis Center (843-785-8388 or 1-800-845-6138; DeAllyon Rd.) 28 courts: 25 hard, 3 clay. Night play available on 8 courts. The center is internationally known for its rigorous teaching programs and camps for kids and pros, as well as serious players. The island's top youngsters often train here.

Van der Meer Tennis University/Shipyard Racquet Club (843-686-8804; Shipyard Plantation) 20 courts: 11 clay, 9 hard. Night play on 8 courts.

SHOPPING

As Hilton Head has grown, it has tried to minimize the visual impact of strip development along its major thoroughfare, US 278—the William Hilton Parkway. As a result, the small shopping centers and larger malls that have sprung up to serve 1.5 million visitors per year are destinations with parking and a mix of tenants that includes restaurants, pizza and ice-cream counters, supermarkets, and boutiques. Here are some highlights.

Harbour Town, in Sea Pines Plantation, remains the only shopping area with a genuine village character, located around the harbor basin, clustered near the lighthouse. There's a $5 gate fee to enter Sea Pines. You can head toward Harbour Town, or pay your gate fee, park your car inside the Sea Pines Greenwood Gate, and take a free trolley (every 20 minutes) to Harbour Town. **South Beach Marina**, a Cape Cod–style village, is also in Sea Pines Plantation.

The Mall at Shelter Cove is a more conventional shopping center, anchored by big department stores like Saks, Williams-Sonoma, Banana Republic, Ann Taylor, and Talbots. There is a food court and the mall is enclosed, making it a good rainy-day outing.

Main Street Village (north island, just inside the entrance to Hilton Head Plantation—no gate fee) feels like a few downtown blocks in a prosperous suburb with its specialty boutiques, pubs and restaurants, and "real" stores that sell ordinary things like beer and diapers. **Village at Wexford** has the most interesting collection of stores, restaurants, and more "arty" locales, like a gallery and a jazz club. Collections of shops around marinas at **Shelter Cove Harbour** and **Palmetto Bay Marina** support the boating and watersport activities located there. **Coligny Plaza** is oriented toward kids and visitors, refreshingly informal, a good place to find beach toys, souvenirs and inexpensive resort wear.

Just off the island on US 278 are Target and other "big box" stores. At **Tanger Outlet Stores 1 & 2**, there are bargains in every category: housewares, toys, shoes, eyeglasses, children's clothing, linens, high fashion, and sportswear. Dozens of name-brand manufacturers including Coach, Brooks Brothers, J. Crew, Donna Karan, Dansk, Waterford, and Nike.

Art and Antiques

Some galleries have limited hours but welcome visitors by appointment. If you're interested in more than browsing, call ahead to check.

America Oh Yes! Folk Art Gallery (843-785-2649; 17 Pope Ave., Executive Park, #4; www.americaohyes.com) More than 250 self-taught and visionary artists have work displayed here, and there are pieces for the beginning or experienced collector of folk art.

Barry Honowitz Gallery (843-686-3100; Village at Wexford) Lowcountry images including wildlife and golf scenes.

Decorator's Wholesale Antiques (843-681-7463; 10 Hunter Rd.) Huge selection of stripped pine furniture, mahogany, and sports memorabilia.

Guggenheim's (843-785-9580; 72 Arrow Rd.) Antiques and collectibles, on consignment. A place you could get lucky.

Alligators are at home in shallow Lowcounry lagoons—on the golf course, in shopping areas, or in nature preserves

Harbour Art Gallery (843-785-2787; Shelter Cove Harbour) Paintings and limited edition works of Beaufort, Savannah, and island scenes by artist R. Bolton Smith.

Hartough Gallery (843-671-6500; www.hartough.com) The official artist of the USGS displays original works, lithographs, giclee prints and golf accessories in her shop.

Moonshell Art Gallery (843-341-3339; 37 New Orleans Rd.) Varied collection of works and styles, from impressionistic Lowcountry scenes to children's portraiture.

Red Piano Art Gallery (843-785-2318; 220 Cordillo Parkway) Lowcountry landscapes, sculpture, and fine art from the 19th and 20th centuries.

Swan House Antiques (843-785-7926; 88 Arrow Rd.) Consignments make the collection eclectic and interesting: rugs, china, silver, paintings and prints, furniture.

Books and Music

Audubon Nature Store (843-785-4311; www.audubonnature.com; Village at Wexford) Field guides, children's guides on local flora and fauna.

Barnes & Noble (843-342-6690; 20 Hatton Place) The superstore for books, with many local authors and events featured each week

Disc Jockey (843-842-2844; Mall at Shelter Cove) Music in all formats; videos and accessories.

Heaven Sent Christian Bookstore (843-837-4727; 1540 Fording Island Rd., Bridge Center Shoppes) Inspirational literature, Bibles, children's books.

Island Bookseller (843-671-3773; Sea Pines Center) Adult and children's titles, local authors.

Paperback Exchange (843-842-5614; Village Exchange, 32 Palmetto Bay Rd.) A wide and constantly changing selection of used books. Books on tape for rent here, too.

Port Royal Bookstore (843-842-6996; Village at Wexford) Local authors, best-sellers, congenial service and recommendations.

Waldenbooks (843-785-4301; Mall at Shelter Cove) Books for beach reading, children's section, history, cooking, and coffee-table books.

Clothing

Camp Hilton Head (843-842-3666; www.camphiltonhead.com; Shelter Cove) Fun, casual beachwear embossed with unique logo of Camp Hilton Head. Locations at Harbour Town and Coligny Plaza, too.

Jamaican Me Crazy (843-785-9006; Coligny Plaza) Wacky resort wear, hip beach accessories.

Knickers (843-671-2291; Harbour Town) Classic outfits in linen, cotton, tweeds, and madras. An institution.

Loose Lucy's (843-785-8093; Coligny Plaza) A little bit of the 60s featuring tie-dye, old jeans, Indian prints, bandannas. For Phish fans and Deadheads.

Outside Hilton Head (843-686-6996; Plaza at Shelter Cove) Top-of-the-line durable sports clothing (Patagonia, Woolrich, Teva), footwear, and accessories. Also at South Beach Marina.

Porcupine (843-785-2779; The Village at Wexford) Designer sportswear for women, lingerie, excellent shoe selection, swimwear. The classiest fashion stop on the island.

S.M.Bradford—Lilly Pulitzer Shop (843-686-6161; www.forlp.com; Village at Wexford) The bright florals for women and children that are the designer's trademark, with accessories and some home goods.

Crafts

Art Cafe (843-785-5525; Coligny Plaza) A hands-on pottery studio, where you select an unadorned object (mug, plate, bowl, something else), choose the glazes and tools, and decorate it until it's unique. A good family project.

Harbour Town Crafts (843-671-3643; Harbour Town) Quality American handcrafts, large and small, whimsical, and functional.

Needlepoint Junction (843-842-8488 Village at Wexford) A boutique with stitchery supplies, threads, yarn, canvas, and kits.

Smith Galleries of Fine Crafts (843-842-2280; www.smithgalleries.com. Village at Wexford) More than 300 American artisans are represented in media such as glass, wood, metal, clay, and textiles.

Gifts

Creative Kitchens (843-785-8516; The Village at Wexford) An excellent kitchen and fine houseware supply store. Cooks love it; anyone who needs a bridal gift should, too.

Favors at Forsythe (843-671-7070; At Forsythe Jewelers, Sea Pines Center) MacKenzie-Childs ceramics, painted furniture, glassware, and a baby boutique.

The Goldsmith Shop (843-785-2538; 3 Lagoon Rd.) Gold charms of dolphins, starfish, and boats, studded with tiny jewels.

Legends Sports Cards (843-681-4444; Main St. Village) Old and new trading cards, autographed memorabilia, and Ted Williams signature items.

Magic Puppet (843-785-3280; Coligny Plaza) Toys, puppets, magic tricks, Playmobil sets, books.

Seasons South (843-785-6280; 38 New Orleans Rd.) Garden furniture, ceramics, tiles, and tools.

Ship's Store (843-842-7001; Shelter Cove Harbour) Everything for the sailor including charts, boat shoes, and nautical accessories.

Gourmet and Fun Food
Chocolate Canopy (843-842-4567; www.chocolatecanopy.com; Crossroads Center, Palmetto Bay Rd.) Homemade chocolates galore.

Cinnamon Bear Country Store (843-661-5558; Main St. Village) Gourmet coffee, candies, and gifts.

Healthy Days Natural Food Store (843-785-7297; Coligny Plaza) Flours, herbal teas, sugar-free items.

Marley's Homemade Ice Cream (843-686-5801; Park Plaza at Greenwood Dr.) Outdoor seating; dozens of flavors and concoctions made fresh daily.

Signe's Heaven Bound Bakery (843-785-9118; 2 Bow Circle) Fresh baked breads, pastries, cakes, cookies, soups.

Truffles Market (843-671-6136; Sea Pines Center) Sandwiches, pâté, salads, breads, pastries and wine.

Sportswear and Sports Equipment
Go Tri Sports (843-842-4786; www.gotrisports.com; Park Plaza) The island headquarters for tri-athletes and a fund of information about races, technique, and new products.

Lowcountry Outfitters (843-837-6100 or 1-800-935-9666; Moss Creek Village) Fly-fishing equipment, fine guns, clothing, and hunting-related gifts and many instructional videos.

Outside Hilton Head (843-686-6996, Plaza at Shelter Cove or 843-671-2643, South Beach Marina) Equipment for windsurfing, canoeing, kayaking, and camping. Patagonia, North Face clothing lines. The island standard for outdoor activity and experienced staff.

Player's World (843-842-5100; Plaza at Shelter Cove) Island's largest sporting goods store. Another branch (843-785-4653; Fresh Market Shoppes) specializes in golf equipment and accessories.

Sportline (843-686-8855; 890 Wm. Hilton Pkwy.) Dozens of models of tennis racquets and same-day stringing; shoes and accessories for runners and soccer players.

Sunny Daze Surf Factory (843-682-3293; 6 Cardinal Rd.) Bodyboards, skimboards, surfboards, and all the accessories and apparel. Rentals and repair, too.

6

INFORMATION
Practical Matters & Seasonal Events

What follows is information to make your visit to the Lowcountry run more smoothly. It's a modest compendium of essentials—what's here and how it works—intended to make planning your trip easier and enjoying your stay simpler. The chapter covers the following topics:

Ambulance, Fire & Police
Area Code, Town Government & Zip Codes
Bibliography
Climate, Weather & What to Wear
Getting There, Getting Around
Handicapped Services
Hospitals
Newspapers and Magazines
Real Estate
Road Service
Seasonal Events in the Lowcountry
Tourist Information & On-line Addresses

AMBULANCE, FIRE & POLICE

The general emergency number in the Lowcountry is 911, whether you're in Charleston, Beaufort, Hilton Head, or Savannah. Outside the cities, most of the counties have basic 911 service. Naturally, in an emergency, you can always dial "o" for the Operator's assistance in reaching the right agency. A selected roster of other numbers, for emergencies or other business, follows:

First Call for Help (Information and referral service):
Charleston 1-800-922-2283
Beaufort/Hilton Head 843-524-4357
Savannah 912-651-7730

Poison Control:
South Carolina . . . . .1-800-922-1117 (from within SC)
Georgia . . . . .1-800-282-5846 (from within GA)

Rape Crisis Hotline:

Charleston	843-722-7273
Beaufort/Hilton Head	843-525-6699 or 1-800-637-7273
Savannah	912-233-7273

Disaster/Hurricane Emergency Preparedness:

Charleston County	843-202-7400
Beaufort County	843-470-3100
Colleton County	843-549-5632
Hampton County	803-943-7522
Jasper County	843-726-7797
Chatham County	912-201-4500

State Police:

S.C. Highway Patrol:

Charleston Area	843-740-1650
Beaufort/Hilton Head	843-524-0163
Ridgeland	843-726-8076

Ga. Highway Patrol:

Savannah Area	912-754-1180

Police (non-emergency):

City of Charleston	843-577-7434
Town of Edisto Beach	843-869-2440
City of Beaufort	843-322-7900
Town of Port Royal	843-986-2220
Town of Hilton Head (sheriff)	843-726-6800
Town of Bluffton	843-706-4550
Town of Hardeeville	843-784-2233
City of Savannah	912-232-4141

AREA CODES, TOWN GOVERNMENT & ZIP CODES

Area Codes

The area code for the South Carolina Lowcountry is 843, with the occasional use of 803. The area code for Savannah, Georgia and its metropolitan region is 912.

Town Halls

The cities of Charleston, Beaufort, Hilton Head, and Savannah are governed by a mayor and city/town council; their outlying lands controlled by county government. The trend in government is toward consolidation of services, whereby the cities or towns and the counties they are part of share in the cost and delivery of these services.

Charleston, Beaufort, Walterboro, Ridgeland, Hampton, and Savannah are the region's county seats. For general information call:

Charleston County	843-958-4000
Beaufort County	843-470-2800
Colleton County	843-549-5221

Jasper County 843-726-7703
Hampton County 803-943-7561
Chatham County 912-652-7175

There are also smaller, scattered municipalities governed by smaller councils. For general information, contact the following town/city hall offices:

Town	Address	Telephone
Beaufort	135 Ribaut Rd., 29902	843-525-7055
Bluffton	P.O. Box 386, 29910	843-706-4500
Charleston	80 Broad St., P.O. Box 652, 29402	843-577-6970
Edisto Island	2414 Murray St., 29438	843-869-2505
Folly Beach	21 Center St., 29439	843-588-2447
Hampton	608 First St., 29924	803-943-2951
Hilton Head	1 Town Center Court, 29928	843-341-4600
Isle of Palms	1207 Palm Blvd., 29451	843-886-6428
Port Royal	700 Paris Ave., 29935	843-986-2200
Ridgeland	108 E. Wilson, P.O. Drawer B, 29936	843-726-3351
Savannah	Bay St., P.O. Box 1027, 31402	912-236-7284
Thunderbolt	2821 River Dr., 31404	912-447-1900
Tybee Island	401 Butler Ave., 31328	912-786-4573
Walterboro	242 Hampton St., P.O. Box 709, 29488	843-549-2545

Savannah City Hall

BIBLIOGRAPHY

Lowcountry life, past and present, is well documented, and bookstores have ever-growing "local history" sections to prove it. Many volumes formerly out of print have been reprinted recently in response to new demand. Originals may be still found in second-hand bookstores, although at premium prices. Here is a suggested reading list of some classics, the books you're likely to find in residents' libraries.

These days, there are more "homegrown" histories available, courtesy of laptop publishing. Don't overlook them and the gems of local lore they contain. And, since the best part of a trip is often reliving it at home, check your local bookstore upon returning for further reading. The boxed quotes scattered throughout the text are taken from books included in the list below.

The list is by no means complete: think of it as a mere guide to the shelves.

Art & Architecture

Cole, Cynthia, ed. *Historic Resources of the Lowcountry.* Yemassee, SC: Lowcountry Council of Governments, 1979, 2nd. ed. 1990. 202 pp., illus., photos, index, $29.95. The definitive four-county survey of historic houses and sites with fine historical and architectural explanation.

Dugan, Ellen, ed. *Picturing the South: 1860 to the Present.* Atlanta, GA: Chronicle Books, the High Museum of Art, 1996. 213 pp., index, $29.95. Based on a 1996 exhibit at the Photographic Galleries of the High Museum in Atlanta, the selection of pictures (from the Library of Congress Collections, private donors, historical societies, and museums) is honed to perfection and the accompanying essays (by several southern writers of the first rank) is excellent. The book is moving without being sentimental.

Lane, Mills. *Architecture of the Old South: South Carolina.* Savannah, GA: Beehive Press, 1984. 258 pp., photos, $75. Exquisite, large format, black and white photos.

———. *Architecture of the Old South: Georgia.* Savannah, GA: Beehive Press, 1986. 252 pp., photos, $75.

Ravenel, Beatrice St. Julian. *Architects of Charleston.* Columbia, SC: University of South Carolina Press, 1992. 338 pp., photos, index, bibliog., $19.95. First published in 1945, a detailed examination of the lives and works of the city's builders, engineers, and architects.

Rosengarten, Dale. *Row Upon Row: Sea Grass Baskets of the South Carolina Lowcountry.* Columbia, SC: McKissick Museum, 1986. 64 pp., photos, $10. A thorough and lovingly documented catalogue of a vibrant Sea Island art. It is the authoritative text on the shapes, weaving style, and uses of island baskets.

Severens, Kenneth. *Charleston Antebellum Architecture and Civic Destiny.* Knoxville, TN: University of Tennessee Press, 1988. 330 pp., photos, index, $49.95. A specialized topic explained in clear prose for the interested amateur or professional architect.

Severens, Martha R. *Charles Fraser of Charleston.* Charles L. Wyrick Jr., ed. Charleston, SC: Carolina Art Assoc., 1983. 176 pp., illus., $14.95. The subject was a miniaturist of the 19th century whose portraits of local gentry, in the collection of the Gibbes Art Gallery, are exquisite and incisive.

———. *The Charleston Renaissance.* Charleston, SC: Robert M. Hicklin, Jr., Inc., 1999. 232 pp., illus., $65. A scholarly, beautifully illustrated chronicle of the artists in early 20th-century Charleston who were inspired by the city's heritage and story and expressed themselves in a variety of media.

Talbott, Page. *Classical Savannah: Fine and Decorative Arts 1800–1840.* Savannah: Telfair Museum, 1995. 320 pp., illus., $24.95. An overview of a period during which Savannah was deeply influenced by English Regency and Continental architecture and interior style.

Vlach, John Michael. *Back of the Big House: The Architecture of Plantation Slavery.* Chapel Hill, NC: University of North Carolina Press, 1993. 236 pp., illus., photos, index, $18.95. A serious, well-written, and fundamental study of the relationship of plantation "spaces"—the outbuildings, the quarters, the "Big House," the *allées* or avenues, fields, docks, and waterways—to the black and white people who lived there and to each other. Numerous plantation plans are cited.

Autobiography, Biography, Diaries & Letters

Bartram, William. *Travels through North & South Carolina, Georgia, East & West Florida.* New York: Viking Penguin, 1988. 452 pp., $7.95. The account of an 18th-century trip through the Lowcountry by the famous botanist.

Chesnut, Mary Boykin. *A Diary from Dixie.* Cambridge, MA: Harvard University Press, 1980. 608 pp., $12.95. A classic account, good on Charleston society.

Daise, Ronald. *Reminiscences of a Sea Island Heritage.* Columbia, SC: Sandlapper, 1986. 103 pp., photos, $18.95. Archival black-and-white photos accompanied by text and stories of Sea Island Gullah culture. Daise and his wife, Natalie, were the creators and stars of the television series for children, *Gullah Gullah Island,* and continue to perform nationally.

Egerton, Douglas. *He Shall Go Out Free: The Lives of Denmark Vesey.* Madison, WI: Madison House, 1999. 272 pp., illus., $34.95. A complete, well-researched and well-argued account of the failed slave uprising in Charleston in 1822.

Elliott, William, & Theodore Rosengarten. *Carolina Sports by Land and Water, Including Incidents of Devil-Fishing, Wild-Cat, Deer, and Bear-Hunting, Etc.* Columbia, SC: University of South Carolina Press, 1994. Illus., $14.95. A reprint of Elliott's 1850s original, it is still funny, easy to read, and as full of suspense as ever.

Forten, Charlotte L. *The Journal of a Free Negro in the Slave Era.* New York: Norton, 1981. 286 pp., index, $8.95. The vivid impressions of a Northern teacher who came to the Sea Islands to educate the newly freed slaves.

Georgia Writers' Project, ed. *Drums and Shadows.* Athens, GA: University of Georgia Press, 1986. $11.95. The collection of oral histories first published under the WPA program in 1940. It allows you to hear the voices of the coast.

Higginson, Thomas Wentworth. *Army Life in a Black Regiment.* New York: Norton, 1984. 279 pp., appendix, index, $6.95. Higginson, a Boston Brahmin, was the white commander of the First South Carolina Volunteers, headquartered in Beaufort, S.C. during the Civil War. Its honest, self-effacing narrative of camp life, countrysides, and skirmishes is invaluable.

Kemble, Frances Anne. *Journal of Residence on a Georgia Plantation in 1838–1839.* Athens, GA: University of Georgia Press, 1984. 488 pp., $11.95. Although the setting is the coastal Georgia plantation of the author's husband, Pierce Butler, her insights into plantation life and the culture of black female slaves make this perhaps the best account of that time.

McTeer, J. E. *High Sheriff of the Lowcountry.* Beaufort, SC: JEM Co., 1995. 101 pp., $19.70. Newly reprinted, it contains the colorful recollections of the author's days as a Lowcountry lawman and his encounters with voodoo and witch doctors, rum runners, and local scoundrels.

Olmsted, F. L. *A Journey in the Seaboard Slave States.* Westport, CT: Negro Universities Press of Greenwood Pub., 1969. Illus., index, $35.00. A reprint of the 1856 edition in which the author acutely observes the coastal region and standards of living there.

Pearson, Elizabeth Ware, ed. *Letters from Port Royal, 1862–1868.* New York: Arno Press, 1969. $14.00. In 1862, dozens of Northern abolitionists flocked to the Federally occupied area around Beaufort, SC to educate the newly freed slaves and manage the abandoned cotton plantations. This collection of letters by the Boston contingent is as forceful and moving a commentary on race relations and liberal expectations as exists.

Pennington, Patience. *A Woman Rice Planter.* Cambridge, MA: Belknap Press of Harvard University Press, 1961. The author was a Lowcountry native who managed her father's rice plantations after the Civil War and wrote about the experience for New York newspapers. The illustrations are by Alice Ravenel Huger Smith, a lyrical interpreter of the rural Lowcountry.

Pinkney, Roger. *The Beaufort Chronicles.* Beaufort, SC: Pluff Mud. 110 pp., $9.95. A new collection of remembrances and essays on small-town life and its simple pleasures.

Towne, Laura. *Letters and Diary Written from the Sea Islands of South Carolina, 1862–1884.* New York: American Bio. Series, 1991. 310 pp., $79. Another wonderful journal of a teacher; she established Penn School, the first school for freed slaves in the United States.

Verner, Elizabeth O. *Mellowed By Time.* Charleston, SC: Tradd St. Press, 1978. $15.00. Sketches and memories of old Charleston by a distinguished artist who favored etchings, pastel, and pencil drawing.

Cultural Studies

Bluffton Historical Preservation Society. *No. II A Longer Short History of Bluffton, South Carolina and its Environs.* Bluffton, SC: Bluffton Historical Preservation Society, 1988. 49 pp., photos, $9.95. An excellent local history with photographs of classic Lowcountry cottages.

Carawan, Guy & Candy, eds. *Ain't You Got a Right to the Tree of Life? The People of John's Island, South Carolina—Their Faces, Their Words and Their Songs.* Athens, GA: University of Georgia Press, 1989. 256 pp., photos, $29.95.

Johnson, Guion G. *A Social History of the Sea Islands.* Westport, CT: Greenwood Press, 1969. 185 pp., index, bibliog., $38.50. A reprint of the 1930 edition of a series in which scholars from the University of North Carolina examined the lives, speech, culture, and folkways of Sea Island natives. Others in the series include *Folk Culture on St. Helena Island* by Guy B. Johnson and *Black Yeomanry* by T. J. Woofter, which, if you can find it, has stirring documentary photographs.

Jones-Jackson, Patricia. *When Roots Die: Endangered Traditions on the Sea Islands.* Athens, GA: University of Georgia Press, 1987. 189 pp., photos, bibliog., $19.95.

Parrish, Lydia. *Slave Songs of the Georgia Sea Islands.* Athens, GA: University of Georgia Press, 1992. 252 pp., photos, musical notation, $19.95. A reprint of the 1942 original by the wife of artist Maxfield Parrish, documenting the islanders' songs from the praise house to the play yard.

Taylor, John Martin. *Hoppin' John's Lowcountry Cooking.* New York: Bantam, 1990. 345 pp., illus., $24.00.

————. *The New Southern Cook: 200 Recipes.* New York: Bantam, 1995. 287 pp., illus., $27.95. A superb follow-up to Taylor's first book, this one ranges a bit further but maintains the author's discriminating judgments and lack of pretension.

Terry, Elizabeth, with Alexis Terry. *Savannah Seasons: Food and Stories from Elizabeth on 37th.* New York: Doubleday, 1996. 340 pp., $30. Recipes and memories, written by mother and daughter, of the family's nationally acclaimed Savannah restaurant, which opened in 1980. There's a useful "source list" for ingredients available from specialty vendors by mail, too.

Vernon, Amelia Wallace. *African-Americans at Mars Bluff, South Carolina.* Columbia, SC: University of South Carolina Press, 1995. 200 pp., illus., photos, index, bibliog., $16.95. A wonderful documentary account of an African American community north of Charleston, SC.

Welty, Eudora. *The Eye of the Story: Selected Essays and Reviews.* New York: Vintage International, 1990. 355 pp., $14.00.

Westmacott, Richard. *African-American Gardens and Yards in the Rural South.* Knoxville, TN: University of Tennessee Press, 1992. 175 pp., illus., photos, index, bibliog., $24.95. One of the most thoughtful and inspired books ever written on African-American rural life (some in the Lowcountry), it focuses on several families and the way they create color, style, whimsy, and usefulness in their immediate landscape. It is part scholarly, part oral history, and the tone is just right.

Fiction

Berendt, John. *Midnight in the Garden of Good and Evil.* New York: Random House, 1994. 388 pp., $22.00. A wild romp in Savannah—and it's all true.

Conroy, Pat. *The Water is Wide.* New York: Bantam, 1972. 320 pp., $4.95. This was the book based on Conroy's experiences as a Beaufort County schoolteacher on isolated Daufuskie Island. His other books include *The Great Santini, The Prince of Tides,* and *Beach Music* and have Beaufort as their setting (even in the movie version).

Griswold, Francis. *Sea Island Lady.* Beaufort, SC: Beaufort Book Co., reprint of the 1939 original. 964 pp., $19.95. A big, fat Southern novel set in Beaufort.

Heyward, Du Bose. *Porgy.* Charleston, SC: Tradd St. Press, 1985. 130 pp., illus., $20. A reprinting of the great tale, set in and around Charleston.

Humphreys, Josephine. *Rich in Love.* New York: Viking Penguin, 1987. 262 pp., $8.95. Set in Mount Pleasant, near Charleston, this novel (basis of the 1993 movie) captures the world view of a precocious 17-year-old girl. The author's other novels, *Dreams of Sleep* (1984) and *The Fireman's Fair* (1991), also have the Charleston area as their setting.

Naylor, Gloria R. *Mama Day.* New York: Random House, 1989. 312 pp., $9.95. A magical story set in a mythical place that nearly mirrors the Georgia/ South Carolina Sea Islands.

Peterkin, Julia. *Scarlet Sister Mary.* Marietta, GA: Cherokee Press, 1991. 352 pp., $18.95. A reprint of the 1928 edition.

Powell, Padgett. *Edisto.* New York: Farrar, Strauss & Giroux, 1984. 192 pp., $11.95. A boy's coming-of-age on a Sea Island.

———. *Edisto Revisited.* New York: Henry Holt, 1996. 145 pp., $20.

Sayers, Valerie. *Due East.* New York: Doubleday, 1987. 264 pp., $15.95. The first novel in a group that chronicles life in a town like Beaufort, SC, where the author grew up. Others include *How I Got Him Back* (1989) and *Who Do You Love* (1991).

Worthington, Curtis, ed. *Literary Charleston: A Lowcountry Reader.* Charleston, SC: Wyrick & Co., 1996. 360 pp., $24.95.

History

Bridenbaugh, Carl. *Myths and Realities: Societies of the Colonial South.* New York: Atheneum, 1963. 208 pp., index, bibliog., $1.25.

Dollard, John. *Caste and Class in a Southern Town.* Madison, WI: University of Wisconsin Press, 1989. 466 pp., index, $14.50. A reissue of the 1937 work which, while not specifically about the Lowcountry, has everything to say about race relations in small towns throughout the region.

Jacoway, Elizabeth. *Yankee Missionaries in the South: The Penn School Experiment.* Baton Rouge, LA: LSU Press, 1980. 301 pp., index, bibliog.

Jones, Katharine M. *Port Royal Under Six Flags.* Indianapolis, IN: Bobbs-Merrill, 1960. 368 pp., illus., bibliog. A good general introduction to the area, with long passages quoting original documents.

Rogers, George. *Charleston in the Age of the Pinckneys.* Columbia, SC: University of South Carolina Press, 1984. 198 pp., index, $9.95. If there is one book you should read about Charleston's heyday, this is it.

Rose, Willie Lee. *Rehearsal for Reconstruction: The Port Royal Experiment.* New York: Oxford University Press, 1976. 450 pp., index, bibliog., $13.95. A beautifully written and meticulously researched account of the Northern abolitionists who went to the Sea Islands of Beaufort at the time of the Civil War. If you have a serious interest in the subject, the bibliography of this book is where you should start.

Rosen, Robert. *A Short History of Charleston.* San Francisco, CA: Lexikos, 1982. 160 pp., illus., photos, bibliog., $8.95. A popular introduction to Charleston by a native son.

Rosengarten, Theodore. *Tombee: Portrait of A Cotton Planter.* New York: McGraw, 1988. 752 pp., index, $15.00. This prize-winning book reproduces the diaries of an antebellum St. Helena Islander, Thomas B. Chaplin, and creates a context of explanation for them. This is the story—not the myth—of life on a cotton plantation, handled in vivid prose by the region's best historian.

Stampp, Kenneth. *The Peculiar Institution: Slavery in the Ante-Bellum South.* New York: Vintage, 1989. Index, $10. A classic study, first published in 1956.

Wise, Stephen R. *Lifeline of the Confederacy: Blockade Running During the Civil War.* Columbia, SC: University of South Carolina Press, 1988. 403 pp., illus., index, $16.95.

———. *Gate of Hell: Campaign for Charleston Harbor, 1863.* Columbia, SC: University of South Carolina Press, 1994. 218 pp., illus., index, $29.95.

Wood, Peter. *Black Majority: Negroes in Colonial South Carolina from 1670 through the Stono Rebellion.* New York: Norton, 1975. 384 pp., index, $9.95.

Photographic Studies

Blagden, Tom. *The Lowcountry.* Greensboro, NC: Legacy Publications, 1988. 104 pp., photos, $49.95. Views of the coastal world by an immensely talented photographer. His words of introduction, of praise for the region's natural beauty, resonate with visitors and locals alike.

——. *South Carolina's Wetland Wilderness: The ACE Basin.* Englewood, CO: Westcliffe Publishers, Inc. 1992. 110 pp., $29.95. A sumptuous study of the land and estuarine ecosystem in and around the Ashepoo, Combahee, and Edisto Rivers; much of the area is protected by federal, state, local and private organizations.

Dabbs, Edith, ed. *Face of an Island.* An album of early-20th-century photographs taken on St. Helena Island by Leigh Richmond Miner and reproduced from the glass plates. A treasure.

Ellis, Ray. *South by Southeast.* Birmingham, AL: Oxmoor House, 1983. 122 pp., $50. Watercolors of the coastal region by noted painter and Hilton Head resident.

Isley, Jane, Agnes Baldwin, and William P. Baldwin. *Plantations of the Lowcountry.* Greensboro, NC: Legacy Pub., 1987. 151 pp., $19.95. Color photographs and histories of historic homes.

McLaren, Lynn, and Gerhard Spieler. *Ebb Tide, Flood Tide.* Columbia, SC: University of South Carolina Press, 1991. 105 pp., $40. Color photographs of favorite Beaufort sites—natural and man-made.

Schultz, Constance, ed. *A South Carolina Album. 1936–1948.* Columbia, SC: University of South Carolina Press, 1992. 143 pp. A collection of photographs taken under the auspices of the Farm Security Administration, and later under the direction of its chief, Roy Stryker.

Recreation/Travel

Baldwin, William P. III. *Lowcountry Daytrips: Plantations, Gardens, and a Natural History of the Charleston Region.* Greensboro NC: Legacy Publications, 1993. 283 pp., illus., photos, index, bibliog., $18.95. The best new guide to the area, written by a Lowcountry native. It is a model of organization (with maps and mileages clearly spelled out), good design, practicality, and a writing style that lends itself to reading aloud. The book you'll lend to anyone who takes your advice and visits the Lowcountry.

Ballantine, Todd. *Tideland Treasures.* Columbia, SC: University of South Carolina Press, 1991. 218 pp., $15.95.

Crowley, Rebecca Kaufmann. *Hilton Head Guidebook.* Beaufort, SC: Coastal Villages Press, 1995. 135 pp., $9.95.

Federal Writers' Project Staff. *The WPA Guide to the Palmetto State.* Walter B. Edgar, ed. Columbia, SC: University of South Carolina Press, 1988. 514 pp., photos, index, $16.95. A reprint of the superb guide.

Georgia Conservancy. *A Guide to the Georgia Coast.* Savannah, GA: The Georgia Conservancy, 1989. 199 pp., illus., index.

Moeller, Jan and Bill Moeller. *The Intracoastal Waterway.* Camden, ME: Seven Seas Press, 1979 (updated 1991). 149 pp., $16.95.

Trask, Fred. *A Guide to Historic Beaufort.* Beaufort, SC: Historic Beaufort Foundation, 1970. 125 pp., maps, illus., photos. The definitive guide, especially good in describing walking and driving tours.

Wright, Cantey Holmes. *The Edisto Book.* Columbia, SC: Mac Kohn Printing, 1988. 109 pp., map, illus. Good local history.

CLIMATE, WEATHER & WHAT TO WEAR

Before spring was celebrated with house tours in Charleston and St. Patrick's Day parades in Savannah, there was just the season to rave about. Tourists came to see the blossoms and they weren't disappointed—azaleas and wisteria bursting into bloom all over downtown, jasmine flowering on fence posts, dogwood and magnolia peeping out from under the shadows of live oaks in the woods. April is the Lowcountry's sunniest month.

In fact, there is something in bloom year-round in the Lowcountry, from late-summer mums to camellias to paper-white narcissus, which scent the air at Christmas. This comes as a result of the semitropical to subtropical climate and the ever-present breezes that characterize the coastal region. There are also micro-climates—as small as a yard, as wide as an acre—which make it possible to cultivate plants that are used to a warmer zone, like oranges and freesia. Rarely do days pass in succession without sunshine. The annual rainfall for the region is about 51 inches.

Endless Summer

From this early spring-time onward, there seemed no great difference in atmospheric sensations, and only a succession of bloom. After two months one's notions of the season grew bewildered, just as very early rising bewilders the day. In the army one is perhaps aroused after a bivouac, marches before daybreak, halts, fights, somebody is killed, a long day's life has been lived, and after all it is not seven o'clock, and breakfast is not ready. So when we had lived in summer so long as hardly to remember winter, it suddenly occurred to us that it was not yet June. One escapes at the South that mixture of hunger and avarice which is felt in the Northern summer, counting each hour's joy with the sad consciousness that an hour is gone.

—Thomas Wentworth Higginson, in his memoir, *Army Life in a Black Regiment* (first published in 1869) New York: Norton, 1984.

The winters are generally mild—maybe 9 days of frost, and a half-dozen hard freezes. Spring comes early. Farmers generally break ground on February 1. In the old days, the cotton crop was finished by "lay-by time" in late August, when slaves, temporarily released from heavy field work, would tend to their cemeteries and families.

By May 1, it's hot, and that heat will penetrate every living thing through the end of September. The mean summer temperature in the Lowcountry runs between 70 degrees and 88 degrees but with the heat index and humidity figured in, it can feel much hotter. If you arrive in summer, be prepared to move slowly, wear a hat, slather on the sunscreen, and drink plenty of liquids. Even on a hazy day the sun will burn you. Take extra precautions if you're planning athletic pursuits: the tennis court is no place to be at midday. The wild cloudbursts that drench the region in summer, and the often-spectacular thunder and lightening shows that accompany them, may cool things off a bit. More likely, they'll just bring mosquitoes.

Then there are the gnats. Just when you're enjoying a creamy autumn day in the 70s, they find you. Insect repellents can be effective, as is staying out of the shade or standing in a breeze.

The seasons each bring their color, their migratory birds, their harvest of fish or shell-fish, duck or deer. And twice a year it seems as if a whole new shipment of air is carted in, too—in late October, when the marsh has turned golden and the clouds pull themselves into exquisitely defined cumuli; and again in late February, when the prevailing northeast winds of winter start to shift south and southwest.

But perhaps the best quality of Lowcountry weather is its subtlety and contradiction: the warm day in January that you were not expecting, the roaring fire in October that banishes the dampness and chill in the morning, but by late afternoon seems an inferno.

For clothing, pack more cotton shirts than you think you'll need. Take comfortable shoes for touring (high-heeled shoes are often forbidden in House Museums and on tours) and a light sweater or windbreaker. An overcoat or parka may be too much in winter; sweaters and shells work better.

The hurricane season lasts from about June to November, with most recent devastating storms having come between late August and October. If you're traveling then, make sure you are aware of evacuation routes and keep alerted to local media for hurricane watch and hurricane warning announcements. The National Weather Service (www.wchs.csc.noaa.gov) provides excellent coverage in the South Carolina and Georgia area on the website.

Sidewalk garden in Charleston

GETTING THERE, GETTING AROUND

The first and most important fact about the Lowcountry is that it is mostly water. Perhaps this is why the old houses of the region's cities and towns—and the dense feeling of permanence they exude—are so venerated, above and beyond their architectural and historic status. They appear—now, as in the past—literally to triumph over their surroundings, as if daring wind, water, and the harsh storms of hurricane season to teach them the lessons of frailty.

The tides, which cast the riches of sea life toward shore and offered the first planters the possibility of harnessed power, bestowed on the Lowcountry a natural abundance of marine and bird life, and enabled the cultivation of rice. The settlements that clustered around what we know today as peninsular Charleston, flanked by the Ashley and Cooper Rivers, grew up there to take advantage of the tidal watercourses. Flat-bottomed plantation barges loaded with rice, bales of cotton, and farm produce plied the rivers and creeks to the city harbor. Throughout the Lowcountry, eight-oared bateaux, made on the plantations and navigated by slaves, clove the marsh from one plantation to another, carrying news, goods, and passengers. The Savannah River offered both protection to an English colony in the Southern wilderness and a commercial avenue.

Quite often, what roads existed were hardly distinguishable from the water. Highways could be covered with washed-up shells, sponges and seaweed, brought and removed by the tides each day. As time went on, people of the Lowcountry took nature one step further: they made roadbeds of oyster shell, fashioning a crown at the "center line" to facilitate drainage. These were the best roads around, and in some towns like Beaufort they were in use well into the 20th century. An unimproved road, such as you'd find—and still find today—on the Sea Islands, was plowed through fine sand, perhaps a foot deep, rutted and banked. More than one elderly Lowcountry resident can tell a tale of pushing a Model T Ford through this sand, or of watching the ice melt through the sawdust when the iceman got stuck.

Perhaps as a result of the reliance on water travel, as well as the sheer isolation of the plantations and their rural dependencies, a thickly veined series of land transportation routes never really developed in the Lowcountry. Instead there evolved a fleet of small packet steamers that made their way from island to island, picking up passengers, mail, produce, and cotton to deliver in Charleston and Savannah. And ox-drawn carts, or horses, or marsh "tackies" (diminutive horses, something like a Shetland pony) serviced them. When, in 1894, the historian Henry Adams visited St. Helena Island, he traveled first by train, then by carriage over a sand road, then on a shell road, then by foot to the ferry crossing, then over the river to board the steamer *Flora*, which carried him to his destination. These days travel is easier but there are plenty of unlit, two-lane roads that are major thoroughfares and require extra time and careful driving. Directions to specific areas are noted near the beginning of each chapter. The mileage charts and marina guides below are provided to give a sense of context.

The only thoroughfare by land between Beaufort and Charleston is the 'Shell Road,' a beautiful avenue, which, about nine miles from Beaufort, strikes a ferry across the Coosaw River. War abolished the ferry, and made the river the permanent barrier between the opposing picket lines. For ten miles, right and left, these lines extended, marked by well-worn footpaths, following the endless windings of the stream; and they never varied until nearly the end of the war. Upon their maintenance depended our whole foothold on the Sea Islands; and upon that again finally depended the whole campaign of Sherman.

—From *Army Life in a Black Regiment,* 1869
by Thomas Wentworth Higginson (New York: W. W. Norton, 1984)

By Car

Unless your visit to the Lowcountry is limited strictly to Charleston or Savannah or to a self-contained Hilton Head resort, having your own car really pays off. The Lowcountry is decentralized; a lot of space separates those "points of interest." What's more, appreciating that very space by finding yourself in it lies at the heart of the Lowcountry experience.

That's where you'll find some of the region's subtle treasures: the view of a marsh at sunset, the sight of feeding pelicans as they hit the water, the faded impression of an abandoned oyster-shell road strewn with wildflowers. It is in these very open spaces, in their linked geography, that the sense of times passed and lives abundantly lived will catch up with you and shape your awareness of what the Lowcountry is all about. US 17, one of the region's oldest roads and still perhaps the most direct, threads its way from above Charleston to Savannah (and beyond) through marshes, old rice fields, and bottomland forests. Turnoffs that access the Sea Islands to the east (Kiawah, Seabrook, Edisto, Port Royal, St. Helena, Hilton Head) and the Ashley River plantations (Drayton Hall, Middleton Place, Magnolia Gardens) to the west (along SC 61) are well marked, as are historic sites, parks, and picnic grounds.

From Washington and points north: Travelers from the north can reach the Lowcountry by approaching it on I-95, which roughly parallels the coast. From there, well-marked exits direct you to downtown Charleston (via I-26), to Beaufort (via US 21), to Hilton Head (via US 278) and Savannah (via I-16). The coastal destinations beyond the big cities, such as Kiawah Island, Edisto Island, Beaufort, and Hilton Head, lie approximately 45 minutes east of I-95. Distance from Washington to Charleston: 512 miles; to Savannah: 616 miles.

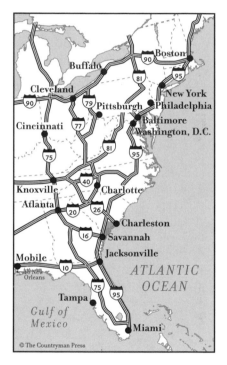

From Jacksonville and points south: Like visitors from the north, drivers from the south approach on I-95 and then turn east to the coast. Distance from Jacksonville to Charleston: 241 miles; to Savannah: 139 miles.

From Asheville and points northwest: Take I-40 to I-26, then follow I-26 toward Spartanburg and Columbia. About an hour out of Columbia, you meet I-95. At that point either continue east to Charleston or turn south. Distance from Asheville to Charleston: 265 miles; to Savannah: 297 miles.

From Charlotte: Take I-77 south to I-20 at Columbia; follow I-20 for a few exits to link up with I-26 east. Distance to Charleston: 200 miles; to Savannah: 240 miles.

From Atlanta: Take I-75 to I-16. When it crosses I-95 go north for Charleston, or continue directly to Savannah. Distance to Charleston: 286 miles; to Savannah: 259 miles.

Lowcountry Access

The approximate distances and driving times to Charleston and selected cities are given in the charts below. The distance between Charleston and Savannah is 114 miles, so depending on the direction from which you are traveling, you should adjust accordingly. If you're touring within the Lowcountry, however, stopping along the way between Charleston and

Savannah in places like Beaufort, Hilton Head, Bluffton, Edisto, or Walterboro, this trip easily may take a day. In general, traveling to specific Sea Island destinations located to the east of the major cities can add up to an hour to your trip.

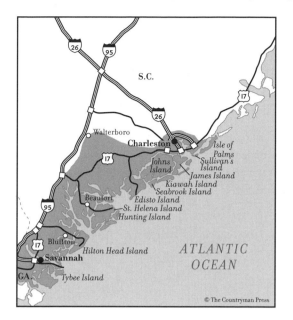

To Charleston from:

City	Miles	Hours
Atlanta	286	5
Boston	929	17
Charlotte	200	4
Chicago	906	15.5
Knoxville	395	7
Miami	590	10.5
New Orleans	784	13
New York	768	13
Washington, D.C.	512	8.5

By Bus

Greyhound (1-800-231-2222; www.greyhound.com) serves Charleston, Beaufort, and Savannah and maintains stations in those cities. It also serves points in between, but here the stops are less formal—perhaps as simple as a crossroads store. As a result, if you're planning to do a substantial amount of traveling by bus, you should consult both a detailed map and the bus schedule. Don't expect to find a taxi or rental-car stand—or even a working pay telephone—at every stop.

The service and price to Charleston and to Savannah from various points are roughly equal; in most cases the same bus goes to both cities. Travel times on longer trips may vary up to three hours, according to the number of stops and the specific route, so it's wise to ask about arrival times and whether or not it's a direct trip.

Charleston Greyhound Bus Terminal (843-744-4247; 3610 Dorchester Rd., North Charleston).

Savannah Greyhound Bus Terminal (912-232-2135; 610 W. Oglethorpe Ave).

Beaufort Greyhound Bus Terminal (843-524-4646; 1307 Boundary St.).

By Train

Amtrak (1-800-872-7245; www.amtrak.com) travels the north-south corridor, making daily stops at North Charleston (843-744-8264; 4565 Gaynor Ave.), about 25 minutes from downtown, Yemassee (about 30 miles west of Beaufort), and Savannah (912-234-2611; 2611 Seaboard Coastline Dr.), about 20 minutes from downtown. On the long hauls from major cities like Boston, New York, Chicago, and Miami, there are generally two trains a day, departing morning and evening and arriving either late the same day or early the following morning. Traveling by night with sleeping accommodations is a nice option for these 10- to 18-hour trips.

By Private Plane

If you're flying on your own, contact the following county or regional airports or services:

Beaufort County Airport. 843-770-2003
East Cooper Airport. 843-884-8837
Hilton Head Airport. 843-689-5400
John's Island-Charleston Executive Airport 843-559-2401
Mercury Air Center-Charleston International. 843-746-7600
Savannah Aviation 912-964-1022

By Boat

The **Intracoastal Waterway** winds through creek and river, ocean and sound, from one end of the Lowcountry to the other, making for some of the most sublime cruising on the East Coast. In Charleston, Beaufort, and Hilton Head, you can dock at a marina right downtown or within walking distance of restaurants and sightseeing. Savannah's marinas are about 20 minutes from downtown. There a dozens of full-service marina options, so choose among them according to your needs, for example, if they provide repair service. If you want to make use of the charter fishing, sailing, or tour services based at marinas, see the **Recreation** section in the appropriate chapter for some ideas. If your main mode of transportation is by boat, check those listings for details on berthing facilities and services. An excellent area map—from the perspective of water—is available for $9.95 from **Coastal Expeditions, Inc.** (843-884-7684; 514-B Mill St., Mt. Pleasant, SC 29464; www.coastal expeditions.com).

By City Transportation

Inexpensive, or free, shuttle bus service to the Historic Districts is convenient, handicapped-accessible, and a great solution to having to deal with a car. In *Charleston*, the attractive trolley-like **Downtown Area Shuttle (DASH)** (843-724-7420; www.ridecarta .com) makes regular stops along five routes in the Historic District and greater downtown area. Board at the Visitor Center (375 Meeting St.; 843-853-8000), where you can park your car ($8 per day; $7 with a DASH pass discount). The DASH maps and schedules are easy to follow and color-coded by route. All-day shuttle passes cost $3; a three-day pass is $7; single rides are $1. Fares for adults over 55 and disabled passengers are $0.25, except at rush hours, and children age six and under ride free. Exact change is required. City buses operated by the **Charleston Area Regional Transportation Authority (CARTA)** service destinations like Kiawah Island, Isle of Palms, Sullivan's Island and Mount Pleasant, some from the Visitor Center, some from nearby stops. Fares begin at $1. Bike racks are available at no charge on most of these routes, and take about 10 seconds to operate. For help in planning a trip outside the Historic District call **CARTA** (843-747-0922).

In *Savannah*, there's **Chatham Area Transit (CAT)** (912-233-5767; www.catchacat.org). A free shuttle bus service within the Historic District, with regular stops at the Visitors Center (912-944-0455; 301 Martin Luther King Blvd.), downtown inns and hotels, the waterfront, and many sites of interest. It connects to most bus routes, with fares of $1 for regional service throughout Chatham County. Parking adjacent to the Visitors Center in a city lot is $1 per hour until 5 PM, with your first hour free.

HANDICAPPED SERVICES

Most of the region's accommodations, museums, restaurants, and touring services provide access and facilities for those with special physical needs—but call ahead to confirm details: problems remain in retrofitting the older historic buildings, and this includes some house museums and inns, for complete handicapped access. Your guides, hosts, or the Visitor Center's staff in each city will gladly assist you—several offer handicap-accessibility guides. See **Tourist Information** at the end of this chapter for addresses of city or county offices of tourism and travel.

HOSPITALS

BEAUFORT
Beaufort Memorial Hospital 955 Ribaut Rd.; 843-522-5200.

CHARLESTON
Bon Secours St. Francis Hospital 2095 Henry Tecklenburg Dr.; 843-402-1000.

Charleston Memorial Hospital 326 Calhoun St.; 843-577-0600.

Medical University of South Carolina 171 Ashley Ave.; 843-792-2300.

Roper Hospital 316 Calhoun St.; 843-724-2000.

Trident Regional Medical Center 9330 Medical Plaza Dr.; 843-797-7000.

Veteran's Administration Medical Center 109 Bee St.; 843-577-5011.

HILTON HEAD
Hilton Head Medical Center and Clinics 25 Hospital Center Blvd.; 843-681-6122.

SAVANNAH
Immediate Med 2014 E. Victory Dr.; 912-234-8466.

Memorial Medical Center 4700 Waters Ave.; 912-350-8000.

St. Joseph's / Candler Health System 11705 Mercy Blvd.; 912-925-4100.

LATE-NIGHT FOOD AND FUEL

The metropolitan areas of Charleston and Savannah, and the resort centers of Hilton Head, stay lit and active well after midnight—especially during the spring and summer—so finding gas or even grits should not be a problem. However, if you're traveling at night, remember that the Lowcountry is largely rural, traversed by long stretches of quiet highway. Unless you plan to gig for flounder and fry them up by the side of the road, it's best to travel with snacks or stop when you can.

BEAUFORT
Huddle House (food) Sea Island Parkway. Open 24 hours.

CHARLESTON
King Street Station (food; beer and wine) 356 King St. Open until 2 AM.

International House of Pancakes (food) 1521 Savannah Highway. Open 24 hours Sunday through Thursday, to midnight Friday and Saturday.
The Pantry (grocery and fuel) 2231 S. Ribaut Rd. Open 24 hours.

HILTON HEAD
Huddle House (food) Northridge Drive. Open 24 hours.

The Pantry (grocery and fuel) US 278 and Arrow Road. Open 24 hours.

Winn Dixie (food) Northridge Plaza. Open 24 hours.

SAVANNAH
BP Gas 7203 Abercorn (grocery and fuel) Open 24 hours.

International House of Pancakes (food) 110 Mall Blvd. Open 24 hours on weekends.

Kettle Restaurant (food) 6801 Abercorn. Open 24 hours. Wheelchair accessible.

NEWSPAPERS AND MAGAZINES

BEAUFORT AND HILTON HEAD
The Beaufort Gazette (843-524-3183; www.beaufortgazette.com; P.O. Box 399, 1556 Salem Rd. 29902) Daily. Local coverage, wire-service features, and columns.

Carolina Morning News (843-524-5448; www.lowcountrynow.com; 818 Bay St., Beaufort 29902) Daily regional offshoot of the *Savannah Morning News*.

The Gullah Sentinel (843-982-0500; 2303 Boundary St., Beaufort 29902) A bi-weekly with an African American perspective, local and syndicated columnists, and provocative editorials.

The Island Packet (843-706-8100; www.islandpacket.com; 10 Buck Island Rd., Bluffton 29938) A good daily paper that has grown as the island has, with local political coverage, a variety of columnists, and wire stories.

Lowcountry Weekly (843-986-9059; www.lcweekly.com; 106 West St. Ext., Beaufort 29902) Listings, reviews, current cultural news.

CHARLESTON

Charleston City Paper (843-577-5304; www.charlestoncitypaper.com; 689 King St., Charleston 29403) Weekly paper, excellent listings.

Charleston Magazine (843-971-9811; P.O. Box 1794, Mt. Pleasant, SC 29465 A glossy bi-monthly featuring stories about the city of Charleston, local politics, development, and some art features. Reviews and columns, too.

The Post and Courier (843-577-7111; www.postnandcourier.com; 134 Columbus St., Charleston 29403) The daily paper of Charleston.

Skirt! (843-883-3281; www.skirtmag.com; P.O. Box 806, Sullivan's Island 29482) Irreverent, fresh, funny, and good-looking, with a feminist slant. Monthly.

SAVANNAH

The Herald (912-232-4505; www.savannahherald.com; 1803 Barnard St. 31401) Weekly, featuring news of the African American community.

Savannah Morning News (912-236-9511; www.savannahnews.com.; 111 W. Bay St. 31401) Daily and Sunday.

Savannah Tribune (912-233-6128; www.savannahtribune.com; 916 W. Montgomery St. 31401) Weekly, featuring news of the African American community.

REAL ESTATE

If you came to the Lowcountry and couldn't bear to leave without owning a piece, take your place in line. Practically every new resident who has settled here recently was once in your position. Even the ones who thought the Lowcountry would be their "retirement home" have quit fighting the urge and moved in early. In Beaufort County alone, the rate of building exceeds 500 units each year and the population has increased 40 percent in the last 10 years. The fastest-growing segment of the market is in traditional, single-family homes and in new "walking communities" which try to reproduce the feel of a small town. Gated communities, glorified subdivisions, really, which may or may not be resorts, are next. If you want to be on the water, be certain about rules regarding dock permits and building in the flood zones.

There are hundreds of real estate agents, many independent, some affiliated with national brokerage firms. One of them might be the proprietor of your bed and breakfast; if not, he or she will have a suggestion. For starters, you should pick up the free, widely available, real estate magazines that are published weekly throughout the Lowcountry. These will give you a general idea of what's out there and how much it costs. Gated communities usually have exclusive sales teams, offering houses or lots that come with a variety of conditions attached. Walk-ins are welcome, but if you can't find what you're looking for, ask for referrals in other towns, too.

ROAD SERVICE

Here is a list of some 24-hour towing and emergency road services.

BEAUFORT
Discount Auto Service Center (843-524-1191).

Port Royal Exxon (843-522-3399 day; 843-379-9607 night).

CHARLESTON
AAA Carolina Motor Club (1-800-222-4357).

Mikell Towing (843-572-9333).

HILTON HEAD
Coastal Towing (843-689-3869).

Driessen's Grocery and Station (843-785-3914).

SAVANNAH
Auto Intensive Care Towing and Recovery (912-355-5388).

Jackson Bros. Car Care Center (912-236-0631).

SEASONAL EVENTS IN THE LOWCOUNTRY

The following list highlights annual events in the Lowcountry. Some of them, like outdoor concerts in a park, offer informal pleasures that you can enjoy on a whim with your family. Others, like house and garden tours, Spoleto performances, or tennis and golf tournaments, require planning. You should purchase tickets and book lodgings in advance, especially in the busy spring season. For specific information regarding dates, schedules, performance times, admission or ticket prices (if applicable), call in advance, check online or in local media. For lodging and dining suggestions, see specific chapters.

January

CHARLESTON
Lowcountry Oyster Festival (843-577-4030; www.charlestonrestaurantassociation.com)
A huge oyster roast, held on the grounds of Boone Hall Plantation in Mt. Pleasant. Games, entertainment, and contests for the whole family.

HILTON HEAD
1st Sunday Jazz (843-842-4457; www.hhjs.org; Hilton Head Jazz Society) An informal jam session held monthly at various island locations.

February

CHARLESTON
Celebration of Black History Month (1-800-868-8118; www.charlestoncvb.com)
Lectures, book signings, special exhibits at Drayton Hall, Caw Caw Interpretative Center, and performances trace the culture of the Lowcountry's African and African-American residents

Lowcountry Blues Bash (www.bluesbash.com; P.O. Box 13525, Charleston, SC 29422) Ten days of concerts and films, many free, and often in intimate venues. The series covers every blues style including electric, acoustic, post-modern, Delta, Chicago. Tickets are usually pay-as-you-go at the venue, but some advance tickets are for sale.

Southeastern Wildlife Exposition (843-723-1748; www.sewe.com; 211 Meeting St., Charleston, SC 29401) A comprehensive, multi-site exhibition of wildlife art in various media, and presentations promoting habitat conservation and wildlife appreciation. A huge, three-day national event that draws collectors, artists, hunters, and bird-watchers.

HILTON HEAD

Native Islander Gullah Celebration (843-686-3472; www.gullahcelebration.com) A month-long look at island culture and its African roots, through concerts, performances by gospel choirs and choruses, storytelling, art exhibits, and gala dances.

SAVANNAH

Georgia Heritage Celebration (912-651-2125; Historic Savannah Foundation) A 12-day celebration of the founding of Georgia and the Savannah colony which features tours, re-enactments of colonial life, lectures, art exhibits, music, dance, and crafts. At various city locations.

March

BEAUFORT

St. Helena's Episcopal Church Spring Tours (843-524-3163 or 1-800-638-3525; P.O. Box 1043, Beaufort, SC 29901) Tours of historic homes, gardens, and churches in Beaufort and on the Sea Islands.

CHARLESTON

Drayton Hall Candlelight Concert (843-766-0188; 3380 Ashley River Rd., Charleston, SC 29414) When this house is lit only by candles, it seems at its height of serene beauty. The concert continues the century-old tradition of piano music in the plantation house.

Festival of Houses & Gardens (843-722-3405; www.historiccharleston.org; 40 E. Bay St. Charleston, SC 29401) The Historic Charleston Foundation's tours of private homes, plantations, gardens, and churches usually start toward the end of the month and last four weeks. A superbly organized event—a tradition for more than 50 years—it will enrich your understanding of the Lowcountry. Although the city may be crowded, it seems warmly accommodating, especially in the narrow streets late at night, where laughter and conversation drift from gardens and homes. A highlight is the oyster roast at Drayton Hall.

HILTON HEAD

WineFest (Hilton Head Hospitality Assoc.; 843-686-4944 or 1-800-424-3387) A big and popular event, part of a month-long series of activities which include musical performances and outdoor celebrations for families.

SAVANNAH

First Saturday Arts and Crafts Festival March—November (Savannah Waterfront Association; 912-234-0295) Once a month in the good weather, live bands, pushcarts, open-air theatre performances, and craftspeople bring excitement to River Street.

St. Patrick's Day Parade (912-233-4804; Parade Committee, P.O. Box 9224, Savannah, GA 31412) Savannah claims a substantial Irish heritage and celebrates it with abandon on this holiday. Mobs of people turn out to watch the downtown parade, which starts at 10 AM and dominates all other city activity for the day and night.

Savannah Music Festival (912-236-5745 or 1-800-868-3378; www.savannahmusicfestival .org) Fifteen days of jazz, blues, international music, and classical performances held in the Historic District. Some 90 performances—a top-notch selection.

Savannah Tour of Homes and Gardens (912-234-8054; 18 Abercorn St., Savannah, GA 31401) For four days, Savannah's historic homes, churches, and gardens are open to visitors.

April

CHARLESTON
Family Circle Magazine Cup Tennis Tournament (1-800-677-2293; www.familycircle cup.com. The Tennis Centre at Daniel Island, Daniel Island, SC 29403) A new tennis stadium in a beautiful resort hosts this top women's professional tournament.

HILTON HEAD
MCI Heritage of Golf (843-671-2448 or 1-800-234-1107; 71 Lighthouse Rd., Hilton Head, SC 29928) Falling about a week after the Masters at Augusta, this premiere golf tournament brings thousands of people and the top PGA players to Hilton Head.

SAVANNAH
NOGS Garden Tour: The Hidden Gardens of Savannah (912-238-0248) A small gem— usually featuring fewer than 10 walled gardens, but all treasures, located north of Gaston St.

WALTERBORO
Colleton County Rice Festival (843-549-1079; www.ricefestival.org; P.O. Box 426, Walterboro, SC 29488) Arts and crafts, cooking demonstrations, and rice-husking celebrate the Lowcountry's rice-growing heritage.

May

BEAUFORT
Garden Tours (843-521-4144; Arts Council of Beaufort County, 1815-A Boundary St., Beaufort, SC 29902) About a dozen private gardens are on display, with an additional program of lectures, workshops, and corresponding self-guided tours of artists' studios.

Gullah Festival (843-525-0628; Beaufort Chamber of Commerce, Box 910, Beaufort, SC 29901) Held in late May, it features a big outdoor market, dance performances, concerts of spiritual and gospel music, and demonstrations of boat-building, net-tying, and other skills related to the West African heritage of the Sea Islands.

BLUFFTON
Bluffton Village Festival (843-757-3855; Bluffton Town Hall, Bluffton, SC 29910) A very small, old-fashioned street festival featuring artisans, food, and entertainment, usually held the second Saturday of May.

CHARLESTON
Confederate Memorial Day Observance (843-722-8638; Magnolia Cemetery Trust, P.O. Box 6214, Charleston, SC 29405) The United Daughters of the Confederacy and other groups sponsor a program honoring the Confederate War dead. (A similar celebration takes place in Savannah.)

Piccolo Spoleto (843-724-7305; www.piccolospoleto.com; Office of Cultural Affairs, 133 Church St., Charleston, SC 29401). The more informal aspect of Spoleto highlights regional artists and celebrates art, music, dance, and outdoor events.

Spoleto Festival U.S.A. (843-722-2764; www.spoletousa.org; P.O. Box 157, Charleston, SC 29402) Beginning in late May and lasting for about 18 days, Spoleto brings the best of international theater, music, art, and dance to Charleston. It's a magical time in the city.

HILTON HEAD
St. Luke's Tour of Homes and Gardens (843-785-4099; St. Luke's Episcopal Church).

SAVANNAH
Scottish Games and Highland Gathering (912-232-3945; P.O. Box 13435, Savannah, GA 31401) Scottish dancing, pipe bands, and traditional games honoring Scotch heritage, usually held in mid-May.

June

COLLETON COUNTY
Edisto Riverfest (843-549-5591; Walterboro Chamber of Commerce, P.O. Box 426, Walterboro, SC 29488) Join a guided canoe and kayak flotilla as it winds down the Edisto River. Food, entertainment, and displays of equipment featured at two state parks along the way. Usually held the second weekend of the month.

HAMPTON
Hampton County Watermelon Festival (803-943-4978; Chamber of Commerce, Box 122, Hampton, SC 29924) The oldest festival in the state celebrating the county's best crop. Held at the end of the month and lasting a week, featuring seed-spitting contests, beauty queens, and a big parade.

SAVANNAH
Concerts in Johnson Square From June to August, enjoy two-hour lunchtime concerts every Wednesday and Friday, starting at 11:30 AM, in one of the city's loveliest settings.

July
Fourth of July Fireworks take place in several Lowcountry resorts as well as these locations: Brittlebank Park (Charleston), Parris Island (Beaufort), Hilton Head, Bluffton, Savannah's Riverfront, and Tybee Beach.

BEAUFORT
Beaufort County Water Festival (843-524-0600 or 1-800-638-3525; Chamber of Commerce, P.O. Box 910, Beaufort, SC 29901) A 10-day festival starting in mid-July that features special events each day and night: croquet, fishing, tennis, ping-pong, and golf

tournaments, a juried art show, antiques show, kid's day, parade, and several outdoor dances. The air shows and acrobatic water-ski demonstrations are especially fun to watch.

EDISTO ISLAND

Edisto Summer Festival (843-869-3867; P.O. Box 206, Edisto Island, SC 29438) A weekend of family-oriented fun on the beach, in the water, on the links. Street dances, local food specialties, and entertainment.

August

HILTON HEAD

Celebrity Golf Tournament (843-842-7711; Chamber of Commerce, P.O. Box 5647, Hilton Head Island, SC 29938; held at Sea Pines, Indigo Run, and Palmetto Dunes) An island tradition to raise money for charities, it attracts movie stars, professional athletes, and media personalities.

Fishing Tournaments (Various locations) Check the "Marina" listings in the **Recreation** section Chapter Five, *Hilton Head* to inquire about tournaments. There are many, for marlin, billfish, and other species.

September

CHARLESTON

Candlelight Tours of Houses and Gardens (843-722-4630 or 1-800-968-8175; www.preservationsociety.org; The Preservation Society, 147 King St., Charleston, SC 29402) More than one dozen different candlelight walking tours of private homes and gardens are offered over a period of about four weeks by the city's oldest preservation organization. Lectures and small concerts are also scheduled.

MOJA Arts Festival (843-724-7305; www.mojafestival.com; Office of Cultural Affairs, 133 Church St., Charleston, SC 29401) A celebration of the African American and Caribbean heritage in the Charleston area. The influence on southern culture is traced through music, dance, art, food, stage performances, and more.

HARDEEVILLE

Catfish Festival (803-784-3606; Chamber of Commerce, P.O. Box 307, Hardeeville, SC 29927) Family entertainment, boat races on the Savannah River, and of course, catfish, are the focus of this festival, which takes place the third weekend in September.

SAVANNAH

Savannah Jazz Festival (912-356-2381; Coastal Jazz Assoc., P.O. Box 8004, Savannah, GA 31412) All styles of jazz played in spots throughout the city.

October

BEAUFORT

Historic Beaufort Foundation Fall Tour of Homes (843-379-3331; www.historic-beaufort .org; P.O. Box 11, Beaufort, SC 29901) A weekend of candlelight and daytime tours of homes and gardens in and around Beaufort; the final day often features tours of outlying plantations, such as the rarely seen Auldbrass designed by Frank Lloyd Wright and meticulously restored inside and out.

CHARLESTON

Holiday Festival of Lights (843-795-7275; www.holidayfestivaloflights.com; James Island County Park) See more than 100,000 holiday lights strung in the park, a dazzling display in a place that rarely knows a white Christmas. Family entertainment and special events scheduled through Christmas.

Plantation Days (843-556-6020; www.middletonplace.org; Middleton Place, SC 61, Charleston SC 29414) The spirit of harvest days on a Lowcountry plantation is recreated through activities such as blacksmithing, wool dying and spinning, candle-making, and pottery. Traditional music and crafts, too, in the stable yards and green at Middleton Place.

EDISTO ISLAND

Edisto Historic Preservation Society Tour of Homes (843-869-1954; P.O. 206, Edisto Island, SC 29438) Day-long tour of homes which are not usually open to the public and not often visible from public roads.

HILTON HEAD ISLAND

An Evening of the Arts (843-785-3673; Chamber of Commerce, P.O. Box 5647, Hilton Head Island, SC 29938) A festive charity auction featuring work by local artists.

RIDGELAND

Gopher Hill Festival (843-726-8126; P.O. Box 1267, Ridgeland, SC 29936) A one-day celebration with arts and crafts, music, and food. The Ridgeland area was long known as Gopher Hill, named for the gopher tortoise, a species that lives a protected life in the sand hills of Jasper County.

SAVANNAH

Savannah Film and Video Festival (912-525-5050; www.scad.edu; P.O. Box 3146, Savannah, GA 31406) Several days of screenings and lectures sponsored by the Savannah College of Art and Design.

Savannah Greek Festival (912-236-8256; 14 W. Anderson St., Savannah, GA 31401) A day-long celebration of Savannah's Greek heritage with food, music, and dancing. November

ST. HELENA ISLAND

Heritage Days (843-838-2432; www.penncenter.com; Penn Center, P.O. Box 126, St. Helena Island, SC 29920) Held the second weekend in November on the historic Penn Center campus, Heritage Days celebrates Sea Island culture in its many forms. Thursday there is a special community sing; Friday there are lectures and presentations followed by an old-fashioned fish fry with musical entertainment; on Saturday, a parade and performances which include Gullah games and storytelling, dance, music, and demonstrations of traditional Sea Island crafts such as basket-making, net-weaving, and boat-building.

December

BEAUFORT

Christmas at the Verdier House (843-379-6335; 801 Bay St., Beaufort, SC 29902) The late-18th century planter's home is decorated during Christmas week as it might have been during holidays of long ago.

Night on the Town (843-525-6644) Join in an informal, local street party as the downtown merchants welcome patrons to partake of holiday snacks and libations. There are decorations everywhere; jazz musicians, carolers, and even Santa make special appearances. An evening of small-town fun.

BLUFFTON
Christmas Parade (843-757-3855).

CHARLESTON
Christmas in Charleston (1-800-774-0006; www.christmasincharleston.com; P.O. Box 975, Charleston, SC 29402) The season brings special tours and holiday events such as a parade of boats strung with lights and open-air marketplaces. Many restaurants and hotels offer holiday specials, too.

SAVANNAH
Christmas in Savannah (1-877-728-2662; Convention & Visitors Bureau, P.O. Box 1628, Savannah, GA 31402-1628) All month long, Savannah comes alive with special holiday events: tours, performances, 19th-century style holiday presentations in old homes, crafts shows, and celebrations at the beach and on the river.

TOURIST INFORMATION & ON-LINE ADDRESSES

Here is a listing of the organizations in the Lowcountry that cater to visitors' needs. You may benefit from them during your stay or when you're planning. In many cases, booklets, videos, and pamphlets are available at a nominal charge; general information is free.

Fishing and Hunting Regulations

Licenses, permits, and wildlife stamps, whichever apply, must be in your possession while in the field or on the water. They may be purchased at tackle shops, sporting goods shops, and from the state. Check for links on the site to maps of boat landings and public hunting preserves.

Georgia Department of Natural Resources Game and Fish Division Route 2, Box 219-R, Richmond Hill, GA 31324; 912-651-2221. www.georgiawildlife.dnr.state.ga.us.

S.C. Department of Natural Resources P.O. Box 167, Columbia 29202; 843-734-3888. www.dnr.state.sc.us.

Visitor Information

Charleston Area Convention & Visitors Bureau P.O. Box 975, Charleston, SC 29402; 843-853-8000 or 1-800-774-0006; fax 843-853-0444; www.charlestoncvb.com.

Edisto Island Chamber of Commerce P.O. Box 206, Edisto Island, SC 29438; 843-869-3867 or 1-888-333-2781; www.edistochamber.com.

Greater Beaufort Chamber of Commerce P.O. Box 910, 1108 Carteret St., Beaufort, SC 29901-0910; 843-524-3163 or 1-800-638-3525; fax 843-986-5405; www.beaufortsc.org.

Hilton Head Island Chamber of Commerce P.O. Box 5647, Hilton Head Island, SC 29938; 843-785-3673 or 1-800-523-3373; fax 843-785-7110; www.hiltonheadisland.org.

Lowcountry Tourism Commission P.O. Box 615, Yemassee, SC 29945; 843-717-3090 or 1-800-528-6870; www.southcarolinalowcountry.com.

The Savannah Area Convention and Visitor's Bureau P.O. Box 1628, 101 E. Bay St., Savannah GA 31402-1628; 912-944-0456 or 1-800-444-2427; fax 912-944-0468; www.savannahvisit.com.

S.C. Division of State Parks PRT, Edgar Brown Building, 1205 Pendleton St., Columbia, SC 29201; 803-734-0156; www.travelsc.com.

IF TIME IS SHORT

The Lowcountry divides easily into three parts: the major cities (Charleston and Savannah), the more rural areas (Beaufort, Edisto, Bluffton, and the Sea Islands), and the beach resorts (on Hilton Head Island, Kiawah, Isle of Palms, or others). Concentrating on one of these locales can make for a spectacular, relaxing, and brief, visit.

Each place has its special qualities; refer to individual chapter openings for a sense of them. In general, the resorts are self-enclosed and limited in terms of history, culture, and sightseeing, yet their on-site recreational resources are exemplary and their use may determine your schedule. Beaufort or Edisto is a lower-keyed destination, where beach-combing and modest shopping might wrap around a day's worth of walking, biking, kayak-ing, or sightseeing. Each place has a superb restaurant. The cities, of course, are full of opportunity for touring and shopping. (A car is not necessary for a weekend trip to either city, although helpful if you want to explore the countryside or visit both Charleston and Savannah, a schedule that really requires four nights.)

I have tried throughout this book to present lots of options with as much impartiality as I could, with explanations to back up my choices so as to make it easier for you to make yours. Of course I have left things out: restaurants, hotels, tours, shops. Sometimes I did this on purpose for reasons of uneven quality or a changed market, and sometimes because my revisions, though regular, can lag behind the dynamic growth of the Lowcountry. What follows here, then, is the biased opinion of one who has lived in the Lowcountry for 25 years, who has visited every place covered in this book many times and is still not bored.

IN CHARLESTON

Governor's House Inn (843-720-2070; www.governorshouse.com; 117 Broad St.) is locat-ed in the Historic District, and waking up there makes you feel as if you're a native. It's an especially good choice for two couples who might want to stay in the carriage house. My favorite large hotel is the **Harbour View Inn** (843-853-8439; www.harbourviewcharleston .com; 2 Vendue Range) located on the river and adjacent to the Waterfront Park, a wonder-ful place for a morning run or a late-night stroll. These inns will be booked months in advance during the annual **Spoleto Festival** (843-722-2764; www.spoletousa.org), a series of music, dance, and theatre performances, and art exhibits, that occurs in late spring.

The house museums and military sites that are most evocative are the **Heyward-Washington House** (843-722-0354; www.charlestonmuseum.com; 87 Church St.) built in 1772 and representing the height of colonial living; the **Nathaniel Russell House** (843-724-8481; www.historiccharleston.org; 51 Meeting St.) completed in 1808 with its gardens and free-flying spiral staircase; and the **Joseph Manigault House** (843-723-2926;

Touring Savannah's Historic District

www.charlestonmuseum.com; 350 Meeting St.), designed in 1803 by a native son and a marvelous example of adapting European taste for the Lowcountry elite. Slightly father afield on SC 61 are two nationally recognized historic sites: **Middleton Place** (843-556-6020; www.middletonplace.org) where the oldest landscaped gardens in America were laid out in 1741; and **Drayton Hall** (843-729-2600; www.draytonhall.org), an 18th-century Georgian home which is a magnificent, unfurnished example of the Palladian style. Military history buffs should visit **Fort Sumter National Monument** (843-881-7337; www.fortsumtertours.com; in Charleston Harbor), where the Civil War began.

Popular shops among locals are along **King St.** from Broad St. to six blocks north of Calhoun (housewares, antiques, and clothing), **Queen St.** (boutiques and art galleries), and **Church St.** (art galleries and antiques stores,). **G&M** (843-577-9797; 96 Broad St.) is a place for a quick bite, **Hominy Grill** (843-937-0930; 207 Rutledge Ave.) for breakfast or lunch, **Il Cortile De Re** (843-853-1888; 193 A King St.) for a simple lunch downtown. For an ethnic dinner (rare in Charleston) try **Basil** (843-724-3490; 460 King St.), which serves Thai cuisine to a hip local crowd. Or try the award-winning **Peninsula Grill** (843-723-0700; 112 N. Market St.) and **McCrady's** (843-577-0025; 2 Unity Alley) with one of the loveliest, quietest bars in town.

In Savannah

The Gastonian (912-232-2869 or 1-800-322-6603; www.gastonian.com; 220 E. Gaston St.) is a sumptuous luxury inn and **The Marshall House** (912-644-7896 or 1-800-589-6304; www.marshallhouse.com; 123 E. Broughton St.) is the luxury/hip alternative. Historic sites of architectural and military interest include: the **Green-Meldrim House**

(912-232-1251; Madison Square), where General Sherman lived during the occupation of the city; the **Owens-Thomas House** (912-233-9743; www.telfair.org; 124 Abercorn St.), a Regency-style urban villa designed by William Jay in 1816; and **Fort Pulaski** (912-786-5787; www.nps.gov/fopu; U.S. 80) a masonry fort that was, in 1847, state-of-the-art, and now is a great place for a picnic. Established in 1865, the **Beach Institute** (912-234-8000; 502 E. Harris St.) includes a permanent display of folk-art sculpture that celebrates the talent of Ulysses Davis and other African American artists.

Antiques stores proliferate downtown on **Bull St.**, **Abercorn St.**, and **Whitaker St.**; there are more touristy spots in **City Market** and **River Street**. Locals eat breakfast at **Clary's** (912-233-0402; 404 Abercorn St., Tybee). The best fancy restaurants are **Georges'** (912-786-9730; 1105 E. Hwy. 80, Tybee Island) and **Sapphire Grill** (912-443-9962; 110 W. Congress St.).

IN BEAUFORT AND THE SEA ISLANDS:

The **Rhett House Inn** (843-524-9030; www.rhetthouseinn.com; 1009 Craven St., Beaufort) is the most gracious inn outside the cities. The innkeepers may also arrange kayak and bicycle outings, prepare picnics, and suggest forays to **Edisto Beach State Park** (843-869-2156), **Hunting Island State Park** (843-838-2011), and other, more out-of-the-way places. For a quick sandwich in downtown Beaufort, head for **Plums** (843-525-1946; 904-1/2 Bay St.) but for a fancy dinner that will equal anything in Charleston or Savannah choose **Saltus River Grill** (843-379-3474; www.saltusrivergrill.com; 802 Bay St.).

On Edisto Island, **The Old Post Office** (843-869-2339; SC 174) is the best place for dinner; **Po Pigs Bo-B-Que** (843-869-9003; 2410 SC 174) for lunch.

For a sense of history, visit the **John Mark Verdier House** (843-524-6334; 801 Bay St.), the home of a wealthy 19th-century Beaufort merchant; **Penn Center** (843-838-2432; St. Helena Island) the nation's first school for freed slaves; and the **Edisto Museum** (843-869-1954; Edisto Island), which reveals the history of the island, from the time of Native Americans to the present. The **Museum** at the **Marine Corps Recruit Depot** at **Parris Island** (843-525-2951) features the history of the Marines and the Corps' training. Beaufort's **Bay St.**, and the narrow streets that lead off it, has a classic main street feeling: plate-glass display windows, awnings, and family-run stores. On St. Helena, **Red Piano Too** (843-838-2241; US 21 at The Corner), an art gallery and store, is a good place to see native and outsider art and understand how those traditions both inspire and reflect today's island culture.

Index

LODGING BY PRICE CODE

DINING BY PRICE CODE

DINING BY CUISINE